Raise Happy Children

Teach Yourself®

Raise Happy Children

Glenda Weil and
Doro Marden

For UK order enquiries: please contact Bookpoint Ltd,
130 Milton Park, Abingdon, Oxon OX14 4SB.
Telephone: +44 (0) 1235 827720. Fax: +44 (0) 1235 400454.
Lines are open 09.00–17.00, Monday to Saturday, with a 24-hour
message answering service. Details about our titles and how to
order are available at www.teachyourself.com

For USA order enquiries: please contact McGraw-Hill Customer
Services, PO Box 545, Blacklick, OH 43004-0545, USA.
Telephone: 1-800-722-4726. Fax: 1-614-755-5645.

For Canada order enquiries: please contact McGraw-Hill
Ryerson Ltd, 300 Water St, Whitby, Ontario L1N 9B6, Canada.
Telephone: 905 430 5000. Fax: 905 430 5020.

Long renowned as the authoritative source for self-guided
learning – with more than 50 million copies sold worldwide –
the **Teach Yourself** series includes over 500 titles in the fields of
languages, crafts, hobbies, business, computing and education.

British Library Cataloguing in Publication Data: a catalogue record
for this title is available from the British Library.

Library of Congress Catalog Card Number: on file.

First published in UK 2008 by Hodder Education, part of
Hachette UK, 338 Euston Road, London NW1 3BH.

First published in US 2008 by The McGraw-Hill Companies, Inc.

This edition published 2010.

Previously published as *Teach Yourself Bringing Up
Happy Children*

The **Teach Yourself** name is a registered trade mark of
Hodder Headline.

Typeset by MPS Limited, A Macmillan Company.

Printed in Great Britain for Hodder Education, an Hachette UK
Company, 338 Euston Road, London NW1 3BH, by CPI Cox &
Wyman, Reading, Berkshire RG1 8EX.

The publisher has used its best endeavours to ensure that the URLs
for external websites referred to in this book are correct and active
at the time of going to press. However, the publisher and the
author have no responsibility for the websites and can make no
guarantee that a site will remain live or that the content will remain
relevant, decent or appropriate.

Hachette UK's policy is to use papers that are natural, renewable
and recyclable products and made from wood grown in sustainable
forests. The logging and manufacturing processes are expected to
conform to the environmental regulations of the country of origin.

Impression number   10 9 8 7 6 5 4 3 2 1
Year   2014 2013 2012 2011 2010

Acknowledgements

Thanks to:

Parentline Plus for allowing us to use the excellent material from their 'Parents Together' courses.

All the parents who have shared their stories with us in groups and courses over the years and taught us so much.

Our colleagues and friends for their thoughtful input and suggestions, and everyone who gave time to listen and discuss ideas with us.

Our husbands for their support and encouragement, and our children, now young adults, who have commented on the work in progress and given us useful reality checks!

Finally, a special thank you to Victoria Roddam at Hodder Education for her patience and positive guidance.

Contents

Meet the authors

Doro Marden

I vividly remember the first parenting course I ever attended more than 20 years ago at a local adult education centre. My eldest (a stepdaughter who had lived with us full time since the age of six when her mother tragically died) had recently started secondary school and my youngest was just two.

In those days 'parenting' was hardly a word, and it was a revelation to actually think about what I was doing and saying as a parent and to learn some really useful skills – I recall the group leader warning me not to do quite so much listening as I plunged into practising at every opportunity!

I have been far from a perfect parent, but I know that my relationships with my three daughters (now all young adults, and one married) would have been quite different if I had not learned so much about how (and how not) to take the initiative and to react in the hurly burly of family life.

In the years since then I have done many different trainings, including as a psychotherapist, but nothing has been as useful as the skills and ideas my long-time colleague Glenda and I have been able to communicate in this book.

Glenda Weil

'Why does one read books?', Nehru wrote to his daughter Indira – later to become Indian Prime Minister. 'To understand life and know how to live it. Our own experience is so limited.'

As a mother of four children aged five to ten I keenly felt the limitations of my experience when the hustle and bustle of real life intruded upon my ideal picture of a peaceful, harmonious home.

My husband and I joined a 'Parentlink' course and found, to our great relief, that we were not alone! Alongside other parents, we saw what worked well, and discovered new strategies for daily difficulties. At the end of the course, we understood ourselves much better, while also having greater insight into how our children felt about things. We came away thinking that even if home life still presented challenges, we had many more ways of dealing with them. What we learned about talking and listening to each other has transformed all the relationships in our family.

Since then I have trained and have run many groups for parents. This book has given me the opportunity to share with you the gems I have gleaned from their experiences as well as my own.

Only got a minute?

Happy children know that they are loved and also know that their parents are in charge. Sometimes you need to step back and think about how you are talking and listening to your children – are they really getting that message of love, trust and firmness?

Taking a few moments to stop and think about what you feel, need and want in any situation is the first step towards changing knee-jerk reactions and choosing different ways to handle potential conflicts. If you also reflect on what is really going on beneath the surface for your children before you speak you are more likely to gain co-operation and avoid confrontations, and your family life will be calmer and easier.

Recalling incidents from your own childhood helps you to understand your children in turn. Research shows that it is not so much what happened to you as a child, but how you have thought about it and talk about it in later life that makes the vital difference to your relationship with your children.

Discussing and agreeing some simple family rules (which can change as children get older) will give you a basis for keeping boundaries.

Consequences for breaking rules should stress making up for any damage, hurt or worry caused. Could someone lend a favourite toy, make their mother a cup of tea or sacrifice pocket money to pay for something broken?

There are times when you as the adult have to say 'NO', and do it with inner certainty.

Remember that play, fun and cuddles are not just 'extras' but a vital element in bringing up happy children. A playful approach and humour can often defuse a situation and lead to a win–win solution.

5 Only got five minutes?

All parents want their children to be happy, but everyday difficulties of family life often make them lose sight of the longer view: that harmonious relationships are the bedrock of a happy childhood and that children develop through repeated experiences of care, joy, understanding, laying down limits and setting goals.

Some parents are lucky enough to be able to draw on their own happy memories, others have to reflect on what they liked and disliked about their upbringing and consciously change some of their automatic responses.

ACT don't REACT is the fundamental formula for connecting with your child. A for Adult is for you to STOP and think 'What am I feeling and what do I want in this situation?; C for Child – you work out what is really going on for your child – what is he feeling? What is he trying to achieve? T stands for Tools: maybe showing you understand is enough, maybe he needs help to solve a problem, or maybe you have to be firm and put your foot down.

Children are happy when their parents are both loving and firm, and you can learn to be this way with your children for more of the time. Looking after your own needs as a person is vital if you are to have the energy and goodwill you need to give out to your children.

Are you having the same clashes with your child again and again? One way to approach this is to imagine a pool and think about what is going on under the surface – there are universal human needs which, when frustrated, give rise to feelings and behaviour which show above the surface. You will get better results by addressing those submerged needs than by dealing with surface behaviour.

Paradoxically, children often try to meet their need for attention by inviting negative reactions – any response is better than none! Often a little focused attention will head off irritating behaviour.

All children need to feel secure and loved, and welcome in the world. The family is one place where they can be accepted for who they are rather than what they achieve. Touch is a fundamental way of showing love: research on other mammals shows that babies who are touched more are braver in exploring their surroundings as they grow up.

Children also need to be challenged. Parents can help by praising effort more than results and treating failures as ways to learn rather than disasters.

Recognizing and naming feelings is the way to help children manage their emotions, so they grow up capable of coping with life's ups and downs. Anger is a feeling which is all too common in families; it can be helpful to be aware of physical sensations warning of rising anger, and to think about what frustrated need is lying under angry feelings before you react.

Boundaries are necessary to enable children to live happily alongside others and to develop self-discipline. You can agree simple family rules, based on values that you feel are important such as kindness, respect and appreciation. Discipline is about learning. Punishment, on the other hand, can lead to anger, fear and resentment rather than learning and growth. You want your children to think about the consequences of their actions and to change their future behaviour: 'What will you do differently next time?' is a good question.

As you understand both your own needs and those of your children and learn how to listen and talk more effectively, you will find that your children become more co-operative and family life will be more enjoyable, light hearted and happier!

10 Only got ten minutes?

Happiness is receiving more attention from researchers these days, and the number one ingredient is connectedness. Children who feel secure and loved have an inner warmth which is the foundation for building future relationships and the springboard to launch them out into the world to achieve their goals.

Research is discovering that the most important pathways in the brain for emotional health are actually created through experiences with parents and carers in the first few years of life. You as the adult can start to make changes in the way you relate to your children which will lay down pathways for happiness in their brains and affect how they feel and behave. Whatever age your children are, it is never too late to make a difference.

All too often in moments of stress parents find that the tone and words which authority figures used on them as children pop out without them thinking. If you can just find a way to stop and think before you speak you will find your relationship with your children improves immeasurably and they will be far more willing to co-operate.

The first step is to **ACT** rather than **REACTING**. **A** stands for Adult. You are the one who can change how things go: so stop and ask yourself, 'What is going on here for me?', 'How do I feel about this?', 'What do I need to happen?'. **C** stands for Child. Before you make a move, wait and think about what is going on for your child: 'How does he feel about this?', 'What need is he trying to meet?' Finally **T** is for Tools. Ask yourself what ideas and skills you can use in this situation.

Research shows that children thrive when their parents are loving and firm, but this is not always easy, especially if you did not experience that kind of childhood yourself. It is important to reflect on how you yourself were brought up: it is not so much what happened to you but how you have thought about it and talk about it now that makes the difference to your relationship with your children.

Remember that to be positive with your children it helps to have your own needs met, and to do things you enjoy with other adults. Giving priority to time with your partner if you have one is really important too: conflict between parents is very bad for children and family break-up is a major cause of unhappiness.

Loving and firm parenting means:

- ▶ plenty of nurturing
- ▶ consideration of your child's feelings, wants and needs
- ▶ interest in your child's daily activities
- ▶ respect for your child's point of view
- ▶ showing you are proud of what your child does
- ▶ giving support at times of stress

together with:

- ▶ moderate levels of control
- ▶ giving reasons for your requests and rules
- ▶ noticing and praising when your child behaves well
- ▶ focusing on ways to repair damage and help victims rather than on punishment.

When your child is upset he may often present the problem in a way that irritates you, or you may get overwhelmed by his feelings and cannot be helpful. The first step is always to acknowledge what the child is feeling; naming feelings helps to bring them into the thinking part of the brain and makes them easier to deal with. Touch is also a powerful way to help children calm down, stimulating the brain to produce soothing neurotransmitters which strengthen relationships. When children are wound up, questions and logic are not useful to them; they need to have what they are saying and feeling made easier to understand. Then they can nearly always find their own solutions.

To make family life run more smoothly, ask for what you want rather than what you don't want, and always separate the 'doer' from the 'deed' by describing what you like or dislike about behaviour rather than saying 'good boy' or 'naughty girl'. It is surprising how small changes in language make a big difference to the atmosphere. A playful approach will often help to avoid confrontations, and giving responsibility for a 'special job' increases confidence.

There will be times when you have to say 'No' to your children and mean it. Being firm does not necessarily mean being harsh. When your needs and values override those of your child you can acknowledge his disappointment while repeating one good reason. It can help to get quieter rather than louder; if you are sure of yourself you will communicate this; watch how really good teachers show their authority.

You can use your skills in acknowledging feelings, listening and setting boundaries to help brothers and sisters get on better with each other and to negotiate, an ability that will stand them in good stead in later life.

It is important to talk about topics that may make you feel embarrassed or worried, such as sex and drugs, before your children encounter the temptations of teenage life. There are ways to bring up the subject naturally, for example by discussing relationships in their favourite 'soaps'.

Communicating well in situations of change and loss such as bereavement or divorce can make all the difference to children's future health and happiness.

Recent research has shown that gratitude or 'counting your blessings' is a potent way of increasing wellbeing. A good idea is to ask your child to say three good things that happened that day as part of your bedtime ritual; you could do the same thing. You can increase resilience and counter perfectionism by making sure to praise effort rather than success, and reminding your child of past achievements: 'Remember when you kept trying and got the campfire going when we had given up.'

When you teach yourself to use the skills in this book you will find that your children become more co-operative, considerate, expressive of their feelings, responsible and independent, and confident. Moreover, they will be happier, and you will be too.

And remember above all to have fun with your children, building up a store of happy memories with them.

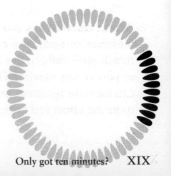

Introduction

Until we become parents, we cannot imagine the strength of the feelings that we have for our children. Our love seems boundless as we gaze into our babies' eyes, and our fury unlimited when we are defied by a truculent toddler or stubborn schoolgirl. We suffer with them when they cry about a grazed knee or a rejecting friend; we delight in their fresh view of the world and celebrate their every achievement, while we worry endlessly about the choices we make on their behalf, from infant feeding to school selection.

> Did you know that some of a baby's cells stay in the mother forever after she has given birth?

We all want the best for our children, but what does that really mean? What *does* create happiness? How much effect do we as parents have on our children's present and future wellbeing?

The ingredients of happiness are these days receiving more attention from researchers, and the good news is that these ingredients are within the store cupboard of just about every family, whatever their shape or circumstances.

The number one ingredient is connectedness. Children who feel secure and loved have an inner warmth which is the foundation for building future relationships themselves, as well as a springboard to launch them out into the world to achieve their goals.

This book is about how we put our love for our children into practice. What we say and how we listen to our children is the stuff of our connection with them and flows naturally from our strong feelings for them. But sometimes our 'Autoparent' takes over, and words come out of our mouths which sound like those used by critical, overbearing parents and teachers from long ago. Sometimes our children don't respond in the way we expect and want, or we can't find out what is worrying them, or they behave in ways we simply don't understand or like very much.

Children nowadays may speak to us in a manner that we would never have done to our own parents (though we might indeed have dreamt of doing so!). In some ways, this is one of the benefits of children knowing that they have rights and entitlements, but in other ways it is confusing for us and for them. Parenting is more difficult now, with external pressures and influences such as brand promotion which translate into 'pester power'. Access to all kinds of virtual worlds is commonplace earlier and earlier in childhood, and there are the demands of an increasingly pressurized academic system. Parents seem to be blamed by the government and the media for everything from obesity to antisocial behaviour, but they don't receive much practical support.

We know that 'authoritative' parenting – loving and firm – is what helps children to thrive and be happy. But how can we do that in practice, especially if we never experienced it ourselves?

Being a parent is more of an art than a science. Each child is a unique individual and our reaction to him or her is also unique. However, few artists would not take every chance to learn new techniques, study the work of others, practise new ways of creating effects and amend them as they go along. Parenting is no different. Having a wider range of colours in your palette will help you to brighten up family life.

We have written this book drawing on the experiences and stories of parents we have worked with and learned from over the years in parenting education groups, many for the charity Parent Network and later Parentline Plus.

When you use the skills that you teach yourself in this book, you will find that your children become more:

- *co-operative*
- *considerate*

- *expressive of their feelings*
- *responsible and independent*
- *confident.*

They will be happier, and you will be too.

Our emphasis is on deepening and strengthening relationships, rather than simply controlling behaviour. Children are not performing animals that need to be trained. They have to be supported to grow into human beings who can discipline themselves, make fulfilling life choices, cope with life's ups and downs, as well as be good friends, partners and parents themselves: the ingredients of happiness.

Children do not acquire these capacities by being told about them, but by learning through their everyday experiences of care, joy, understanding, laying down limits and setting goals. Indeed, research is discovering that the most important pathways in the brain for emotional health are actually created through experiences with parents and carers in the first few years of life. Of course children inherit some aspects of their temperament, but parents have a huge impact on how they grow up to greet the world.

You as the adult can start to make changes in the way you relate to your children which will lay down pathways for happiness in their brains and affect how they feel and behave. We have heard from countless parents about how their family life calms down and becomes more enjoyable when they work on changing the way they listen and talk with their children. Whatever age your children are, it is never too late to make a difference.

And don't worry if you sometimes forget to use your new skills. Your children will give you plenty more opportunities to practise them!

You will see that this book often asks you to reflect on childhood experiences before working on a new technique. Remembering how we felt as children really helps us to understand our children more and also makes us less likely to overreact when certain buttons are pressed.

Researchers have found that the key to the quality of our relationships with our children is not so much what actually happened to us when we were little, but rather how we have thought about it and how we talk about it in the present.

So making sense of our own childhoods is the first step towards breaking any negative patterns from the past.

Overview

Chapter 1 – ACT don't REACT introduces the fundamental formula for connecting with your child. Based on traffic lights, it is an easy way to remember to stop and think about what is going on for you and for your child, and then decide what approach or communication tool to use.

Chapter 2 – Understanding yourself as a parent looks at the pressures on you as a parent, and introduces four parenting styles as a way of thinking about what your parents were like and how you are yourself as a parent now. It also includes a section on what you need to do to nurture yourself. Being a parent requires lots of positive energy, and adult activities which you enjoy are essential if you are to have the vitality and goodwill to be a positive parent.

Chapter 3 – Understanding your child's behaviour introduces the 'Needs Fountain', a way of illustrating the link between feelings, needs and behaviour and looking underneath the surface for what is really motivating your children to do what they do.

Chapter 4 – Valuing your child. Feeling loved and valued just for being you is the basis for security. The chapter lists some of the ways parents show how they value their children, with a section on the importance of touch. As well as nurturing, children need stimulation. Parents can help build confidence through encouraging and finding fitting challenges. Lastly, this chapter includes a light-hearted quiz to test the temperaments of everyone in the family and appreciate their similarities and differences as well as their uniqueness.

Chapters 5, 6 and 7 – Recognizing feelings, Dealing with feelings and **Anger and tantrums** are all about emotions. Of course relationships are made up of feelings. One of the best gifts we can give a child is the ability to recognize and think about feelings. We know that 'emotional literacy' is even more important than the '3Rs' for a successful and happy life. In these chapters, you will learn and practise ways of expressing your own feelings and acknowledging how children feel – the results can be miraculous!

Chapter 8 – Encouraging co-operation and positive feelings looks at the power of what we say and how we say it, and ways of going for what we want rather than what we don't want. This is the chapter which tackles the mess and everyday niggles which can ruin family life.

Chapters 9 and 10 – Skilled listening and **Problem solving**. In these chapters you will learn a way of listening skilfully which will encourage your children to open up to you and then empower them to sort out their own problems. You will practise the kinds of questions which will get children talking rather than the grunted 'Yeah yeah' which is all too often the response to 'Did you have a good day?'

Chapter 11 – Boundaries and freedom. This chapter guides you in thinking about the values and rules in your family so that you are clear about where you draw the line. You will learn ways to stand firm while maintaining mutual respect.

Chapter 12 – Tackling sibling conflict explores common causes of fighting between siblings. It brings together the communication skills you have learned and adds a model for negotiating solutions to conflicts.

Chapter 13 – Time to talk about difficult issues gives ideas about how and when to start talking about topics which may make you feel uncomfortable and worried, such as sex and drugs. It also tackles communicating about the change and loss which come with bereavement and family break-up – handling these well can make all the difference to your children's future health and happiness.

Chapter 14 – Happiness. The book ends with a chapter exploring the ingredients of happiness both in childhood and the rest of your life.

Before you begin

Our experience of running parenting groups has shown that people learn at least as much from each other as from us. After the first session, they usually heave a huge sigh of relief and say 'I'm so glad to see that I'm not the only one ...'.

In writing this book, our aim has been to let you be part of that vast community of parents whose experience of bringing up children is very similar to your own. You will learn from their difficulties as much as their successes, which is why we have included so many of their stories. In a parenting group, the weekly 'check-in' helps people to share ideas and encourage each other. You might think of working through this book with a friend who would be your 'learning companion'. You could do this face to face, by phone, text or email. It's amazing how simply knowing that you are going to report back to someone encourages you to actually try things out. On the other hand, you may prefer to read it alone, or with your partner if you have one. There are parts where your children can join in too, especially the fun activities at the end of each chapter. These are there to remind you that an essential part of bringing up happy children is simply to have fun!

In any case, see this book as a companion, writing on it (you may like to keep a notebook too) and carrying it around while you are working through it.

If you were learning to drive, the Highway Code on its own would not be enough. You would also need the hours of practice, including the stalling and bumpy starts!

Similarly, when you read this book, you can take your time.

It is structured so that you learn and practise skills which build on each other, and it is divided with headings so that however busy your life is, you can read it in small chunks. Just like learning to drive, some of the things you try out may not come effortlessly at first, so we have included some 'ready phrases' as an aid when you want to try a new tactic but can't find the words. The more these new approaches become part of your parenting style the more natural they will feel. This book has not been written by 'experts'. When you become a parent, you embark on a journey of discovery which lasts a lifetime – we have 'L' plates on all our lives. However, we can share with you the ideas which have helped countless parents to build greater happiness and harmony in their family relationships.

As a parent, you have much wisdom and know your children better than anyone else. You already have many skills and 'tools'. We would like to give you greater confidence in using them at the same time as adding new ones to your 'toolkit'.

Anyone in a caring relationship with a child can learn from this book. The families featured are fictional, but we include stories based on those told to us by mothers, fathers, grandparents, step-parents and childminders. We have used 'he' and 'she' in alternate chapters for convenience, not because certain topics are more suitable for one gender or the other.

Before setting out, write down your answers to the following questions to give you a clearer idea of your starting point and what you are aiming for.

What do I like about being a parent?

As a parent, what do I find difficult?

What would I like to get out of reading this book?

We hope you enjoy this book! Many parents say that they find the skills you will learn just as helpful with colleagues and friends as in family life.

1

ACT don't REACT

In this chapter you will learn:
- *a strategy to help you think more clearly under stress*
- *a way to stop and think of your own needs*
- *to pause and think about what is going on for your child*
- *then decide what to do.*

In the heat of the moment

Penny, mother of Mia and Abby:

'HELP! When I'm stressed, I find Mia and Abby really get on my nerves and then I snap at them, which only makes us all feel miserable! I keep on promising myself that I'll handle things better next time, but you know what it's like ... When they fight or refuse to come home from the playground, I revert to shouting. I really want to find a more positive way forward to understand what's going on and what I can do to avoid these flare-ups.'

Celia, mother of Grace, Adam and Finlay:

'Yes ... I know what you mean ... It's hard being a parent! I often feel really frustrated with Adam. He's so reluctant to try anything new ... There's a great karate class after school but he simply refuses even to go and watch.'

Penny's cry for help has been echoed by many a frazzled parent. There may be moments in your family life when you, like Penny and Celia, feel frustrated with a situation but can't think how to change it.

Parents are often juggling so many different things that it can be hard to think clearly. You may be trying to cook supper after a long day, with one child demanding your attention while the other two are squabbling over the remote control. At times like these, you could find yourself just reacting – saying or doing the first thing that comes into your head. It's easy to say something in the heat of the moment and regret it later on.

The ACT formula

ACT – the strategy described in this chapter comes first because it is an effective way to stop and think, and not just react. This will give you that vital moment to calm down and engage the brain rather than the vocal cords – or hands.

By using **ACT** you are more likely to respond in a way that helps rather than making things worse.

ACT stands for:

Adult – *your own feelings and needs*
Child – *your child's feelings and needs*
Tools – *the skills and ideas you can use to make family life easier and more enjoyable for everyone.*

This book will give you an array of tools and techniques to choose from, and the ACT model will help you to use them as part of your repertoire in day-to-day life.

It is a three-step process, like traffic lights, which will help you to communicate more effectively with your children. Figure 1.1 shows how it works.

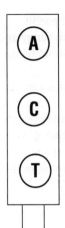

A (adult) – is the red light that tells you to **STOP** and **THINK**.

Ask yourself: *'What's going on here for me?'*
'How do I feel about this?' 'What do I need to happen?'

C (child) – is the amber light reminding you to **WAIT** and think of what is going on for your child.

Ask yourself: *'How does she feel about this?'*
'What does she need to happen?'

T (tools) – is the green light that indicates you can **GO** ahead and use your tools.

Ask yourself: *'What skills and ideas can I use here?'*
'What can I say or do that will help us get what we need?'

Figure 1.1 The ACT formula.

Children can push your buttons in many different ways. Say you've just cooked your daughter's favourite meal, and she says 'Yuck! I hate spaghetti!', you may find all sorts of feelings welling up inside you. The button she pushed might be the 'I don't feel appreciated' one, and your knee-jerk reaction could be to retaliate with 'Don't be rude! You're lucky I cooked at all for such a fuss-pot!', which doesn't solve the problem, and will probably make things worse.

Insight

We have found that ACT is a good way to remind ourselves that we are in fact the ADULT in the family situation. It is so easy to react to a child by descending to his level and getting locked into an argument which no one can win.

The 'Autoparent'

Mothers and fathers sometimes discover their own parents speaking through them in moments of stress. Whatever ideas you have about how to bring up your children, they can go out of the window when your feelings overshadow your rational thinking.

'Autoparent' – the model imprinted on your mind from your earliest infancy – can take over at these times. You may think to yourself: 'I sounded just like Mum then' or 'Those are the very words Dad would have said about me.'

> **Insight**
>
> I always swore that I would never say 'Because I say so' – remembering how frustrating it was to hear that from my father – but sure enough it popped out on numerous occasions, with a similar response of fury from my children!
> – *Doro*

ACT in practice

Using ACT will enable you to pause for long enough to think for yourself, take stock of the situation, and see the wood for the trees.

You may be wondering how this strategy can work for you in practice. Julie's story will illustrate this process.

A parent's story

Julie, mother of Anna and Jake, was in her local John Lewis department store buying a present for her Mum, and it took her a very long time. It wasn't much fun for Jake, but he was remarkably patient on this occasion, so she rewarded him by taking him to the toy department.

He was having a great time in the play house, and Julie let him stay and enjoy it for a while. He was so absorbed in a pretend game that when she finally took his hand to leave, he snatched it away, and refused to budge. 'We must have looked the picture of a parent–child power struggle,' she said, 'and I imagined everyone thinking: "Why doesn't she just control her child?!"' Jake was shouting at the top of his voice and as his mother tried to reason with him, his protests escalated to: 'You're mean! I hate you!' Julie was horribly embarrassed, and was about to drag him screaming from the house, when she remembered **ACT** and managed to put it into practice.

A = (Adult) – She took a very deep breath and dropped her shoulders, using the 'red traffic light' to STOP for just long enough to get her thinking back. She tuned in to her own feelings and needs. 'I recognized how mortified I felt when I saw the disapproving looks of the staff and customers. I also realized that I was worried I might be late for collecting Anna from her club, and needed to leave straight away.'

C = (Child) – Remembering the yellow traffic light, she tried to put herself in Jake's shoes and think about what he might be feeling. She saw how hard it was for him to tear himself away when he was enjoying the house so much. After all, children don't really understand time pressures.

T = (Tools) – The green light – She decided to acknowledge how they were both feeling, so she said: 'Jake ... I can see you're having a wonderful time, and I'm worried we might be late for Anna. I feel really embarrassed that you're shouting in a shop!'

Amazingly, it worked like magic! He sighed, shrugged and took her hand to leave.

Because Jake saw his mother understood how he was feeling, he was prepared to co-operate, and a pitched battle was avoided.

> Parents are 100% important
> Children are 100% important *and*
> The relationship is 100% important

WAYS TO STAY CALM

No one finds it easy to stay calm when they are stressed. At those moments when you throw your hands up and think: 'What on earth can I do now?!', a formula can be very helpful. 'ACT don't react' is easy to remember, and traffic lights are a simple yet powerful image to call upon.

Often the most difficult thing is to *stop* – the **A** of **ACT**. As you work through this book, you will discover ways which help to give you that split second to put the brakes on rather than hurtling into a confrontation. You will also explore the reasons for your child's behaviour, and a better understanding will reduce the irritation you may sometimes feel about it.

A good place to start would be to consider what helps you to stop at the red light.

It might be enlightening to talk this over with someone else, maybe your partner, or a friend who also has children – perhaps your learning companion.

Exercise: How do you put the brakes on?

In moments of stress, what helps you to stop and think before reacting to the situation? Make a list of the things you and your friends find helpful.

Here are three ways other parents have managed to stop and think:

▶ *deep breathing*
▶ *counting to ten*
▶ *walking into another room.*

Don't be too hard on yourself when you jump in with both feet instead of pausing for thought. New ways of doing things take time to assimilate, and your children will provide you with plenty more occasions to practise that moment of calm before speaking.

Insight

I remember creating an 'affirmation' to say in my head in moments of stress – 'I am a calm and loving parent'. Affirmations are positive statements which are used to consciously replace the negative 'self-talk' which so often goes on in our minds. – *Doro*

How to remember ACT

ACT is a theme which runs through all of the following chapters. It is a formula which works for all human relationships as you consider and respect yourself and the other person before deciding what to say or do. This is why many parents have found ACT just as helpful with their mothers, fathers, brothers, sisters and work colleagues, as they do with their partners and children.

Thinking about what is going on for yourself and your child and putting all this into words will build closeness and empathy between you. You will be able to sort out problems as they arise in ways that work for both of you. ACT is a useful reminder when feelings are running high to stand back rather than jump in.

Having given yourself time to think, you will respond to what is
happening in helpful ways rather than adding fuel to the fire.

Chapter 7 on anger and tantrums will explore this principle
further, looking at scenes from your own family and giving you
opportunities to practise helpful strategies.

PARENTS' COMMENTS

Ingrid, mother of Eric:

'I've struggled with ACT. Sometimes I don't want to think about
what my child is feeling. I just want him to do what I say and not
talk back. But I have to say that since I've been putting myself in
Eric's shoes and seeing things from his perspective, I do understand
him better, and lately he's been far more affectionate.'

Suresh, father of Asha and Hari:

'I find the most difficult thing is to STOP; but when I remember
the red traffic light and think before I speak, the rest just falls into
place. The other day I was getting terribly annoyed with Hari
because he kept getting down from the table. When I paused and
thought about it, I realized that it's important to me that we sit
down together as a family; and at the same time, when I looked at
Hari, I could see that he was uncomfortable; his chin was only just
level with the table and his feet were dangling.

So we got a 'special' cushion to bring him up to the right height, and found a box to put his feet on. I said he was like a prince sitting on his 'throne' and that made the meal much more exciting for him.'

Things which have struck me in this chapter

Make a note of anything which particularly struck a chord with you in this chapter.

Something I am going to try out

HAVE SOME FUN

'Simon Says'

One of the joys of having children is their ability for fun! Having a good laugh together and playing games is a wonderful way to let go of the seriousness of adult life.

'Simon Says' is a great game for practising listening and self-control – both important ingredients for ACT. The leader gives quick instructions saying: 'Simon says: "touch your toes", "scratch your head", "hop round the room"' – or whatever comes into their mind. If the leader gives an order without saying 'Simon says', the followers must remain still. Anyone who moves is out. The last remaining person is the next leader. Younger children can be given more chances.

10 THINGS TO REMEMBER

1   *In the heat of the moment, parents often say and do things that they later regret.*

2   *The ACT strategy is a way of thinking about how you respond to your children. It helps clarify what you can say and do, so that you 'ACT rather than react'.*

3   *A for Adult means that you first stop to think about what is going on for you, how you feel, what you need and what you want to happen.*

4   *C for Child leads you to put yourself in your child's position to empathize with her feelings and needs.*

5   *T is for Tools – a choice of strategies which will be expanded in this book.*

6   *The most vital step is the first one – to stop and be aware of your feelings and thoughts. Think about ways of doing this that work for you.*

7   *A good reminder is to buy red, yellow and green stickers and put them up as traffic lights on your fridge, mirror, front door, or anywhere that will remind you to ACT not REACT.*

8   *Remember that adults are 100% important, children are 100% important AND the relationship is 100% important.*

9   *New ways of doing things take time to become automatic. Don't despair if you forget at first; next time you will be more prepared.*

10 *ACT don't REACT is a way of approaching all relationships, not just those with children.*

2

Understanding yourself as a parent

In this chapter you will learn:
- *about the pressures on you as a parent*
- *how to identify different parenting styles*
- *a way to think about what your parents were like with you*
- *what you can do to nurture yourself and feel more positive.*

The most powerful role models for your parenting are your own parents. What was their style? Do you emulate aspects of what they did or do you react against it at all costs?

The first step in learning new approaches is to be aware of what you are doing (thinking about the 'A' for adult in ACT). When it comes to parenting, bringing into awareness how you were treated as a child is important too. It is not so much what happened to you, but more how you have thought about it and explain it to yourself now which makes a difference to your own parenting style. Many thousands of parents have successfully worked to change and improve the way they relate to their children, and you can too.

The last part of this chapter looks at how you look after your own needs for fun and fulfilment. Being a parent is hard work, and you will feel more positive about being with your children if you can find ways to do things that you enjoy.

Parenting pressures

Being a parent in the twenty-first century is perhaps more demanding than it has ever been. The old certainties of 'children should be seen and not heard' and 'spare the rod and spoil the child' have gone. Or have they? You know that you should not be using the harsh punishments of the past, but you still feel – and the media and government still give the message – that you should be able to control your children's behaviour. People 'tut' in the supermarket both if you smack or scold a child and if your child is being noisy or running around or pestering for sweets.

As well as these uncertainties, parents are having to cope with an unprecedented level of technological change in the home, where children often know more about electronic gadgets and social networking on the web than their parents do. Advertisers are using these channels to reach children at younger and younger ages.

Insight

Reading recently that 16 per cent of 8–11-year-olds in the UK can use the internet in their bedroom, we realized it would be extremely difficult to supervise what they are playing or looking at. Soon internet connections on mobile phones will open up even more avenues for advertisers and others. We've included some websites which will help you keep your child safe on the web on page 310.

Children themselves are more anxious about achieving at school and are the most tested generation ever. And the background to all this is high housing prices, leading to long working hours and less time to just be around each other.

Parents are told that what they do and say to their children has an impact on their future happiness and health. They are blamed for antisocial behaviour, obesity, teenage pregnancy, truancy and exam failure, but they are not given much support unless things go badly wrong, and in the meantime are given a lot of contradictory advice.

You can feel guilty that you are not living up to some ideal, and compare yourselves and your children to a mythical perfect family that exists only in advertisements. In fact, children don't need perfect parents; in the words of the renowned paediatrician and psychoanalyst Donald Winnicott, parents need only to be 'good enough'. You are the one who cares most about your own child, no one knows him and your particular circumstances as well as you or cares as much about his future happiness.

But what is 'good enough'? There is no doubt that how you parent has an effect on your children. A recent overview of research found links between parenting style and levels of aggression, depression and anxiety, high-risk behaviours, a child's view of himself, social competence, academic outcomes and even number of accidents. So what should you be aiming for to give your children the best start in life?

The parenting style graph

One way of thinking about parenting is to look at two scales – from firm to soft and cold to warm (see diagram opposite).

If you are at the **Warm** end of the scale, you would find it easy to show love, enjoying hugs and cuddles, giving lots of positive messages and slowing down to a child's own rhythms of play and learning. This does not come naturally to all parents. Some may find it easier to have those feelings for babies than older children and vice versa.

Nearer the **Cold** end of the scale, you might find it easier to stick to rules and routines, and find it hard to understand and sympathize with the messiness and unpredictability of babies and small children. But caring is a basic human – indeed mammalian – instinct. Touch and physical contact helps the production of oxytocin, the neurotransmitter of love and security. Oxytocin is present in all humans, and plays a vital role in labour and breastfeeding.

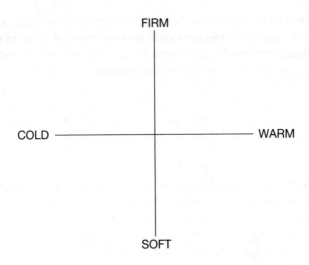

Recent studies are indicating its importance in building close family relationships and reducing stress. The very fact of having children will make many parents move along this scale towards warmth.

Looking at the other line, **Soft** parents are easygoing, have few hard and fast rules and give in to nagging, even when they are not really comfortable about letting their children do something that inconveniences them or others.

Firm parents at the top end of the scale don't negotiate – they give orders and make rules that they expect to be obeyed.

Where do you think you might be on the **Cold** to **Warm** line? And on the **Firm** to **Soft** line? If you mark where you think you are on each scale, then draw lines up or down and across from each place, the spot where they meet will show your 'parenting style' (see diagram on page 16).

Parents and carers who are **Loving and Firm** (sometimes called 'authoritative' in psychological research) are able to say what they want to happen without putting their children down. Their children know that they are loved, and also that there are limits and why. They are gradually trusted to make their own decisions and to accept the consequences, so that eventually they learn self-discipline. They tend to be able to get on well with other people, which is an important element of happiness.

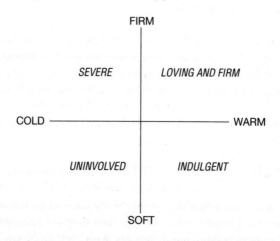

Some parents find it easy to be loving and firm, probably because they have experienced this from a parent or parent figure themselves. But many parents have to work at it by learning skills of empathy, communication and assertiveness. They need to reflect on what in their own childhood can pop up and make them react without thinking. This book will give you lots of ideas for ways of being a parent who is warm and firm.

Severe parents are more like the picture of an authoritarian father from long ago. They may be fearful that their children will not achieve their full potential. In turn, their children may feel that they can never live up to their parents' expectations. Children brought up like this may behave themselves out of fear, but act thoughtlessly when they are not being told what to do, as they are used to being controlled and have not developed self-control.

Indulgent parents are the ones who find it hard to refuse their children anything and who give in to nagging for a quiet life. They may feel guilty that they don't spend enough time with their children because of working long hours, or they may be trying to make up for something that they did not get as children; or perhaps they are just not able to bear their children's disappointment. As a result, their children may act more and more wildly as they try to find where the boundary is.

Parents in this category often 'snap' and swing into the **Severe** box, regret it, feel guilty and give way even more, see-sawing between indulgence and severity. For example, you might give in to begging for an ice cream while you are out, then lose your temper when your child won't eat his meal soon after, send him to bed without his tea and finally relent and give him a sandwich in the bath.

Uninvolved parents are often too bound up in problems and concerns of their own to be able to give their children the love, thought and energy that they need. Many parents go through phases of being uninvolved, usually when they are extremely stressed or depressed. Even if they are with their children, they are not really present and 'there for them'. Parents in this category need to get support for themselves quickly. Long periods of uninvolved parenting are bad for children.

Insight

We both know from experience (and research backs it up) that bereavement can have an impact on a parent's relationship with a young child, so plenty of support needs to be put in place when there has been a death in the family.

You will probably recognize elements of all these styles in your parenting at one time or another. The important thing is not to feel guilty about it, but to think how you can have more times in the **Loving and Firm** box of the graph.

It is never too late to make changes in the way you relate to your children, whether by finding new ways to show them affection and to appreciate their good qualities, or by agreeing rules that reflect your values and sticking to them.

An example of different parenting styles might be:

Mia says she can do her homework in front of her favourite 'soap'. It is an important episode and all her friends will be watching and want to discuss it.

A **Severe** response would be: 'No way! You must be crazy to think you can concentrate like that! I'm turning the TV off this minute.' Here the parent is criticizing the child, dismissing her feelings and allowing no negotiation.

An **Indulgent** parent might say: 'Oh, is it really important? I suppose I can give you some help with your homework later if you need it.' This is responsive to what the child wants, but gives no structure and inconveniences the parent.

An **Uninvolved** parent would probably not really focus on the implications of what was being asked and just say 'OK'.

The **Loving and Firm** parent might say: 'You really want to find out what is going to happen and discuss it with your friends, but the rule is homework done before the TV is on. I will record the programme and you can watch it later in your pyjamas.'

She recognizes that the request is important for Mia, and finds a way for her needs to be met within the family rules.

So loving and firm parenting means:

▶ *plenty of nurturing*
▶ *consideration of your children's feelings, wants and needs*
▶ *interest in their daily activities*
▶ *respect for their point of view*
▶ *showing you are proud of what they can do*
▶ *giving support at times of stress*

together with

▶ *moderate levels of control*
▶ *giving reasons for your requests and rules*
▶ *noticing and praising when they behave well*
▶ *focusing on ways to repair damage and help any victims rather than punishment.*

Working through this book will support you in getting the balance of parenting right.

If you feel you are too severe, you will want to work on the 'soft' skills of valuing, empathizing and listening. If you feel you need to be more firm, there are lots of ideas in the chapters on gaining co-operation and setting boundaries.

Your own experience of parenting styles

Like it or not, your own parents are the most potent influence on how you act as a mother or father. Reflection about your own childhood is surprisingly important as a first step to being the kind of parent you want to be. Remember, it is how you think about and process your childhood rather than what actually happened that makes the difference to the relationship you have with your own children. So if you think that your parents made mistakes, you are not bound to repeat them!

Exercise: What were your parents like?

Thinking back to your childhood:

1 *Which box of the parenting style graph were your parents in most of the time? Your father and mother may have been different.*

2 *Can you remember an incident in your childhood when your mother or father reacted in a warm and firm way?*

(Contd)

3 *Can you remember an incident when they reacted severely, neglectfully or indulgently?*

4 *What do you imagine was going on for them? What were they feeling and thinking?*

5 *What was going on for you? How did you feel?*

This is a useful exercise to work through with a learning companion, and also with your partner. Your memories may spark off stories for them and vice versa.

Shanti, mother of Asha and Hari:

'I remember being so ill with chickenpox and my mother sitting with me till I fell asleep singing to me and dabbing my itchy spots with calamine lotion; she knew I wouldn't be able to resist scratching them. I felt special and loved, even though it was so uncomfortable.'

Warm and firm parents give support in times of stress. What might be indulgent in some circumstances is appropriate when a child is ill.

Patrick, father of Callum, Sean and Logan:

'My Dad would read to me at bedtime. He was a brilliant reader who acted out all the characters – but I had to be ready in bed on time for it to happen. I remember once pleading with him when I was too late, and him saying: "I want to know what happens too. Get to bed earlier tomorrow and we can have two chapters then!" Even though I was disappointed, I could see he really knew how I felt, and the penalty for dawdling came without him getting angry.'

A boundary was kept here with consideration of the child's feelings and avoiding an argument.

John, stepfather of Grace and Adam and father of Finlay:

'I was regularly hit by my father. One time, I remember, it was for losing my school blazer. He was severe, but in some ways uninvolved as well – he never bothered to find out what had really happened; in fact my blazer was stolen by a bigger boy who was bullying me. I can still remember how despairing I felt that no one would take my side. I know he had been beaten by his father and I don't think he knew how to react in any other way.'

This authoritarian father used harsh discipline to try and teach his son a lesson, but failed to find out what the real problem was.

Over 90 per cent of parents in the US and the UK use physical punishment, so it is highly likely that you were hit as a child. Parents did their best with the knowledge they had at the time, but today research shows that, although physical punishment results in short-term compliance, any form of hitting tends to lead to more problem behaviour rather than less.

This might be because anger and fear are natural responses to being hurt by the person you love and depend on, and a lesson is being taught that violence is an acceptable way of tackling a problem. Indeed, there is a strong link between being physically punished as a child and violence in later relationships.

Research in the US has shown higher levels of depression in adults who were hit as teenagers too. (Chapter 11 covers some more helpful ways to set limits.)

If you have painful memories, make sure you look after yourself and ask for understanding from your partner or a close friend who will be supportive. Remind yourself that thinking and talking about difficult things in your childhood makes you less likely to repeat them with your children. Other sources of help are at the end of the book.

Your own parenting styles

Exercise: What are your parenting styles?

Think about your interactions with your children in the past week. Can you think of a time when you were:

Strict?

Indulgent?

Uninvolved?

> Loving and firm?

> What was going on for you? What were you thinking and feeling?

> What was going on for your child? What were they thinking and feeling?

This is what two parents who did this exercise thought.

Laura, mother of Rory and Owen, said:

'Owen is always pushing the limits. On Saturday, in the shopping centre buying trainers, he went on and on until I ended up buying him a more expensive pair than I had planned on. I was cross with myself and irritable with him. I suppose I was indulgent and then regretted it. When I thought about it, I realized I should have discussed with him what was a reasonable amount to spend before we went, and then stuck to it.'

Gloria, mother of Jasmine, Chantal and Nathan, remembered:

'I wouldn't let Chantal stay over with her best friend on Thursday. She was really upset in the playground, but I reminded her of the rule: "not on a school night", without shouting, and said I could see how disappointed she was. So I managed to be warm and firm.'

It is important to remember that children vary – within the warm and firm 'box' there is room for manoeuvre to provide firmer boundaries for some children and a lighter hand for others.

You may act differently with different children: it may be easier to be warm and firm with one child, whereas another is more challenging for you. Being aware is the first step towards changing how you act and react with your children. It is never too late to make those steps.

Insight

It can be a comfort to remember that traits which are difficult and worrying in a child can be useful in adult life. Both of us had children who were 'stubborn' and never gave up if they wanted something – now as young adults this gift of clarity and persistence is standing them in good stead!

The oxygen mask

Have you ever been on a plane when the announcement about oxygen masks is made? The stewardess always tells you to put on your own mask before helping your child. This is a stark message – if you fall unconscious, you will not be able to keep your child alive. There is also some truth in it for everyday life. Being a parent demands energy, attention and a positive attitude. Nurturing yourself and your adult relationships will help you to remain loving and firm with your children and avoid feeling resentful towards them.

However much you love and enjoy your children, being a parent means giving up a lot of freedoms. Research shows a reduction in satisfaction with the marital relationship during the more demanding period of parenting preschool children, though satisfaction does go up once they start school. Time, money, sleep and sex are all in short supply and couples have to be creative to keep romance alive.

'No entertainment licence required', as the late great psychologist Haim Ginott put it. Parents can sympathize with their child's feelings about being left behind, but should not feel guilty about going out for some grown-up fun.

It can be helpful to think about different levels of 'me' time and 'us' time. Going away for a few days or a weekend with your partner and/or friends might be possible as your children get older and can spend a night with trusted carers, related or not. Being at home without the children is another option if they can stay elsewhere. A day or an evening out is easier to arrange. Breaks like this are good to look forward to and back on when things feel dull and unremitting.

Parents' stories

Penny was lucky enough to live in an area where the local council paid for a babysitting service for lone parents. She said: 'You get the same sitter every time, so you and your child get to know them. Going out to the pub or the cinema with my friends once a month kept me sane when Mia and Abby were little – I really do think it stopped me going mad.' Being able to go out and knowing that your children are enjoying contact with another adult is an extra pleasure.

***

Last winter, Peter was ill and off work for more than a week. He found that everything his sons Rory and Owen did was annoying him. When he talked it over with his wife, they realized that they had been hard at it every weekend for months decorating the house. They made a resolution to have some more breaks, bought concert tickets in advance and asked Laura's mother to babysit every other week.

Time and money may not always permit you to have a day or an evening out. So how else can you nurture your body and spirit in ways that fit in to a normal day? Examples might be going for a walk and appreciating nature, listening to your favourite music, having a long soak in the bath, painting your nails, reading a book instead of work reports on the train, doing some yoga or weight training.

The human brain is programmed to remember painful and frightening incidents – where the sabre-tooth tiger jumped out at you perhaps.

You can train yourself to be aware of the pleasurable moments in life, and remember them as vividly. This is important for happiness. You can help your children to remember special times too by talking about them together.

Before you do the next exercise, think about the things you do that make you feel good inside, the ones that make you smile.

Exercise: What do you enjoy doing?

List ten things you enjoy doing.

1

2

3

4

5

6

7

8

9

10

Note by each one when you last did it.

Circle the activities you can do in the course of a normal day or week.

Look at the list to see if there are any patterns or surprises.

What stops you doing each activity more often?

Celia, mother of Grace, Adam and Finlay:

'When I looked at my list, I realized that I enjoy a lot of physical activities, like swimming and yoga, though I never thought of myself as being 'sporty'. I was quite surprised really.'

Patrick, father of Callum, Sean and Logan:

'I saw that some of the things on my list I hadn't done since before my children were born, like country walks and country pubs, and there's really no reason why we shouldn't all do that together now they're a bit older.'

Insight
Doing this exercise for the first time was a revelation!
I realized that making time for things that gave me pleasure and satisfaction is not self-indulgent: it's important for my children to be around a happy mother, not a disgruntled one! In addition, when we look after our own needs we are teaching our children to do the same. – *Glenda*

If there are things you wish you could still do which now seem impossible, you may be able to find another way to fulfil the same needs. For example, eating out with friends may have satisfied your need for friendship and company in the past. Now you might be able to go to the playground with them and chat while your children are having fun together. Some couples have a candlelit dinner at home one night a week when they focus on each other without the children or the television.

THE FULL CUP

Looking after yourself is especially important when you are a parent. One way to think about it is to imagine a cup – a beautiful goblet or a cup of tea, depending on your style! Over a normal day, you are constantly giving out from your cup. Unless you replenish it, you can't nourish those around you, including your children. As an adult, you are responsible for making sure that your cup is kept filled by doing things that give you happiness and satisfaction. Your children will learn about looking after themselves by watching you. If you model healthy ways to unwind, you are giving them a good start in life. Coming home and saying 'I could do with a drink' may be giving the wrong message about alcohol, for example.

If you are stressed, your children will pick it up even if they don't know what exactly is going on. Australian parenting writer and speaker Steve Biddulph puts it like this: 'kids are like corks being tossed around on the ocean of adults' emotional lives'.

So think about what 'fills your cup' and work out how to do more of it. Ideally, every day should have some moments that lift the heart and spirits. The good moments will help you through times when everything seems to be going wrong and make it easier to look on the bright side.

PARENTS' COMMENTS

Shanti, mother of Asha and Hari:

'It was hard looking at myself as a parent. I had such high ideals about how I would be, and now I find myself doing the kind of thing my mother did – being a martyr!

The other day Asha asked me if we could go to the park to ride her bike. When I said I was too tired she said: "You're always too tired!" and flounced off. She was right, I don't have much spare energy at the moment. I now realize I need to "fill my cup"!'

Penny, mother of Mia and Abby:

'At first I thought – "but I don't have time to do anything for myself". Then I found out that there is a public pool near the girls' drama class, so instead of rushing to the supermarket or sitting chatting to the other mums, I go for a swim during that time.'

Things which have struck me in this chapter

Something I am going to try out

HAVE SOME FUN

Cinnamon toast
With your child, make a joint creation that is good to eat.

The smell of cinnamon will linger in the mind linked with happy family times.

Make cinnamon toast together for tea. Someone can butter the toast, someone else can add a sprinkling of sugar, and another can shake the cinnamon over it.

Then place it under the grill for a few moments and enjoy the treat!

10 THINGS TO REMEMBER

1 *Parents are pressurized by the media and government to make their children behave, but the old harsh methods of control are increasingly discredited.*

2 *Although physical punishment may bring quick results, in the long run it can lead to more problem behaviour rather as opposed to less.*

3 *What you do as a parent does affect your child, but you are the expert on your own child. You do not have to be perfect, just 'good enough'.*

4 *Making sense of your own childhood is important and affects how you are as a parent – try to think back to specific incidents and talk them over with a friend.*

5 *A parenting style which is both loving and firm is best for your child and for you. Notice when you manage to do this and analyse what went well.*

6 *Having fun is a vital part of being a parent, with and without your children.*

7 *Bringing up small children is stressful. Remember to find ways to nurture your relationship with your partner too.*

8 *Children will pick up on your stress; it is hard for them to be happy if you are not.*

9 *Think what you can do during the course of a normal day to lift your spirits.*

10 *Consciously register, deepen and bring back happy memories and help your children to do the same.*

Understanding your child's behaviour

In this chapter you will learn:
- *a way to understand your child's behaviour*
- *how to identify needs underlying behaviour.*

A parent's story

Julie just can't see what's got into her daughter. When they walked to school, Anna, who is six, always used to hold on to the pushchair without any problems. But now she doesn't just refuse to hold on; she runs ahead and scares the living daylights out of her mother – it's such a busy road. She can't possibly catch up with her daughter with Jake in the pushchair. 'I've tried reasoning with her ... I've threatened punishments ... I've shouted, but nothing works,' says Julie. 'We have the same old battle every morning. It's such a bad start to the day.' They both end up at the school gate in a foul temper.

Scenes such as this are familiar to many a parent. If it's not the walk to school, it could be fighting, name-calling, dawdling when you are in a rush to leave the house, getting up after bedtime, or arguing over the computer.

With the pace of life getting ever faster, and so much being done at the flick of a switch, you might well want a quick tip which will 'sort' the offending behaviour in an instant. But unlike computers, which shape so much of our twenty-first century lifestyle, your children are alive, with all the complexities which make them human: mystifying, sometimes infuriating, and often enormously gratifying. In today's busy lives, it is hard to find time to pause for reflection, but when it comes to understanding your children's behaviour, there is no substitute for really thinking things through. You will discover that there is much more going on beneath their actions than meets the eye.

Julie's attempts to control her daughter all ended in failure because she couldn't understand what Anna was thinking and feeling, and was therefore tackling the problem from the wrong angle. If you find yourself having the same clashes again and again, it can be worth asking yourself what your child is really trying to achieve: what is the source of this behaviour? The good news is that this book will give you greater understanding of why children (and adults!) behave as they do, and you will develop strategies for bringing about some positive changes.

Insight

Somehow I kept reacting the same way when my children persisted in doing something I didn't like – even though it didn't work. Stepping back and asking myself what was really going on and what I could do differently was the first step in changing things. 'If you do what you've always done, you'll get what you've always got.' – *Glenda*

Your starting point for dealing with difficult moments is to look at what is going on behind the scenes. An awareness of causes will give you a much better grasp of where to begin.

The link between behaviour, feelings and needs

Looking back at Julie's story, you might be wondering what lies behind Anna's difficult behaviour (think of the C of ACT in Chapter 1). What might she be feeling?

If she were able to put it into words, Anna would probably reveal that she is embarrassed and frustrated that her mother still holds her hand as if she were a baby. She feels trapped and wants to be trusted to walk on her own. She's angry with her mother for shouting at her. So she runs ahead to be independent and find some peace. Anna longs to be seen as more grown-up than her little brother. She needs a sense of achievement, responsibility and independence. She feels capable of walking safely on the pavement without running out into the road and needs respect and recognition. Looking at the picture below, you will see that the link between behaviour, feelings and needs is rather like a fountain. Anna's behaviour – running ahead of her mother – is the expression of a number of different feelings which spring up from some deep-seated needs.

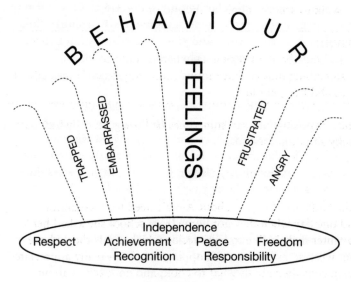

Figure 3.1 Needs Fountain.

Once Julie has considered the emotions underlying her daughter's 'unreasonable' behaviour, she can see that Anna is not running ahead simply to annoy and frighten her. In fact, Julie has just observed the C (child) stage in ACT (see Chapter 1) and paused to see the picture from her daughter's perspective. She wonders whether Anna might also need reassurance that she is still loved and valued after the birth of her brother, and to have status as the big sister.

To bring about a change in the problematic walk to school, Julie must address the needs behind Anna's defiant behaviour. This could be done in various ways. She may choose to show respect for Anna's growing up by giving her independence and responsibility in small things while not risking her safety on a busy road. She can find opportunities to give her daughter recognition for her achievements. She may honour Anna's need for peace by discussing the walk to school calmly at the end of the day.

> **Insight**
> Talking about a tricky issue when it is not so 'hot' is something that we have found really important, especially as children get older.

And, surprisingly, it can sometimes be little gestures which turn a tricky situation around.

A parent's story – continued

Julie had been thinking about Anna's need for recognition, and one day when they got home from school she asked her daughter if she'd like to help decide which meals they'd have that week so as to make a shopping list. Anna really appreciated being consulted about what to cook, and got excited about choosing all her favourite things. The funny thing is that since that time she has held on to Jake's pushchair on the dangerous road without another word. Julie said: 'It's as if my asking her views about meal planning has given her the freedom to co-operate with my wishes on road safety.' A bit of respect on both sides.

The fountain of needs

The important principle behind Julie's story is that people will behave in a certain manner as a result of their needs, and that these can be met in all sorts of different, creative ways. This story illustrates a cause and effect process which you will recognize in your children's actions as well as your own.

Behind every smile or giggle, every shouted insult or tantrum there are **feelings** welling up inside. Often a child may not become conscious of these feelings or even have the words to name them, so they tend to spill out in actions. This is sometimes called 'acting out'. Just as behaviour springs from feelings, these, in turn, arise from very deep **needs**. Everyone has needs – for love, acceptance, attention and much more. Understanding what you need and what your children need is a key step in resolving problems and helping you all feel happier and more satisfied with life.

The fountain image will help you to visualize this process.

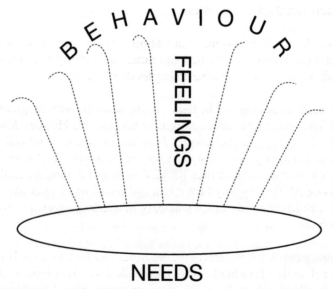

Figure 3.2 Needs Fountain for you to fill in.

The jets of water represent your feelings, which spring out of the pool of needs and spill over into behaviour – the droplets at the end of the jets. Your needs lie in the pool, which represents your deepest inner being.

Think of your feelings as the signal pointing to what you need. Having your needs met brings joy, happiness and satisfaction. When you don't get what you need, you may feel upset, angry, frustrated or disgruntled; and these feelings will come out in one way or another in your behaviour.

Here are some simple examples of this process, where the need is easily met:

NEED	FEELING	BEHAVIOUR
I need to be comfortable	I feel cold	I put on a jersey
I need nutrition	I feel hungry	I eat an apple
I need companionship	I feel lonely	I call a friend

When needs are not met

While almost all behaviour is an attempt – often unconscious – to meet a valid human need, there are times when it may fail to reach its objective, as the following examples demonstrate:

Eric **needs** to belong and he **feels** left out when he hears laughter and fun coming from downstairs after his bedtime. He goes down and asks for a drink (**behaviour**). How his parents respond will depend on their parenting style as well as their mood and stress levels at that moment. If they **REACT** without thinking (instead of using **ACT**), they may blame Eric and send him straight back to bed with harsh words which will leave him feeling rejected as well as left out.

Naomi **needs** love. She **feels** that her Mum and Dad love the baby more than they love her because they smile and coo at him, so she starts talking in baby language in an attempt to be as loveable as her little brother (**behaviour**). A typical reaction of parents might be to tell Naomi not to be silly. She will then feel even less loved.

In both these scenarios, the child may well **behave** in more extreme ways since their **feelings** will become increasingly acute as long as the **need** is unfulfilled.

As you progress through this book, you will learn how these parents could respond more constructively. You will have a chance to reflect on the value of feelings and how best to manage them. You will be able to explore strategies which will help you look after your own needs (remember the oxygen mask in Chapter 2) as well as those of your children.

When needs are not met, people experience uncomfortable feelings which drive them into action. On the other hand, when the need is fulfilled, pleasant feelings ensue, indicating that everything is fine, as you can see in the following example:

Peter is hungry on leaving work and feels grouchy when he arrives home; but after eating with his family he's laughing and smiling, lying on the floor with his children, making a house out of cards. His needs for food, love and fun are all met, so he feels happy and satisfied, and it shows in his behaviour when he laughs, smiles and plays.

Exercise: What is really going on here?

Think about some behaviour in your child that you find difficult.

Describe the behaviour here:

What feelings might your child have?

Beneath these feelings, what might your child need?

You might find it helpful to write these on the Needs Fountain diagram on page 36.

A parent's story

Laura's ten-year-old son Owen was often answering back and refusing to do anything she asked. Things came to a head when he wouldn't get down to his maths homework one Saturday morning and was just whining on and on about wanting to go to McHamburger Heaven. Laura shouted; he slammed the door; and the weekend felt ruined.

That night she discussed it with her husband, Peter, and they thought about what the feelings and needs might be behind his behaviour. Perhaps the emotions being expressed were to do with feeling left out in some way – which might explain the whining – and the need would be for attention.

She came up with one breakthrough – it was to do with being together as a family. McHamburgers was a child-centred place where they all sat round the table and chatted. Now that she was working more hours and Owen's big brother, Rory, was often out at meal times they didn't manage to eat together very often. Laura made a plan to have a proper family dinner on a Monday, the day she gets home early, as pinning Rory down at the weekend was too hard.

Looking at the questions in the exercise can be helpful whenever you are faced with behaviour you find upsetting or irritating, whether in a child or another adult. Many parents have found the **'Needs Fountain'** useful in understanding friends, partners, in-laws or work colleagues. You can also use this 'tool' to unravel your own strong feelings: 'How am I feeling? What do I need?' – the **A** part of **ACT**.

> **Insight**
>
> I can easily get caught up in strong feelings – especially if I'm angry. It's much harder to stop and think: what needs lie behind these feelings? When I do, it becomes clearer what course of action I should take, and then I feel calmer. – *Glenda*

Bearing needs in mind

There will always be occasions, however, when you haven't the luxury of thinking things through: those times when you're late for school, your child's behaviour has upset Granny, or you are trying to get some quarrelling children into the car in a hurry. Then, even if you don't understand why your child is acting in a certain way, just knowing that her behaviour arises from feelings and is an attempt to meet a valid human need can help you stay calm and deal more positively with the situation.

Chapters 7, 8 and 11, on anger, co-operation and boundaries, show how you can help your children meet their needs in ways that are acceptable to others.

Basic human needs

All too often deep human needs go unrecognized because they don't show on the outside. Only behaviour can be seen or heard. Needs lie invisibly in your heart of hearts, in the pool beneath the fountain.

This is true for you as much as for all the people who cross your path. Whether you are confronted with an obstinate child or a surly traffic warden, an overbearing boss or a withdrawn eight-year-old, their actions will spring from feelings and needs which may never be acknowledged.

Here are some universal human needs:

Love,
food, drink, sleep,
shelter, warmth, relaxation, exercise,
stability, protection, routine, predictability, structure,
fairness, boundaries, economic security, independence,
affection, physical closeness, friendship, belonging,
recognition, respect, acceptance, achievement, being valued,
understanding, creativity, personal growth,
mental stimulation, spiritual nurturing,
freedom.

You may want to add other needs to this list as they occur to you. The most fundamental of all these, however, and the one which drives much of your children's behaviour, is the need to feel loved and valued, and to express love in return.

A child might act out an inner feeling in all kinds of ways to get her parents' attention and love which she so deeply needs. The more a child acts out, the more parents may show their displeasure with the child. The more displeasure is expressed, the worse the child will feel about herself, and the worse she will act out. You can see the vicious circle. The following story illustrates this problem and shows how it can be resolved.

A parent's story

Shanti complained that, on returning home from school, her son would pester her while she was trying to cook the evening meal. 'Hari kept coming in to the kitchen moaning about something, or else disrupted his sister's games. I used to scold him and tell

(Contd)

him to stop bothering me. He would go away for a few moments and then come back asking me to look at something, wanting help with a game, or complaining that he was bored.' After attending a parenting group, Shanti learned about the power of listening, and thought she'd give it a try. On getting through the front door, she sat down for five minutes and gave Hari her undivided attention.

'I put my preoccupations on hold and really focused on him. For the first time, Hari told me about his friends and his teacher. I was so happy that he was opening up to me. After a little while, he went off and played happily and I got on with cooking the supper.'

Shanti could not believe how much calmer her son was once she had shown him that he was important to her. Those few minutes of undivided attention conveyed the message 'You matter to me', and Hari no longer had to repeatedly seek that affirmation from his mother. His need to be loved was met and he was freed up to play peacefully.

Often we hear parents say 'He's just looking for attention!'

Attention is a really basic need for children, and if they do not get positive attention they will seek negative attention – any attention is better than none. In the natural world it is a question of life or death. If a mother's attention wanders, her offspring is in danger of becoming a predator's next meal!

Exercise: How do your children express these needs?

What do your children do when they need:
Attention

Love and affection

A sense of belonging

To develop their own sense of identity/independence

PARENTS' COMMENTS

Celia, mother of Grace, Adam and Finlay:

'I always used to think my children were misbehaving just to annoy me, and I would get angry and shout. Now I've got a whole new perspective on their behaviour. I've come to see that when they do irritating things their behaviour stems from their own needs and may have nothing to do with me at all. Even if I don't understand what's going on exactly, I feel much less wound up.'

Ingrid, mother of Eric:

'Before I started thinking about feelings and needs behind behaviour, it never really occurred to me that Eric might feel left out when he was alone in his bedroom at night. That explained why he kept coming downstairs. He and I have talked about it, and he decided to put a few of his favourite teddies and toys on the shelf by his bed. He said he'll make up stories as he goes off to sleep about all their adventures.'

Things which have struck me in this chapter

Something I am going to try out

HAVE SOME FUN

Fly a kite

It is not difficult to find simple kites, even ones which will fold up and fit in your pocket. If you are feeling inventive, there are websites which show you how to make them.

On a windy day, take a kite to a large open space away from trees. One person may need to hold the kite while the other lets out the string until the kite can be released to fly up into the air. Then lengthen the string and watch it fly higher and higher. It is a wonderfully uplifting experience! Sometimes a kite will nose-dive to the ground, and you may need to run to get it airborne again.

10 THINGS TO REMEMBER

1 *Long running battles with your children require a fresh approach, and can rarely be resolved by a 'quick fix' solution.*

2 *It is worth asking yourself what your children are trying to achieve by their behaviour.*

3 *Children (and adults) behave as they do to try and meet universal, deep-seated needs.*

4 *These needs give rise to feelings, and then to behaviour. A good way to visualize this is as a fountain: the pool of needs, the jets of feelings and above these, the behaviour.*

5 *If needs are not met, behaviour becomes more extreme.*

6 *Unpleasant feelings are a useful signal that a need has not been addressed.*

7 *If you can find a way which is acceptable to you to meet your child's need, she is more likely to change her behaviour.*

8 *There are many creative ways of attending to needs.*

9 *Basic human needs range from the physical, like food and sleep, through love and belonging, to creativity, achievement and a sense of freedom.*

10 *If you think about what your child does in order to meet her needs, you will gain a better understanding of her behaviour.*

4

Valuing your child

In this chapter you will learn:
- *ways to show your children how important they are to you*
- *about the importance of touch*
- *approaches for building confidence and resilience*
- *a way of understanding differences in temperament.*

Valuing your children

As you were reminded in the last chapter, feeling loved and important to someone is a universal human need. It gives that inner warmth and strength that makes children feel that they are welcome in the world – the basis for happiness. Your family is one place where you want to be accepted for who you are rather than what you do and achieve. However, in the hurly-burly of family life it is all too easy to give children the message that they are all wrong rather than all right, and to discover that the majority of your communications with them are:

commands – 'Get ready for bed NOW!'
criticism – 'You clumsy oaf, you spilt it again!'
nagging – 'Don't forget your lunch box.'
preaching – 'You'll never amount to anything if you don't knuckle down to it.'

This chapter looks at what you can actually do and say to let children know that you cherish them – you know you love them, but do they? What would your child say if someone asked him: 'What does your Mum or Dad think of you?' Would he come out with some of the words that you had used about him in annoyance – 'a pest', 'a pain in the neck' – without any of the counterbalancing, loving words?

When your child comes into the room, do you see the light in his eyes or the stain on his T-shirt?

Maya Angelou

Showing you care

If you think back to the parenting styles graph in Chapter 2, this section helps you work on being warm. This is not the same as being soft. Parents worry that they will 'spoil' their children if they give them too much attention. 'Spoiling' happens when it is the child rather than the adult who is in charge of the allocation of time and resources in the family. How to balance everyone's needs has to be something that the parents decide. This includes the need for the grown-ups to have time and space to be more than just a Mum or Dad, and the changing needs of children as they grow up. Children can have input, which should increase as they get older, but the final decision is not with them. Chapter 11 covers ways of being firm in this way.

Exercise: Memories of being valued

Can you remember times when you felt valued as a child?

Who was the adult involved and what did they do or say?

Gloria, mother of Jasmine, Chantal and Nathan:

'My grandmother was always pleased to see me. She would smile, hold out her arms and her eyes would light up with joy when she opened the door and saw it was me. She hugged me and when she called me her 'treasure' I knew she meant it!'

Daniel, father of Zach, Martha, Naomi and Ben:

'I had a game with my Dad when I was little that he would throw me on the bed and then scoop me up again – I would shriek and laugh and beg him to do it again and again.'

It can be easier to remember times of being punished and told off than times when you felt valued. This is because people often remember frightening events more vividly than happy ones. Also, parents tend to be much more intense when they are angry than when they are pleased. Repeated positive experiences like those in the two memories above are what makes a happy childhood as much as the special occasions, like going to Disneyland.

> **Insight**
>
> In fact sometimes special treats are more for the adults than young children – I well remember having to leave pantomimes because they were too frightening, or getting to the front of the queue for the roundabout and a child bursting into tears and refusing to go on it. They were often much happier playing in the sandpit in the park. – *Doro*

Children can also benefit from the interest of another adult, a teacher or the parent of a friend, for example, who values them and notices their strengths.

Exercise: Valuing

Write down things that you do and say to show your child that you care about them.

Here are ways which some parents came up with when discussing this topic.

CUDDLES, HUGS AND KISSES

Children need touch to grow and thrive. If they seem to be growing out of cuddles, a shoulder, neck, hand or foot massage is often acceptable (more on touch later in the chapter).

SMILES AND EYE CONTACT

Smiling eye contact says: 'I love you'. Remember gazing into your baby's eyes? The eyes are the 'windows of the soul'.

BEING AWARE OF YOUR EXPRESSION AND TONE OF VOICE

One parent caught sight of her frowning face in the mirror. Another parent set up a tape recorder and was shocked by the sharpness of his tone during the evening meal.

GIVING TIME

Time is one of the strongest messages of love for a child. One-to-one time without other siblings is extra special. If this can be a time when you play on their terms, following their lead rather than your own agenda, so much the better.

SAYING 'I LOVE YOU', USING PET NAMES

Families have their own loving terms, often passed down from grandparents. Just be careful individual pet names don't have a teasing edge – 'fatty pumpkins' or 'baby baboon' may give a lasting message!

SAYING 'YOU ARE THE BEST AT BEING YOU IN THE WHOLE WORLD'

Every child is unique, no one else can be exactly like them. Even identical twins have different personalities. There is enough testing and comparing in their lives. Sometimes they need to hear 'I love you because you are you'.

PUTTING UP PICTURES, KEEPING THEIR CARDS AND NOTES

Showing you care about what they create, sticking up pictures and keeping Mother's and Father's Day cards, special pieces of school work, programmes of school plays and other records of achievement to look back at.

SWITCHING OFF THE PHONE

What message does it give a child when special times are invaded by others who are given priority?

LISTENING TO THEM AT BEDTIME

Asking them to say three things they liked about the day and what they are looking forward to the next day. Give them a chance to say what they didn't like too. You can also share good things and bad things that happened to you.

Insight

Parents have told us that when they do this regularly, their children start looking for good things during the day to remember and tell them about: an effective way to encourage a positive attitude.

WORK/HOME TRANSITION

Slowing down when you come home from work to get into 'child time' is really important and often requires a deliberate effort. A US survey asked children themselves about parents and work. The results showed that they were remarkably tuned in to the stresses and strains in their parents' workplaces, even when their parents said that they did not discuss work in front of them! Children's messages to parents included: 'Leave your work at work and put on your parenting suit at home' and 'Not to be angry and so grumpy when you get home from work and don't be so stressful at work.' Interestingly, children did not say that they wished their parents were not working, just that they should be less stressed.

A parent's story

Peter, father of Rory and Owen, made a conscious decision to make the transition between work and home a smoother one. He realized that his first utterance on coming through the door was usually critical, something like: 'What's all this mess on the table? I've had a long, hard day and I don't want to see this disgusting clutter when I get home!' He decided to take a deep breath and calm down before he came in through the front door, deliberately changing gear from work rhythm to family time. He subsequently said: 'Things are much better. I listen to the children telling me what they are up to, and I give us all some slack before we clear up. The boys are pleased to see me, and I just don't feel as irritable. The whole evening goes better.'

Difficult times

It can be hard sometimes to show your children you love them. If your parents were not ones to show affection, being demonstrative won't come naturally to you. Maybe you never got off on the right foot with your child after a difficult birth. Maybe you have 'fallen out of love' with them during a particularly stressful time for them or for you. Maybe you are looking after a child who is not your own (for example as a step-parent, foster-carer, adoptive parent), and so have missed out on the memories and baby milestones which help to build up a loving relationship.

You may have to make a conscious effort to change your habits, to express positive emotions and give more cuddles. Remember, the sense of touch increases levels of oxytocin, the internal chemical that is linked with love and attachment. Other ways of awakening loving feelings about a child are:

- ▶ *looking at them when they are asleep, and having the internal thought: 'You are loveable'*
- ▶ *remembering their more charming moments – perhaps looking at photos or a video*
- ▶ *making a list of the things you like about them*
- ▶ *thinking about yourself when you were their age*
- ▶ *talking to someone, maybe a grandparent, who does love them*
- ▶ *think about who they remind you of – are you mixing up feelings for someone else with feelings about them?*

Doing these things will help you start a 'virtuous circle' where positive attention leads to more loving behaviour between you. If you are still having problems, you may benefit from some professional help. Suggestions are included in the back of the book.

Insight
As a stepmother, I learned at first-hand about the importance of staying positive while a relationship develops over time. The skills absorbed in parenting courses were invaluable for building understanding and closeness. – *Doro*

FEELING VALUED

When children feel valued by those around them, they learn to value themselves – to have a sense of self-worth. Children with a sense of self-worth are more likely to:

- ▶ *co-operate and care about others*
- ▶ *care for themselves*
- ▶ *cope with the ups and downs of life*
- ▶ *achieve well at school or in other activities*
- ▶ *develop their potential.*

These are all important ingredients of happiness.

Chapter 8 covers gaining co-operation and going for the positive in family life. If you can increase the number of positive interactions and decrease the negative ones, everyone in your home will be happier.

The importance of touch

Touch is the first of all the senses to evolve and the skin is the largest organ of the body, developing from the same layers in the embryo as does the nervous system. Touch is known to be vital for babies: for example, premature babies who are gently massaged put on weight more quickly.

The classic experiment showing that touch is a basic need was carried out by Professor Harry F. Harlow in the 1950s. Baby monkeys were taken from their mothers and given the choice of two surrogate mothers built of wire – one had soft cloth around it and the other did not, but had a nipple providing milk. The babies spent much more time with the cuddly cloth-covered surrogate, even though the wire one was the source of food. Research on other mammals shows that when mothers give more physical contact, their babies grow up to be less fearful of exploring, even as adults. So, far from being mollycoddling, cuddles are the springboard for courage.

Touch is the instinctive human way of comforting when someone is in distress. When you think of TV footage of disasters, it is almost automatic to picture strangers with their arms around each other.

You are no less a source of comfort to your child. Loving touch produces natural feel-good chemicals in the brain – oxytocin, which is the neurotransmitter for love and attachment, and opioids, one of whose functions is to relieve pain. They help the body and brain to produce less of the stress hormones, so that your children can cope better with anxiety and fear. Touching raises your oxytocin levels too, so that you feel more loving towards your child.

One single parent who had a conflict-ridden relationship with her 11-year-old son reported that he became calmer and more affectionate when she managed to get into the habit of putting her hands casually on his shoulders when he was sitting down. Another mother found that her anxious eight-year-old loved to be rocked in her arms while she sang to her. Try to find the kind of touch which suits you and your children at the stage they are, and increase the amount you give it. Let 'I want a hug' be a common phrase in your family.

Touch says: 'You are beautiful' and 'You are safe'. Of course, sexual touch is not at all appropriate for children. There is more about this in Chapter 11 on boundaries and Chapter 13 on talking about difficult issues.

Building confidence and resilience

As well as inner warmth, happiness requires inner strength. How can you help your child to approach the world in a positive frame of mind? Knowing he is loved is a great start and gives confidence. Alongside showing warmth, parents often need to support their children to try new things. Studies of mothers show that they naturally make small challenges for their babies as they grow up, helping them to walk, for example, by putting something just out of reach. The same principle applies to older children – they need to be stretched, but not so much that they feel discouraged.

NOTICE WHAT GOES WELL RATHER THAN WHAT GOES WRONG

Aim to 'catch them being good' and give nine positive messages for one negative one. Try to be specific rather than saying 'good girl' or 'clever boy!'

You could say:

'I really like the way you mixed blue and green paint for the sea.'

'I appreciated your reading to your little sister while I cooked.'

PRAISE EFFORT AS MUCH AS RESULTS

This is a way to challenge perfectionism. Elder children particularly are prone to being perfectionists and can give up if they do not meet their own high standards.

You could say:

'You didn't give up on that model, even when you had to take it apart and start again.'

'You're getting the ball through the hoop much more often now. That shows how much you have practised. Well done!'

TREAT MISTAKES AND FAILURES AS WAYS TO LEARN

Ask 'What did you do? What went well? What went wrong?', and most importantly, 'What can you do differently next time?' Many business tycoons had failures before they found the right formula – it is really vital that children see learning as a process to try things out. Children who are afraid of failing stop themselves from trying out new things. Their learning becomes restricted and their lives are the poorer for it.

BE A 'TREASURY OF MEMORIES'

Remind your children about past achievements when they are lacking confidence in the present.

You could say:

'Remember when you managed to light the camp fire when we had all given up?'

'Remember when you were scared of going in for the tennis tournament and then won a prize?'

FIND QUICK WAYS TO SUCCESS

Sometimes it can be helpful to engineer some instant gratification, for example, in a project which will make your child feel good about himself. Cooking is a great way to do this, as everyone eats and praises the results.

LEARNING A SKILL TO ACHIEVE 'FLOW'

'Flow' is a concept which features in much literature about happiness. It is the experience of deep involvement in a task which is challenging and requires skill. Time stands still and the sense of self vanishes. This could be the sensation young children experience in play. Research on US teenagers found that those who frequently experienced 'flow' in playing music, sport or absorbing hobbies had higher scores on nearly every measure of psychological wellbeing. If your child has a passion in life, encourage it all you can.

FIND WAYS FOR THEM TO HELP OTHERS

Being a helper is a good way for children to feel more competent. Perhaps they can help a younger child to do or make something.

Being involved in charities and campaigns helps children to learn about the world and makes them feel that something can be done about global or local problems. Helping others is one of the pointers for happiness in later life too.

HELP THEM TO MAKE FRIENDS

Sometimes children need a bit of support to make friends. To have a friend, you have to be a friend. Discuss what that means; for example, taking an interest and listening, taking turns. Sometimes you have to take the lead in inviting a potential friend home, you can plan ahead with your child what they could play, and talk about being a host. Sometimes younger children can be good playmates for a child who finds his own age group difficult. If your child is going into a new situation, discuss possible questions to start a conversation, see if he wants to take a simple game or toy to break the ice.

Insight

Adults can underestimate the strength of feelings that children have about friends. They can be a 'buffer' to help children during stressful events such as the birth of a sibling or starting school.

Celebrating difference

To value your child for who he is and to understand his sometimes bewildering behaviour, it is essential that you first realize that your child is not you. Frustration with children often arises because parents implicitly assume their children are carbon copies of themselves or their siblings, particularly if they look alike. This fundamental misunderstanding can lead to a great deal of distress on both sides.

If your daughter is easygoing, you may be surprised and irritated when your son resists every instruction or suggestion. If one child loves variety, you may be taken aback when another finds new experiences a struggle, or if you were a daredevil and your daughter clings to your skirts, you may not know quite what to do.

How easy it is to assume that everyone thinks and operates in the same way!

Many parents unconsciously want their children to be an improved version of themselves, perhaps wishing to see their own unfulfilled potential given full expression in their children. They have learned life's lessons, and want to prevent their children making the same mistakes that they did. Wanting to pass on their wisdom wholesale, they are surprised when children want to learn about life in their own way. However, forcing a child into a mould that doesn't fit is a recipe for unhappiness.

You will find it much more helpful to recognize your child as an individual and encourage him to learn for himself and fulfil his own promise. A good place to start is to understand his personality type. Companies get the most out of their workforce by personality tests which show how each individual works best, and there is no reason why this method should be any less helpful in the home. There are many ways of categorizing personality which trace their roots over 2,000 years back to Hippocrates, who came up with the concept of the four 'humours'.

One test which is simple and easy to use gives each of the personality types an animal name:

▶ Lion
▶ Beaver
▶ Monkey
▶ Golden Retriever.

Taking an example of a father and son who have distinct character traits, you will see how differently they function, and how disappointed the father will be as long as he expects his son to be just like him:

Daniel is a **Lion**. Lions are motivated by power, have the ability to move from point A to point B and get things done efficiently. They like to achieve and excel. Zach, his son, is a **Monkey**, whose main motive is fun. Monkeys do things just for the joy of doing them, and are not interested in achievement or results. They live for the moment.

Daniel loves classical music and wishes he had the talent to play well. Zach is very gifted musically, and his father just can't understand why he won't practise more regularly: 'If I had half his talent, I'd be working on it every day! I get so frustrated seeing him waste such an immense gift!' Zach, on the other hand, is a very sociable type and is popular. Although he enjoys playing in the school orchestra and likes his teacher, a game of football with his friends is more important to him than the violin when he's finished his homework. He can't understand why his father keeps on nagging him to practise when it's not a priority for him.

This example shows how upset and frustrated parents can become when they expect their children to think and act in the same way as they do.

Their children will also feel like a disappointment because they don't fit into the pre-ordained shape.

> *Variety is the very spice of life that gives it all its flavour.*
> William Cowper

Your child will be happier when you value him for who he is rather than who you want him to be. You and your family may enjoy a light-hearted way of looking at your differences by doing the following 'Who's Who' personality test for yourselves. Be clear with your children that the animal types are not labels which define you, but rather 'tendencies'. Being aware of your tendencies helps you all to understand each other better.

WHO'S WHO?

Instructions: For each animal choose the words that best describe your personality. Count them, double the number and then record it.

LION

Likes leading	Takes charge
Confident	Determined
Firm	Enterprising
Enjoys challenges	Competitive
Problem solver	Productive
Bold	Purposeful
Goal driven	Loves choice
Strong willed	Independent
Self-reliant	Controlling
Likes freedom	Action oriented

'Let's do it now!'

Double the number chosen _____

BEAVER

Enjoys instructions	Accurate
Consistent	Controlled
Reserved	Predictable
Practical	Orderly
Factual	Conscientious
Perfectionist	Discerning
Detailed	Analytical
Inquisitive	Likes thinking-time
Persistent	Scheduled
Sensitive	Likes routine

'Let's consider this carefully'

Double the number chosen _____

MONKEY

Enthusiastic	Takes risks
Visionary	Impatient
Energetic	Talkative
Promoter	Friendly
Fun-loving	Likes variety
Spontaneous	Enjoys change
Creates new ideas	Group oriented
Happy-go-lucky	Initiator
Infectious laughter	Inspirational

'Trust me! It'll work out!'

Double the number chosen _____

GOLDEN RETRIEVER

Sensitive feelings	Loyal
Calm	Idealistic
Non-demanding	Gives in
Avoids confrontations	Tolerant
Loves friendship	Dislikes change
Optimistic	Sympathetic
Thoughtful	Nurturing
Patient	Likes appreciation
Good listener	Peace maker

'Let's see what everyone wants'

Double the number chosen _____

	Mark your score under each animal.		
Lion	Beaver	Monkey	Retriever

```
50 _____ 50

30 _____ 30

20 _____ 20

10 _____ 10

 0 _____  0
```

If you join up each score with a line, you will see your personality 'pattern'.

You can photocopy this chart for each member of your family, or else mark each person's scores and lines in different colours. You will see from doing this test that no one fits exactly into one category; so you can't pigeon-hole your children! Neither you nor your children will be only one animal type. People have many different aspects to their personalities, but have greater tendencies in one direction or another. It is also worth noting that different aspects of personality come to the fore at different times in people's lives.

Insight

One of my children found it hard to join in playground games as a small child and would linger on the edge of things. As an adult, he is the life and soul of the party! – *Glenda*

Lions – This personality likes to lead. Lions are good at making decisions and like to achieve. They enjoy challenges and are competitive. They like freedom and prestige.

Strengths: They bring gifts of vision and leadership, are decisive and direct. They get things done.

Weaknesses: Because Lions are thinking of the goal, they can step on others to reach it. They may not understand that directness can hurt people. Lions need to learn not to be too bossy or take charge in others' affairs.

Beavers – Thoughtful and mature, Beaver personalities are creative. They find rules and routine helpful. They desire to solve everything and take their time to do it right. They do not like sudden changes. They need reassurance.

Strengths: High standards, reliability, order and respect.

Weaknesses: Unrealistic expectations of self and others. Lack flexibility.

Beavers need to learn to relax and see the optimistic side of things.

Monkeys – Charming, inspiring, they like company and enjoy motivating others. They love fun and will hurry to finish jobs, which are therefore not always done well. They are the life and soul of the party, and often act impulsively. They are popular and trusting. They are notorious for messy rooms.

Strengths: Sociable, open, positive.

Weaknesses: Can be too talkative and not listen enough. Disorganized and slap-dash.

Monkeys need to learn to think before they act, remember commitments and follow things through.

Golden Retrievers – Reliable, stable, they are good at making friends and are loyal. They look for security, and do not like big changes. They can be very sensitive and caring. Retrievers have deep relationships, but usually only a few close friends.

They want to be loved by everyone and look for appreciation. They work best in a limited situation with a steady work pattern.

Strengths: Accommodating, calm, affirming.

Weaknesses: Indecisive; difficulty expressing emotions; too soft on other people.

Retrievers may need to learn to be more assertive, and to hold others to account.

While you will be very different in some aspects, you may be pleased to discover that you have some traits in common even with the person you consider to be your opposite in the family. Everyone wants to be loved, for example, and everyone desires freedom, to some degree. It is rather like being right or left handed – even somebody who is strongly right-handed will use their left hand for some things, such as holding a fork, or playing a piano bass line.

So here's where temperament theory is valuable. Although it is not an exhaustive study of character, it does give you some clues about yourself and why you behave as you do, and in observing those around you – particularly your children – you can become aware of their core needs and what motivates them.

As you become a little clearer about your children's characters, you can empathize with them and recognize what is likely to motivate them to co-operate. This enables you to bring out the best in them by building on their strengths, while avoiding some of the personality clashes which can drive you apart. It is important to note that personality profiling does not give an excuse for any weaknesses, but rather points to the areas which you and your children need to work on.

For example, Monkeys might need help with prioritizing, and Retrievers with standing up to peer pressure.

Penny, mother of Mia and Abby, said:

'After doing the animal test, it suddenly became clear to me why Mia gets so fraught about being late for school. In that way, she is a typical Beaver. Abby drives her crazy because she's so laid back – she's still vaguely looking for her socks when it's time to leave home. In so many ways, I can see the Monkey in her. They just don't function the same way; so now I realize I'll have to find different strategies for each of them in order to get out of the house in a calmer way.'

ALL CHILDREN ARE UNIQUE

While it may be possible to classify people into different personality 'types', ultimately every single human being is unique. Your child can never be the same as you or anyone else. At present, there are well over six and a half thousand million (6.5 billion) people on Earth, with more being born every second. Each one is unique. There never has been and never will be anyone else like your child.

Even identical twins – brought up with the same values, the same surroundings, hearing the same stories and sent to the same school – will be different, because although their genes are the same, their individual experience of the world is different.

Many misunderstandings arise when mothers and fathers fail to recognize that everyone in their family sees things from their own unique point of view.

Hari (4): 'Mummy, can you time me running to that tree and back?'

Shanti: 'Sorry, I can't. I haven't got a second hand.'

Hari: 'But, Mummy, you have got two hands!'

Perhaps this chapter will have opened your eyes afresh to the variety in your family. Enjoy the differences for all the richness they bring to life. As someone once said:

> *Diversity is the one true thing we all have in common. Celebrate it every day.*

Anonymous

Practising **ACT** and thinking about the **Needs Fountain** will bring greater closeness and harmony between you and your children. In the following chapters, on feelings and listening, you will learn further ways to enhance understanding and empathy with them.

PARENTS' COMMENTS

Celia, mother of Grace, Adam and Finlay:

'On Mothers' Day at school every child gave their mother a card and said what they loved about them. My daughter said she loved me because I helped her with her homework! Everyone else's children said things like 'Mummy hugs me and sings at bedtime'. It was a wake-up call to me to find more loving ways to be together.'

Sarah, mother of Zach, Martha, Naomi and Ben:

'The animal test was helpful for me. I saw that my eldest son and I had far more in common than I'd realized. I'm going to keep everyone's uniqueness in mind and stop saying: "You children ...", which pops out of my mouth far too often.'

Things which have struck me in this chapter

Something I am going to try out

HAVE SOME FUN

Interesting questions
You can write the following questions on small slips of paper and put them into a box or bag. In turn, each person closes their eyes and draws out a question.

- *Where would you go for your perfect holiday?*
- *You are on an aeroplane. Out of anyone in the world, who would you choose to sit next to?*
- *What is your all-time favourite article of clothing?*
- *If you could be any character from a story, who would you be?*
- *If you could take up a musical instrument, what would it be?*
- *What is the job you least like doing?*
- *What is the most beautiful place you can remember?*
- *If you could be any animal, what would you be?*

Either: only the person who draws out the question answers it, or: everyone playing the game can answer each question.

You choose. It is very important to remain silent and listen while each person is speaking. Of course, you can add your own questions.

10 THINGS TO REMEMBER

1 *Feeling loved and valued is vitally important for a child's wellbeing. You may have to work at loving a child, but all children deserve to be loved. Get help if this is hard for you.*

2 *Try to make sure you have given a surplus of positive versus negative messages to your child by the end of a day.*

3 *Time is the strongest message of love a child can receive. Protect 'special time' from interruptions by phone calls and messages.*

4 *Touch is vital for all mammals, including humans. It produces the brain chemicals of attachment that make love grow and guard against stress.*

5 *Think of ways in which you can have more touch and cuddles in your family life, whatever age your child is.*

6 *Confidence comes from feeling competent. Stretch your child enough for a challenge but not so much that he is discouraged by failure.*

7 *Encourage by praising effort and treating mistakes as useful ways to learn. Be a 'treasury of memories' to remind your child of past successes.*

8 *Help your children to make and keep friends by discussing what friendship means.*

9 *It is useful to observe the traits and habits of your children to see which approach will work best for each child; but don't see them as being set in stone: they can change as they grow up.*

10 *Remember that children are different from each other, and from their parents, and value those differences.*

5

Recognizing feelings

In this chapter you will learn:
- *about basic emotional operating systems that all mammals have*
- *ways to recognize and name feelings*
- *how one feeling can overlay another.*

A parent's story

One evening Gloria is sorting laundry outside the bathroom door while Chantal and Nathan are brushing their teeth. Suddenly shouts and screams break out: 'I hate Chantal. She is always bossing me around, I don't have to do what she says!'

'Well, you are such a baby you can't even brush your teeth properly, eurgh, you're spitting on my hand!'

'Chantal and Nathan, I am getting really fed up with this bickering at bedtime, just get finished in the bathroom and get to bed.'

'Waaah, she pushed me, my mouth is bleeding, look!'

'Cry-baby, that's not blood, it's toothpaste!'

'I am bleeding, I hate you, you are so mean!'

'CHILDREN, INTO BED NOW! IT'S STORY TIME!'

(Contd)

To Gloria's amazement, five minutes later, the two children are cuddled up together listening to a story as if nothing had happened, while her nerves are still jangling from the row.

Feelings are so strong in children because they live in the moment, and have not yet developed the higher parts of their brain which help to regulate and give a perspective on strong emotions. Your pre-frontal cortex, the part of the brain that works out consequences and controls impulses, is not fully developed until you are in your early twenties. Parents make a vital contribution to this development. Sometimes you have to act as a kind of pre-frontal cortex for your child, keeping her safe, giving names to sometimes overwhelming feelings and providing routine and structure for her life until she learns to do it for herself.

It is important for parents to bear in mind that girls can be as much as four to six years ahead of boys in verbal abilities, so they can put their feelings into words earlier and more easily. This makes it even more important to help boys understand their emotions!

Emotional literacy

Emotional literacy – the ability to recognize and understand emotional states in yourself and in other people and to respond constructively to them – is strongly linked to mental health and wellbeing. It can be more important than IQ for career success too, because it is the bedrock of good relationships which smooth the way for learning and managing in all kinds of situations. Simply showing you understand and care, acknowledging feelings and giving them a name is a good start to helping your child along the road to emotional health.

You cannot stop feelings any more than you can stop a sneeze, but you can help your children learn not to act on them before due consideration. As a parent, one of your most important tasks is to help your child to recognize and handle strong emotions and to develop ways of thinking about feelings. Helping with emotion regulation starts when you soothe your baby, or play with her until she laughs and shrieks and then calms down. It continues into the teen years, when you comfort her distress and share her joyful moments.

Neuroscientists have found that the way a child is parented actually makes a difference to his or her brain. Pathways are created and then strengthened between different parts of the brain through repeated everyday interactions, be they laughing together or giving comfort. Though these pathways grow more quickly before the age of three, the brain is not fully developed until a person's early twenties. Research shows that parts of the brain can grow even up to old age through conscious practice: through meditation, for example, or – famously – learning all the streets of London as black cab drivers have to do.

Insight

Recently neuroscientists have found that adolescence is a time when the brain is growing and being 'rewired' too. We find this useful for parents of teenagers to bear in mind!

RESEARCH ON FEELINGS

Until quite recently, feelings were not considered to be a worthy topic for scientific research. Psychologists and neuroscientists put more emphasis on the study of thinking and reasoning. Now, discoveries about the biochemical basis of emotions and ways of studying the living brain through functional Magnetic Resonance Imaging (fMRI) have put feelings at the centre of the study of mind and behaviour.

Feelings are essential for survival, in today's world as much as in the days when mammoths roamed the countryside. If you cannot build and repair relationships, or have a good idea about who to trust and who to avoid, or predict someone's probable reactions, it will be hard for you to survive and thrive. People with Autistic Spectrum Disorder, for example, have problems because of their difficulty in recognizing their own emotions and those of others.

Basic feelings in mammals

Researchers since Darwin have argued that there are basic emotions common to all humans, and indeed all mammals – though they do not always agree which emotions these are!

Professor Jaak Panksepp is an eminent researcher in the field whose work brings together the study of behaviour, psychology and neuroscience. He makes the case that emotions arise from patterns of neural and chemical responses that are rooted in the evolutionarily ancient parts of the brain, shared by all mammals and, to some extent, reptiles as well. Although learning and culture affect how we express and understand our emotions, it can be helpful to bear in mind these basic 'emotional operating systems' when we are trying to understand our children's behaviour – and indeed our own.

Here is his list of primordial feelings. Capital letters are used to show that these are words used for systems which may be the wellspring for a range of related emotions:

FEAR – Triggers for this emotion include pain or threat of pain, darkness, angry faces and voices, snakes and spiders. It leads to fight or flight, or for some children 'freezing' (shutting down and hiding their faces).

RAGE – Set off by frustration of a need or expectation, being restrained and prevented from doing something. It can lead to attacking, shouting, biting; think of a toddler resisting being strapped into a pushchair.

SEEKING – Includes curiosity, anticipation, interest in exploring and novelty, learning new things. It is linked with the distress system, so that, for example, toddlers are braver about exploring when they feel secure, and something which interests them can soothe their distress.

SEPARATION DISTRESS – Activated by the absence of a loved one with whom you feel safe and loving; for young children being apart from such a person causes panic, mourning and despair. Distress at separation from parents gradually diminishes as children get older, but can be revived at times of anxiety or illness.

LOVE/CAREGIVING – The urge to nurture and comfort others. This is not exclusively female and is evident in young children. Professor Panksepp's brain research seems to show that humans are a caring species, not a selfish one!

PLAY – Linked with both physical and social learning, rough and tumble play is vital for all young mammals – children as much as puppies. Professor Panksepp put forward the theory that attention deficit disorder can in certain cases be caused by lack of opportunity for this kind of play in children between the ages of three and six. Playfulness encompasses play on words and jokes as children get older, and is an important part of adult relationships too.

LUST – A strong feeling which is not relevant to children until puberty – except that they would not exist without it!

Insight

Parents sometimes ask us: 'Where is happiness in this list?' Happiness has many dimensions: feeling safe, being able to act freely without being frightened; caring and being cared for but also learning new things; the pleasure of being playful and the satisfaction of being creative and achieving.

RECOGNIZING EMOTIONS IN CHILDREN

Bearing in mind these universal underlying feelings can help parents to show understanding and avoid overreacting to some of the things their children do and say. As you saw in Chapter 3, feelings arise out of basic needs, which are sometimes met and sometimes frustrated. If you can understand your child's feeling, you can often work out the underlying need and how to calm things down.

A parent's story

Amina reported that her daughter Noor was finally going in to school without crying and clinging, after months of distress for them both. Amina had felt desperate. She was anxious to get off to work on time. At the same time she felt sad herself at seeing Noor so upset, and embarrassed as well, because she felt other parents were judging her. She was also irritated, as she knew from the teacher that when she finally did go, Noor was fine.

After talking things over in her parenting group, Amina saw that it was natural for Noor to feel upset when she left, and also natural that she then got interested in other things and calmed down.

She said: 'I told her that I understood how much she missed me. I gave her a little hankie with my favourite scent on it to keep in her pocket. And I found out what she was doing that day in school to help her focus on something she was going to enjoy.'

Noor's separation distress was replaced by her curiosity about new things, her seeking system – she was interested in what was happening in school. Her mother putting words to her feelings at the moment of parting and showing understanding rather than irritation also helped her out of her panic at being left. Having the handkerchief was a reminder of her mother's love all day.

A child will learn to think about feelings and to deal with them through a parent or carer's communication – their tone of voice, touch and words. If she has been told not to be 'silly' when she is upset, or angrily commanded to 'calm down' when she's excited, she will never be at ease with her emotions. If, on the other hand, she has been responded to sensitively, she will gradually be able to calm herself in stressful situations, work out what she needs in order to feel better without hurting anyone else and ask for help if she needs it. She will also be able to handle positive emotions without over-excitement.

It is easy for an adult to react to 'over the top' behaviour in children by being 'OTT' themselves.

A grandfather's story

Gerard was playing around with a football in the park with his grandson's friends and their Dads. One little boy, Leon, started getting over-excited. He was rushing around shouting and being rough with the younger ones. His own father reacted by getting angry and shouting at him, which made him even more 'hyper'. Gerard took him off with his grandson and got him to practise shooting goals on the next door pitch. Gerard said: 'When he had to concentrate, he calmed down. I knew he would!'

In this case, another grown-up who was less emotionally involved was able to focus Leon, engaging his seeking system so that he had to think about what he was doing, and that quieted him. Children really need an adult to make sense of what is happening to them and help them to find strategies to cope with it. Adults need to be able to think about feelings, their own and their child's, if they are going to teach their children by example.

Insight

I know how difficult it is to stop and think when in the grip of strong emotions. Everyone will have their own ways to get into the thinking part of their brain, and I learned from another parent that taking one deep breath really helps; breathing out for longer than breathing in is particularly calming. – *Doro*

Identifying feelings

You have a wealth of words to describe how you are feeling; they refine and elaborate on the primary emotions. One of the ways you help your children deal with feelings is to increase their vocabulary of feeling words so that they can talk about them accurately.

Exercise: Your vocabulary of feeling words

Write down all the words you can think of which are variations of:

Happy

Sad

Angry

Frightened

Now take two words from each of the categories of feeling and ask yourself: 'Where do I feel this in my body? What is the physical sensation that I associate with this emotion?

If you compare notes with a friend or your learning companion, you may be surprised to find differences as well as similarities.

Teresa, mother of Callum, Sean and Logan:

'When I am getting wound up by the boys I find that my fists are clenched and I am digging my nails into my palms. I know then that I need to leave the room for a few minutes.'

Celia, mother of Grace, Adam and Finlay:

'I remember once when I was really happy on holiday by the sea, walking on the hard sand by the waves and I felt so light I was almost bouncing in the air.'

Insight

I often get a sensation coming up from the pit of my stomach when I feel anxious, and hum to get rid of it! My husband pointed this out to me years ago; I hadn't even realized. Now when I find myself humming I stop and ask myself what the matter is. – *Doro*

It must be significant that the word for feeling is the same for an emotion and a physical sensation. Indeed, receptors for the chemical messengers for feelings have been found all over the body, not just in the brain. So being more aware of your bodily sensations and linking them with feelings is a useful way of identifying what is really going on for you in any situation.

As children get older, they begin to feel and understand more complicated social emotions such as jealousy, guilt, embarrassment and pride. These are feelings which are linked with our relationships in a group and how we feel about ourselves vis à vis others. There are probably more feelings than there are words for – indeed, other languages have words such as the German '*Schadenfreude*' – joy in another's misfortune, or the Yiddish '*nachas*' – pride in your child's accomplishments, which are instantly recognizable as feelings even though there is no equivalent noun in English.

FACIAL EXPRESSIONS

Facial expression is the primary way that other people tell how we are feeling.

Charles Darwin was a pioneer in the field of researching feelings, studying facial expressions for emotions in humans and animals.

He suggested that six primary emotions – fear, rage, happiness, sadness, surprise and disgust – were universally recognizable.

Have a look at the 'feelings faces' on these two pages which illustrate various emotions, some simple and some more complex.

Aggressive	Angry	Anxious	Apologetic	Arrogant
Bashful	Blissful	Bored	Cautious	Cold
Concentrating	Confident	Curious	Demure	Determined
Disappointed	Disapproving	Disbelieving	Disgusted	Distasteful
Eavesdropping	Ecstatic	Enraged	Envious	Exasperated
Exhausted	Frightened	Frustrated	Grieving	Guilty
Happy	Horrified	Hot	Hungover	Hurt

You may find yourself copying some of these expressions. Interestingly, scientists have found that making a facial expression can actually lead you to feel the emotion you are showing. So if you smile you'll feel happier, and if you scowl you'll feel annoyed. Maybe then, if a builder shouts: 'Smile, love, it may never happen!' as you walk by, he is doing you a favour!

Hysterical	Idiotic	Indifferent	Innocent	Interested
Jealous	Loving	Lonely	Lovestruck	Meditative
Mischievous	Miserable	Negative	Obstinate	Optimistic
Pained	Paranoid	Perplexed	Prudish	Puzzled
Regretful	Relieved	Sad	Satisfied	Sheepish
Shocked	Smug	Surly	Surprised	Suspicious
Sympathetic	Thoughtful	Turned-on	Undecided	Withdrawn

It is worth noting that, around puberty, children lose some of their ability to 'read' facial expressions, perhaps as a result of the changes in their brains at this time. They may mistake fear for anger, for example. This skill gradually returns as they go through the teenage years.

People with varying degrees of autism find it difficult or impossible to 'read' facial expressions or understand other people's emotions. This means that their social relationships will be problematic. In life people need to be able to make a good guess at others' feelings and motivations in any given situation. Even driving is difficult if you cannot work out what someone else is likely to do next.

All children, and especially those with ASD (Autistic Spectrum Disorder), can benefit from some coaching about facial expressions. When you are looking at a story book with pictures, or watching a favourite 'soap', ask: 'What do you think they are feeling? What can you tell by looking at their face?' Find real life situations to ask the same question.

A parent's story

Sarah realized that her daughter Martha had grown a lot bigger than her friends. One day, when she was in the school playground, she saw Martha picking up a much smaller friend. This girl obviously didn't like it, but Martha seemed oblivious. Sarah went up close and said, in an enquiring rather than critical tone: 'Martha, look at Marie's face – is she happy or unhappy when you pick her up like that?' The two girls ended up laughing, and Sarah noticed that Martha didn't do this again.

MICRO-EXPRESSIONS

Some people are very skilled at disguising their facial expressions (a hard thing to do, maybe this is why we admire good acting so much). However, careful study shows milliseconds of fleeting expressions which can be very revealing.

Laura, mother of Rory and Owen:

'When my youngest was about to throw a tantrum, I sometimes saw just a little smile before the screaming started. I knew then that he was trying it on rather than being overwhelmed by his feelings!'

Teresa, mother of Callum, Sean and Logan:

'Logan came home from school seeming very cheerful, but I saw a sad expression cross his face when he thought I wasn't looking at him. It turned out that the teacher had shouted at him for not having his football boots with him, and he knew I was putting off buying him a new pair till the start of next month when our pay-checks came in.'

Look carefully at faces and you will be amazed at what you can spot. It will often back up a gut feeling that you have anyway about a situation.

Layers of feelings

Of course, feelings are not always simple – sometimes one feeling can overlay another one. For example, at the end of a school year, you may feel proud of your child's achievements, but underneath that there may be sadness that she is growing up so fast, and anxiety about how she will cope with the challenges to come. The classic 'top' feeling is anger, which can often overlay fear. An example is when your child runs near a busy road.

There is a longer discussion of layers of feelings in Chapter 7 on anger and tantrums.

Insight

I know that when I have very intense feelings they are almost always a tangle of emotions, which can be very uncomfortable. I have found that looking at the 'feelings faces' and working out the strands one by one can help to resolve this knot. – *Glenda*

Awareness of feelings

This chapter has given you opportunities and different approaches to think about feelings. This is important, because if you and your children are not aware of your feelings, they may emerge in other ways. For example, it is all too easy to mistake anxiety for hunger and try to damp down feelings through constant snacking. Children will often 'act out' feelings in behaviour if they cannot communicate them in words. There will be more about this in the next chapter.

It is also important to be fully aware of positive feelings. The human brain remembers negative feelings more easily and vividly than positive ones. You can help yourself and your children to be happier by fully savouring moments of joy and contentment. Make a point of stopping and thinking about what you will remember about that special time, and consciously store happy memories in your head and your heart.

Talk about happy memories with your children too.

PARENTS' COMMENTS

Amina, mother of Hussein and Noor:

'If I think about where I feel sadness, I realize it is in my heart and behind my eyes. If I have a bit of a weep I do feel better.'

Travis, father of Jasmine, Chantal and Nathan:

'I used to get annoyed with my kids for wrestling on the floor and jumping on the beds. Now I understand that playing like that is natural and good for them. They love it if I join in, and sometimes I just keep an eye on them to make sure they don't hurt each other or damage anything.'

HAVE SOME FUN

The 'Mmmm' game
See if you and your children can communicate without using words,
by just saying 'mmmm' for five minutes. It is surprising how much
you can pick up from tone and facial expression alone.

10 THINGS TO REMEMBER

1   Children's brains are still developing their pre-frontal cortex, the part that helps to manage strong emotions and plan ahead.

2   Basic feelings which all mammals have include separation distress, playfulness and seeking/curiosity. Understanding these natural feelings will help you to sympathize with your child and help her to make sense of them.

3   Everyday interactions with your child, the way you soothe her or incite her curiosity, actually affect her brain. Early patterns are strongest, but the brain can develop new pathways throughout life.

4   You can increase the vocabulary of feeling words that you use yourself and with your child, and link them to physical sensations so that you become quicker at recognizing them.

5   Coach your child to recognize emotions in others through their expressions, using TV or real life situations.

6   Watch out for 'micro-expressions' in others. They can reveal hidden emotions.

7   Looking at the feelings faces can help your child identify her emotions.

8   Children will often 'act out' feelings through behaviour if they cannot communicate them in words.

9   Remember that feelings can be layered, one strong feeling can overlay another.

10 Try to 'imprint' happy times in your memory and remind your child of happy times too.

6

Dealing with feelings

In this chapter you will learn:
- *what happens when feelings are contradicted*
- *ways to react to strong feelings – your own and your children's*
- *approaches to common worries*
- *how to express your feelings without blaming others for them.*

Families are full of feelings. You might describe families as the cauldrons in which the substances that make us human are mixed and boiled up. Sometimes wonderful aromas of love and happiness steam out, other times they boil over and the smell of burning fills the air! How you deal with your own and your children's feelings – both the negative and the positive ones – is a really important part of helping them grow up to cope with life's ups and downs. Showing you understand how someone else is feeling and being able to explain your own feelings to another person are essential abilities to build trust and intimacy in families and friendships, which in turn are fundamental for happiness in life. Parents are sometimes frightened that naming a feeling will make it stronger and that children will get entrenched in it. On the contrary, naming and acknowledging a feeling helps to dissipate it, as the child feels he is being heard and understood.

In this chapter, there is a section on ways to tackle common anxieties in childhood, some tips about whining, and finally some hints on expressing feelings helpfully.

Anger and tantrums are covered in the next chapter, as these very strong emotions are often the most difficult for parents to handle – both in their children and in themselves.

_____

Denying feelings

Children's feelings can be inconvenient. In situations where your child is expressing a feeling that is going to cause trouble, your first reaction is probably to contradict and hope the situation will go away.

'Mum, I don't feel well, I can't go to school' when you are rushing to get to work may be responded to with a brusque: 'You look fine and you haven't got a temperature, on with your coat!'

'I hate Rufus, I don't want to play with him anymore!' can raise your stress level when you depend on Rufus's mother to pick up your child from after-school club twice a week and you are likely to say: 'But you were so keen to go to his house, you do like him really!'

'This book is so boring, I can't read another page' causes tension when you have to sign your son's homework diary to say he has finished the chapter and you may coax: 'Come on, you know you love reading about stars and planets.'

These reactions are all too easy, but, as an adult, how do you feel when someone, maybe your partner, friend or colleague, denies your feelings? How would you feel if you said something similar to the quotes above and your feelings were contradicted?

For example:

'You can't be feeling too sick, you've just been on the exercise bike.'

'Rufus has always been your best mate, you don't really mean that.'

86

'Well you've got to get that assignment finished, boring or not!'

Having feelings contradicted in this way can make adults and children alike feel worse. You may feel:

Angry – the other person is assuming superiority: how do they know what is going on inside you better than you do?

Disrespected – you can't be trusted to recognize your own sensations.

Manipulated – the other person wants you to behave in a way to suit them.

Uncertain – maybe you can't trust your own feelings?

Sad – the other person doesn't care about how you feel.

Exercise: Denying feelings

Think back to your own childhood.

Remember a time when you were upset about something and an adult who was important in your life said: 'Don't be silly'.

How did you feel?

And then think of a time when your feelings were listened to and accepted.

How did you feel then?

Julie, mother of Anna and Jake:

'I remember I was going to a new school when I was seven. The night before, I couldn't sleep and told my Mum I was scared.

She just said "There's really nothing to be scared of." I felt even worse, as if I'd been told off.'

Patrick, father of Callum, Sean and Logan:

'I came back home after we'd lost a match. My Dad didn't ask me questions, he made me tea and toast. Eventually, I told him all about it. And felt better.'

Feelings which are denied, criticized or mocked do not go away. They may show themselves in physical symptoms or be 'acted out' in other ways – for example, through hurting others or even self-harming. If you find it hard to remember times when your feelings were valued, it may be more difficult to tune in and accept your child's emotions.

A parent's story

Sarah realized that she became much more irritable and intolerant of her older two children's feelings if they were upset or made a fuss about something.

When she reflected on her own childhood, she realized that she had been sent off to boarding school as a nine-year-old. 'There was no one to sympathize with me. I just had to get on with it, and I was expecting the same of them, which wasn't really fair.' After she became aware of her attitude she found it easier to be understanding when they were distressed.

Acknowledging feelings

So what can you do when your children are showing strong feelings, in words, tone or actions?

The first step is to stop and think – the **A** in **ACT**. You need to be grounded if you are to react skilfully.

The next step is to be attentive, to show that you are listening. 'Oh' or 'Mmm' or 'Really?' are fine responses, as long as they communicate interest rather than fobbing off. Stopping what you are doing, turning to look at the speaker, and focusing give the message that you are interested.

The last step is to give a name to the feeling. Naming a feeling legitimizes it and turns it into something which can be thought about and dealt with.

The right side of your brain is where emotions, deep feelings and bodily sensations are processed. The left side is where language and logic are developed. The link between the two parts of the brain, the corpus callosum, develops during infancy and childhood. Parents can help this important process through giving words to feelings.

Very often, to communicate a feeling is enough for a child. Sometimes, especially if the feeling has been acted out rather than spoken, you can show that you understand by saying something which expands on the feeling word and describes what you think is going on for him.

A parent's story

John was tidying up after his son Finlay's second birthday when he heard shrieks from the sitting room. He went in to find Adam, his stepson, was riding on the new sit-on car. The resulting dialogue went like this:

'Adam! What are you doing taking the baby's birthday toys? You're far too big for the car, get off this minute or you'll break it!'

(Contd)

'I'm not too big, and you can't tell me what to do!'

'Don't you talk back to me! After we've had such a nice party for Finlay you go and spoil it all! Go to your room!'

'Waaah!'

But later, when John thought about it, he realized he had reacted too quickly. When he put himself in Adam's place, he guessed he was jealous of Finlay being the centre of attention all day. If he had curbed his irritation and empathized with Adam's feelings he could have dealt with the situation very differently by saying:

'Hey, off the car, it's built for two-year-olds and I'm worried it will break.' And then: 'It looks like you wish you were still little enough to play with all Finlay's great toys. Perhaps you're feeling jealous after an afternoon when everyone has been giving things to Finlay; jealous feelings really hurt inside.'

If he had said this, there might have been a very different outcome. Adam might have felt understood and able to understand himself better; he could have felt positive about his half-brother rather than resentful. And finally, he and his stepfather would have felt closer.

John was guessing at Adam's emotions. It is important to be tentative when naming emotions, as you might get the wrong end of the stick completely. Adam could have been playing 'catch me if you can' with Finlay, for example.

Insight

My experience is that siblings have to be nearly grown up before they can cope with a brother or sister's birthday with equanimity! It is as well to be prepared, and talk about feelings beforehand if possible. Depending on the age gap, giving older siblings a helping role can work well. – *Doro*

Often children express their feelings through the way they behave. You can expand on the feeling word and say what you think is going on for your child.

You have probably found out that asking a child what he is feeling and why seldom elicits a clear response. Questions distract during emotional exchanges. Young children often can't recognize their feelings and fear disapproval from an adult. Jealousy is a good example of a common emotion which is not easy to admit to and is often criticized.

Top tips for acknowledging feelings

▶ *Stop and engage your thinking brain.*
▶ *Show your attention.*
▶ *Name what you think your child is feeling.*
▶ *If appropriate, expand to show you recognize what is going on for him.*

It is not always easy, on the spur of the moment, to think of a response that acknowledges feelings. Sometimes you may end up thinking about what you could have said instead afterwards, as John did. If this happens, don't worry too much. Your children will give you plenty more opportunities, and next time you will be better prepared! If you guess the feeling wrong, your child will correct you, and doing that in itself will help him to think about his emotions.

Exercise: What is the feeling?

Write down what the underlying feeling might be and what you could say to your child if he said:

'I hate Jasmine, she took my pencil case and she's really mean.'

'We had a stupid assembly in school today.'

'I don't want to go to my swimming lesson with the new teacher.'

(Contd)

'I can't do my English homework, it's too hard.'

'I really want to go to the cinema with Grampa, but it will mean missing football practice.'

Bear in mind that acknowledging a feeling does not mean that you are permitting any particular behaviour. Saying: 'You sound really angry with Jasmine' does not give permission for retaliation; responding: 'Maybe you feel nervous about what the new teacher will make you do' does not mean your child skips the swimming class. What it does mean is that your child feels that you and he are on the same side. Sometimes just naming the feeling is enough. Other times you may want to help him move on and find a solution – there will be more about this in Chapter 10.

Mixed feelings

Mixed feelings can be very confusing. You can helpfully acknowledge mixed or even contradictory feelings.

You could say:

'It sounds to me like part of you wants to spend time with Grampa, and part of you doesn't want to let the team down.'

Changes in the family, such as new babies or new step-parents, often give rise to mixed feelings, and it can be a comfort to put these into words.

You could say:

'Perhaps you feel two things at once, happy to be a big brother and sad not to be a baby anymore.'

'It looks like you had fun today, and at the same time you're worried about Mum being on her own on a Saturday.'

There is more on talking and listening to children about family change in Chapter 13.

Verbal and non-verbal approaches

TOUCH

However old your child is, a touch or a hug says more than a thousand words when there is real upset. Remember, touch from a loved one stimulates the brain to produce soothing neurotransmitters which help children (and adults) to calm down and strengthen relationships.

PUTTING SILENT SIGNALS INTO WORDS

Some children are not good at expressing their feelings, and withdraw rather than asking for help. You can show your empathy by noticing these silent, non-verbal signals:

You could say:

'I can see you have a sad expression in your eyes.'

'You look as if something heavy is weighing you down.'

MATCHING INTENSITY

It is important that you try to match the intensity of the feelings, using tone of voice as well as choosing the right words. Matching his intensity is a way of getting through to a child who is too overwrought to hear your words; when you have his attention you can gradually calm down your response.

> ### Insight
>
> I know that I used to communicate feelings this way when my children were babies (and still do with my cat!). Toddlers whose language skills are not so developed will respond well to your exaggerated tone and repetition in acknowledging feelings – for example 'You REALLY REALLY HATE your car seat, HATE HATE!' – *Doro*

GIVING IN FANTASY

Sometimes children's feelings are so strong that they really can't listen to you acknowledging them. They find it impossible to move on. One approach that works is to join in with them and fantasize an exaggerated solution. John could have done this with Adam by saying, for example: 'Wouldn't it be great if it was your birthday today as well!' He could have gone on: 'If it was your birthday every month, every week, every day!'

Even though children know that this couldn't actually happen, the underlying message seems to be: 'I hear how very strongly you feel and I wish I could do something about it', and this gets through to them.

A parent's story

Amina was on a train with her son Hussein. He had seen an advertisement for an expensive computer game and was going on and on about it, saying how bored he was with everything she had brought to entertain him on the journey. He just wouldn't let the idea go, and in the end Amina said: 'I bet you wish this train could leave the rails and drive straight to the biggest toy shop in the world and you could choose any game you liked!'

The fantasy worked; Hussein felt that his strong feelings were heard. He relaxed and asked if he could put the game on his birthday list.

Worries

When someone is described as being 'moody', it usually refers to negative rather than positive states of mind – being irritable, withdrawing and wanting to be alone, getting upset over the slightest breath of criticism. Children who behave like this may be suffering from anxiety. An underlying worry can also affect their sleep, school work and social life.

> *My life has been full of catastrophes, most of which never happened.*
>
> Mark Twain

If you think that your child's moodiness is a symptom of worrying, you may have to do some skilful investigating, avoiding direct questions which rarely elicit straight answers. The number one step in helping a worried child is to calm down yourself.

A parent's paramount concern from the first moment they hold their baby is to keep him or her safe, so a son or daughter's worry and tension can be very infectious. Also, the way children express their anxiety can be extremely irritating – getting up in the night, for example – but showing annoyance will only make things worse. So the A for Adult in the ACT reminder – focusing on your own feelings and thoughts – is especially important here.

RELAXATION TECHNIQUES

You may have your own ways of slowing down the racing thoughts and pounding heart that come with stress. It is important to teach children a method to calm themselves too. Here are some simple ideas:

7/11 breathing – Breathe in slowly counting to seven and out counting to 11. This helps to slow breath and gives the mind something to do at the same time. It can be done unobtrusively in many situations.

Putting a teddy to sleep – The child lies on his back with a teddy or soft toy on his stomach, and tries to put it to sleep with the gentle up and down movements of breathing in and out.

Tense and relax – Starting with the face, tense up muscles and then relax them. Work down through your body to your calves and feet.

Visualization – Imagine a beautiful place where you are completely safe – a tropical island, a flower meadow with a tinkling stream, a warm sofa by a crackling fire.

A song – Make up words or use an existing song, like 'My Favourite Things' from *The Sound of Music*. Singing is a great way to lessen anxiety and increase happiness.

FINDING THE CAUSE OF THE WORRY

When you are both a bit calmer, you can acknowledge the feeling and make a very tentative guess at what might be going on. It is important to be tentative because some children will agree with your suggestions whatever they are and this can cause real muddles. They often find it difficult to put their fears into words, and may be frightened that they will be criticized, teased or embarrassed, so you may need several sessions before they will open up.

You could say:

'It sounds like you have a big worry filling you up, can you let it spill over so I can hear what it is?'

'You look all tensed up these days, can you tell me what's the matter? I promise not to be angry with you, whatever it is.'

'It seems as if you are scared about something when the lights go off. What comes in to your head then?'

COMMON WORRIES

Real occurrences

Maybe they are being bullied, have an overly strict teacher, or are concerned over competitive exams. Maybe they have a learning difficulty which is making school an unrewarding place to be. To go beyond acknowledging the feeling, use the skilled listening and problem-solving skills covered in Chapters 9 and 10 to work out the next steps. Some things children can tackle themselves with your support, others need your intervention, for example by organizing an assessment for learning problems.

Imaginary horrors

These could be ghosts, monsters from a book or a strong visual image from a scary film or computer game. Imaginary horrors are rarely vanquished through logic. Try to fight them on their own ground, through fantasy.

Penny, mother of Mia and Abby:

'I remember I told Abby that dragons hated garlic, and ceremoniously put cloves of garlic in the doorway, windowsill and fireplace. It seemed to break the spell!'

Misinterpretations

Children may overhear parents arguing and think they are going to split up, or get the wrong idea about a health issue and imagine that they or a family member is seriously ill. Misinterpretations are sometimes the most difficult to find out about since children may have picked them up through eavesdropping and may be unwilling to admit to that.

You could say:

'It seems that worry is making your tummy hurt, I wonder if you were upset by hearing me and Daddy shouting last night? We did argue but we have made up now.'

News stories

Terrorist attacks, nuclear proliferation, pandemics, tsunamis, global warming – the news is full of potentially life-threatening events which children can find terrifying. Television news with its graphic images and sounds is probably best indulged in by adults after young children are in bed (a good argument for keeping TVs and internet access out of children's bedrooms) but some news events are impossible to avoid.

Talk about how far away some disasters are, and the safe aspects of where you live. Older children can join campaigns to tackle some of the issues they worry about in the news. Actually doing something like running an information stall at school, or raising money for a disaster fund will make them feel less like victims.

'Nameless dread'

What can you do if your child seems to be suffering from 'nameless dread' and you really cannot find a cause? It can be helpful to ask him to describe the worry as an actual thing – for example, a weight in the pit of the stomach, a black cloud in the head, a high-pitched buzz. Then you can help him to do one of the relaxation techniques and imagine the worry getting lighter and lighter, flying away into the sky or quietening down to nothing.

When the worst happens

What if you can't reassure your child? If you are splitting up with your partner, a loved one has been diagnosed with cancer, you have been made redundant? Strangely, most children do already know what is going on at some level. When problems are out in the open in an age appropriate way they seem to be able to cope more easily. There is more about talking and listening to your children in difficult situations in Chapter 13.

***

Top tips for worriers
▸ *Guess at the causes in a 'wondering' way.*
▸ *Teach your children ways to relax their bodies and minds.*
▸ *Give feelings a name, and if possible find a concrete way to describe them.*

***

Self-talk

Just as children benefit from having a name put to their feelings, so you as an adult can use this technique as a way of engaging your thinking brain when your feelings are running high. Looking at the **A** of **ACT**, reflecting on your own mental state is vital if you are to respond skilfully to your child. Start by going through your physical sensations and seeing if they give a clue to your emotions. Some have found it helpful to look at the chart of feeling faces in the previous chapter and marking those that resonate with their state at that time. You may find that your feelings are amplified by a memory of past hurts which are no longer relevant.

A parent's story

Laura was on her way home when she felt her head spinning and her stomach churning. She remembered these sensations from the run up to exams and recognized that she was feeling panicky. By saying the word 'panicky' to herself and breathing slowly, her head cleared and she realized that she was dreading opening the post at home. The family was waiting for the letter to see if ten-year-old Owen had got in to his first choice of secondary school. She had not been aware of quite how anxious she was and how this transfer brought up memories of her own unhappy school experiences. Laura reminded herself that Owen was a very different character to her, much more sociable and good at sports. He was likely to do well wherever he went to school.

Getting in touch with the part of your brain that observes what is going on in your mind and body is the key to this healthy way of talking to yourself. Try asking: 'What are my physical sensations? What am I feeling at this moment? What does this remind me of? Is that really pertinent now?' Wounding memories become less intense when you think about them calmly, and your reactions to your children can then become more considered. If a memory is really overwhelming, it can help to imagine it as a film which you can stop or fast-forward at any time.

Insight

We found a Chinese proverb which we really like: '*Two thirds of what we see is behind our eyes*'. In other words it is what is going on inside us and our past experiences which colour our views now. Being aware of what is 'pressing our buttons' is really important for us as parents.

When you have learned from a painful memory, you can let it go. Write it down and then burn the paper, tell a trusted friend (with the intention of letting go), picture it fading into black and white and sepia and then disappearing. If painful memories persist, it is worth seeking help. Resources are listed at the end of the book.

Expressing feelings

Being able to tell someone else how you feel is a gauge of how much you trust them and in return how much they trust you. Learning ways to talk about feelings in a family is a good start for children to build strong relationships in the future. People are not mind readers, and they often need help to know what is going on inside your head. Children need to be taught how to express their feelings in acceptable ways. Adults too become closer to each other by expressing their feelings, thoughts and beliefs in ways that others can understand and take on board.

> **Warning!** Just because you feel something very strongly, it does not mean that you will or should necessarily get your own way. People who shout and sulk are still stuck in toddler mode, thinking that because they feel something everyone else will have to fall in with their wishes.

HELPING CHILDREN TO EXPRESS FEELINGS

Naming and acknowledging feelings with your children helps them increase their vocabulary of feeling words. You are helping them to think about their emotions and become more emotionally literate.

Creative approaches

'Say it with words' is a useful response when children are acting out strong feelings, but sometimes before they reach the stage of using words, children can be helped to express their emotions in creative ways. Receiving a homemade Mother's or Father's Day card with a heart and 'I love you' in shaky letters is a high point for parents. But what about expressing other emotions in safe non-verbal ways? Drawing, painting, making up a song, kneading playdough, tearing up old newspapers to mix with flour and water for papier mâché; all can be used to communicate feelings. You may also be laying the foundations for an artistic career in the future!

A parent's story

Celia noticed that Adam had come back from school one day looking miserable, and wouldn't say what was wrong. In the end, she gave him some playdough on a kitchen board and he kneaded it and bashed it flat and eventually rolled it into a torpedo shape. Then he told her that the teacher had shouted at him, and his best friend had laughed at him for being upset. They had a cuddle and he was off to play in the garden.

WHINING

Children usually go through a phase of whining – communicating that they feel hard done by through their tone of voice. Most parents find this extremely irritating, and the child therefore elicits an intense reaction – perhaps what they were unconsciously aiming for.

Sometimes a child uses whining to get a response of any kind. Sometimes it is a way of communicating an underlying feeling which they suspect their parent will not be sympathetic towards. Sometimes it has simply become a habit.

Often children are neither sure what whining is nor are they aware that they are doing it. Get your child to practise speaking in a normal voice so that he knows the difference, or record him and play it back. Then you can ask him to speak differently rather than saying 'don't whine'.

You could say:

'Ask me again in your grown-up voice.'

One mother agreed a code word to use with her daughter when she used her 'baby' voice. They chose 'purple ponies', which made them both giggle. You could also ask your child to repeat what he said with a smile (it is hard to whine while smiling). Then you can ask him to say what he feels, needs and wants more clearly.

EXPRESSING YOUR OWN FEELINGS

It would be strange if your children did not provoke strong feelings in you, both positive and negative ones. This chapter and the previous one have looked at recognizing and acknowledging feelings in yourself and your children. The next stage is to consider how you can communicate these feelings effectively – in a way which helps your children to respect how you feel but avoids blaming or overwhelming them.

The first step which is in all the assertiveness courses is to use 'I' to start your sentence. Saying 'I feel' rather than 'you make me feel' is a way of taking responsibility for your feelings and not 'dumping' them on someone else. The best way for your children to learn this is to see and hear you owning your feelings.

Insight

I have heard many a stressed parent say 'You drive me mad' or 'You are a pain in the neck' or worst of all 'You'll be the death of me'. Apart from the fact that small children can take these things literally, no useful information is given on which a child can act. All they hear is that they are 'all wrong' in some way. That is the underlying message we give off when we express our feelings through blaming others. – *Glenda*

There is more about expressing anger safely and effectively in the next chapter.

When you say clearly what you feel, think and want, your children understand what is going on for you and are more likely to change their behaviour, and you are less likely to say hurtful things to them.

TALKING TO CHILDREN ABOUT YOUR FEELINGS

Naturally there are times when you may wish to protect your child from major concerns. However, your children will know if you are worried or upset about something, so it is nearly always better to let them know that something is going on and that it is not their fault. Children often blame themselves for family difficulties.

If your feelings are running really high, you need a time for some 'self-talk' or talk with a partner or friend before you tackle things with your children. You are the adult and your children depend on you; to see you really out of control is frightening for them.

If that does happen, make sure you find some support for yourself and then talk about it afterwards to let them know that you are OK.

A parent's story

Penny described how, a couple of months after her husband left, Mia, her elder daughter, walked in to the kitchen when she was with her own mother in floods of tears. They had a three-way hug and Penny calmed down. She sent Mia off to watch a film while she talked things through with her mother. That evening she had time with Mia and they talked about how they both felt. Having discussed things with another adult, Penny was able to tell Mia what had triggered her tears – a relatively minor thing – and reassured her that she had support from family and friends to work things out. Mia understood her mother's feelings and behaviour and was a lot more co-operative after the conversation.

NON-VERBAL COMMUNICATION

Another important thing to remember when you are expressing your feelings to children is to make sure that your body language, tone and expression back up what you are saying. You can probably think of people who use nervous laughter when they are telling you about some disaster that happened to them. Look at the number of comedy programmes, newspaper and magazine columns which present minor disasters as humorous. In fact, people often say the very opposite of what they mean and feel! This may be a useful defence mechanism outside the family, but inside can be a barrier to true communication, and very confusing to young children. Remember also that children can be frightened by loud voices and someone towering over them.

VENTING FEELINGS

Expressing our feelings is not the same as venting – that is when feelings come out thoughtlessly and unorganized, like steam from a volcano. Venting without thinking can hurt those around you, and can also make you feel worse. Even allowing feelings to overflow constantly, by grumbling and complaining, can make you more discontented. Instead, you can use your awareness of how you feel to take action, change things if that is possible and make the best of them if not.

Remember that emotional literacy is being able to identify your feelings and use them, to know your own internal states, to recognize emotions in others and to communicate them in ways that strengthen relationships rather than undermine them.

Top tips for expressing your feelings

▶ *Start your sentence with 'I'.*
▶ *State clearly what you feel, think and want.*
▶ *Take care that your child is not overwhelmed by your feelings.*
▶ *Make sure your expression and tone match your words.*

PARENTS' COMMENTS

Sarah, mother of Zach, Martha, Naomi and Ben:

'After thinking about needs and feelings underlying behaviour, I wondered whether Martha was really worried about moving schools. I'd been thinking all that stroppiness was because of pre-teen hormones, and I was getting really annoyed with her. Since I've bitten my tongue a few times, she has opened up and we've been able to talk, for example, about how she feels about travelling independently for the first time.'

Gloria, mother of Jasmine, Chantal and Nathan:

'When I thought about my own feelings, I realized that I was still really grieving for my sister who died in an accident a year ago. And that's why it's been hard to focus on my children's ups and downs recently. I've decided to find some bereavement counselling to help me.'

Things which have struck me in this chapter

Something I am going to try out

HAVE SOME FUN

First memories
Ask your children what their earliest memory is and tell them about yours. What do they remember feeling? What did you feel all those years ago?

10 THINGS TO REMEMBER

1 *Families are the place where children learn to deal with their feelings, laying the basis for intimacy and trust.*

2 *Children's feelings are often inconvenient, but denying them leads to problems and affects your relationship with them.*

3 *Attending to your children's feelings and giving them a name teaches them to think about their emotions and creates a connection between the right and left halves of their brain.*

4 *Children (and adults) often express feelings through the way they behave. Remember all feelings are permissible, but not all behaviour is. Strong feelings don't necessarily mean you can or should get what you want.*

5 *Bear in mind that feelings can be mixed, even contradictory, and it can be helpful to acknowledge this.*

6 *When your child is stuck in a strong emotion, you can give in fantasy what you cannot give in reality.*

7 *Find physical and mental relaxation techniques which work for your child when they are worried.*

8 *Try to be aware of your own emotions. Check out linked physical sensations.*

9 *Help your child to express their emotions safely, with words or through creative activities.*

10 *Think before you vent your feelings on others. Try starting sentences with 'I' rather than 'You' to avoid blaming and criticizing.*

7

Anger and tantrums

In this chapter you will learn:

For yourself:

- *what is going on when you or your children are angry*
- *the dangers and benefits of anger*
- *helpful ways to express anger*
- *strategies for preventing anger and calming down.*

For your children:

- *how to help your children deal with their anger*
- *how to respond when you're on the receiving end of anger*
- *how to understand and deal with tantrums.*

> *Anybody can become angry – that is easy; but to be angry with the right person, and to the right degree, and at the right time, and for the right purpose, and in the right way – that ... is not easy.*
>
> Aristotle, 384–322 BC

Anger is so common in families that it deserves particular attention. If you ask parents to make a list of feelings, anger will almost invariably be at the top. Why should this be?

In the family, you are all rubbing up against each other every day, so even relatively minor irritants can sometimes wear you down. You also care deeply about how your children behave, and when they don't live up to your expectations they can touch a raw nerve in you. What's more, both parents and children feel safe to vent their frustrations in the context of the family. If you did this with friends or colleagues, you might lose the relationship; but family is always family, so home is where anger is unleashed.

Insight

It does seem to be a paradox that we express most anger towards those we really love the most – a sign of our deep feelings for them. Being on the receiving end of these strong emotions does not feel good! If we can learn to use this anger constructively we can deepen relationships rather than harming them.

Those who find it hard to control their anger may lash out physically or verbally, shout or slam doors. This can be frightening for children, and fear sets stress hormones going which affect their brain and influence their own patterns of behaviour. They may feel humiliated and resentful, comply out of fear and not develop their own sense of right and wrong.

Penny, mother of Mia and Abby:

'When we were little, my sister and I argued a lot and sometimes Mum would just fly off the handle and shout at us. It was really frightening, and I felt as if I was somehow a bad person. Now I can see there was probably something else worrying her, and our fighting was just 'the last straw'. But that wasn't clear to us at the time, and it meant we lived in fear of an explosion and weren't so close to her as to Dad.'

It is common for people to 'dump' their frustration on others and blame them instead of recognizing its true source.

This chapter will help you to understand what is going on when you or your children become angry, and recognize that this feeling is there to tell you something important. The emphasis will be on learning what to do about anger – without damaging self or others – as it has a useful function in helping to protect everyone's needs and boundaries. A happy child is not a child who never experiences anger, but one who knows it can be well handled.

What is anger?

Anger can vary in intensity from mild irritation to extreme fury, and is not a subject that most people like to talk about. On a biological level, anger is a natural response to perceived attack, injury or violation. It is an evolutionary adaptation to help human beings survive, giving them the strength to fight back or run away when threatened. Psychologists point out that, like all emotions, anger is accompanied by physiological changes. When you get angry, the amygdala (the emotional centre of your brain) reacts by releasing neurotransmitters and stress hormones – adrenaline and noradrenaline – causing your heart rate and blood pressure to go up and giving you instant energy. This energy serves a useful purpose when faced with outside threats in the wild; it prepares you to fight to the death or run for your life. But how useful is it in civilized society? How does it translate into your own experience?

EMOTIONAL FLOODING

When someone is in a calm mood, there is a balance between the rational and emotional parts of their personality as in Figure 7.1.

When someone becomes angry, on the other hand, feelings rise up and virtually 'squeeze out' the thinking part of the brain. You could say a person becomes emotionally flooded as in Figure 7.2.

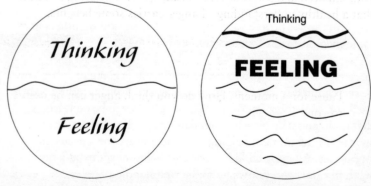

Figure 7.1 A balanced state.   *Figure 7.2 An emotionally flooded state.*

This makes it very hard to act rationally when you are angry. Most parents have experienced this.

Sarah, mother of Zach, Martha, Naomi and Ben:

'I don't think of myself as an angry person, but sometimes I blow my top for something relatively trivial. It feels like a volcano boiling away which suddenly erupts. I can shout and say hurtful things which I really regret when I've calmed down. I feel so guilty about it when I see the effect it has on the children.'

Sarah regrets these outbursts, and apologizes to her children afterwards.

There are some people, however, who become almost addicted to the 'high' they experience when flooded with the adrenaline which accompanies anger. Adults who feel a lot of anger do not usually express it in a situation where there are people more powerful than they are (for example, their boss), but let it out on their children because they are smaller and less powerful. This can be really damaging, and is likely to lead to angry teenagers later on.

___

In what ways is anger useful?

Having seen how detrimental unprocessed anger can be both for your children and for your relationships, it is reassuring to know that a healthy understanding of anger carries some benefits.

Exercise: The benefits of anger

Pause for a moment. How do you think anger can be useful to you?

EARLY WARNING SIGNAL

Thinking back to the fountain of feelings and needs (see Chapter 3), you will remember that negative feelings point to unfulfilled needs. Feelings could be described as friends: when you listen to them, they tell you what's going on for you, like a barometer showing when the weather is fine, rainy, windy or changeable. Anger is perhaps your closest friend, because it lets you know in no uncertain terms when important needs are not being addressed.

The harder the truth to tell, the better the friend who tells it.

So this widespread, yet unpopular, human emotion has a very real use.

A parent's story

Patrick, father of Callum, Sean and Logan, was really pleased that the boys were being creative and making a tree house. The first time they left his tools in the garden, he was only mildly irritated. However, as this kept happening, his annoyance built up and he got really furious one day when he needed his hammer and couldn't find it. He started feeling resentful about the whole tree house project. Having talked it over with some other parents, Patrick has come to realize that his anger is about what he doesn't want. If he sees his anger as a mirror, he can see what he does want:

'I don't want my tools rusting in the long grass; I do want them put away where I can find them.' Now he will heed the early warning signal of his irritation, to make clear to the boys the conditions for borrowing his tools and then enforce them, to avoid any resentment.

A FORCE FOR CHANGE

Anger is a strong energy, and as such, it is a powerful force for change. Having given you that warning signal, it prods you into taking action.

If you want to avoid the sense of powerlessness that Laura speaks of in the following story, it is important to take action when you feel angry and find a solution (see Chapter 8 on gaining co-operation).

Laura found the only way she could get Owen to do his homework was to shout at him. Although it worked, she hated the bad feelings this created. One day, she decided just to keep quiet. He left it until later and later, and she felt completely powerless to get him to bed on time. She said: 'I got so frustrated, I realized something had to change.' After a quiet word with his teacher, Laura decided to hand over the responsibility to Owen. If the homework wasn't done in time, he'd just have to go to bed without doing it, and face the consequences when he got to school. 'Since then, we've avoided the daily battles, and somehow, miraculously he's now getting it done on time!'

HELPS YOU GET WHAT YOU NEED AND PROTECTS YOUR BOUNDARIES

If your own parents were very strict, you may be reluctant to be firm with your children when they encroach on your own time and space. However, when boundaries are being eroded, it is common to feel anger. You could see this as a reminder to be warm and firm – to be the authoritative parent described in Chapter 2 on parenting styles.

A parent's story

Because Amina's father was very harsh with her as a child, she tried asking Noor nicely to stay in bed. But this didn't work at all – Noor just kept on coming down and disturbing her after bedtime. Amina said: 'Something clicked last night. When Noor came down for the third time, I was ready to explode! I'd read her two stories and we'd had a nice chat before I tucked her up with her teddies.

(Contd)

I so badly wanted that time simply to be me, not Mummy, just to relax and read the paper.' It dawned on Amina that this scenario had been going on for far too long, so when Noor's face appeared round the door Amina said: 'If I'm going to be a nice Mummy I need some time on my own.' Her voice was very firm because she really meant it! She took Noor back to bed and kissed her goodnight. She doesn't know if Noor read a book or played with her dolls' house – but she didn't come down again.

> **Insight**
>
> We agree with Dr Haim Ginott (a US based psychologist whose ideas have been popularized in the excellent books by Adele Faber and Elaine Mazlish). He said: '*Our genuine anger is one of the strongest means we have for changing behaviour.*' Anger certainly gives us the energy to challenge unacceptable behaviour with conviction.

THE DANGERS OF IGNORING ANGER

As you can see from the parents' examples above, suppressing anger leads to a sense of powerlessness or resentment, and then to increasing fury. Also, as long as you do not address the source of the anger, nothing changes and needs are not met. On top of this, doctors report that ignoring anger can have negative effects both physically and mentally. It can affect your:

▶ *digestion – causing heartburn, ulcers, colitis, gastritis, irritable bowel syndrome*
▶ *heart and circulation – causing blocked arteries*
▶ *immune system – more liable to catch infections and take longer to heal*
▶ *blood pressure – driving it up high*
▶ *joints and muscles – arthritis.*

Bottling up anger can affect your emotional wellbeing leading to:

- *depression (when anger is turned inwards)*
- *bullying behaviour*
- *addictions and compulsive behaviour.*

If you are not sure what to do with your own angry feelings or those of your children, read on. You will learn how to recognize the early warning signal, and deal with the causes of your anger in a constructive way.

Using – not abusing – anger

The first step in knowing what to do about anger – whether you're furious with your children, enraged with a parking attendant, or someone else is cross with you – is to understand your own reactions. Even if your main concern is your children's flights of temper, your starting point in helping them cope with angry feelings is to understand your own style of dealing with anger.

LOOKING AT YOUR OWN PATTERNS

How you respond to anger will be affected by your personality type (see Chapter 4) and what you heard and saw in your own childhood. It is enlightening to consider how these early experiences have influenced your present attitude.

Exercise: The messages you carry about anger

Take a few moments to picture your childhood home. Close your eyes and imagine an angry scene. Then think about the following questions, and write down your answers. This will give you a better understanding of your own reactions.

(Contd)

How was anger expressed in my family when I was a child?

(Those around you may have been angry in very different ways.)

What did I think and feel about this? How did I react?

Was I allowed to be angry?

What spoken or unspoken messages about anger did you receive when you were a child which could affect your own pattern of behaviour?

▶ *If anger was frowned upon, you may blame yourself or other people when this strong feeling erupts, and try to push it down: 'Of course I'm not angry!' (thinking: 'I'm absolutely livid!'), or 'How can you tell Chantal you hate her! She's your sister! You're supposed to love her!'*

▶ *If anger was laughed at, or not taken seriously, you may try to make light of it: 'Come on, cross-patch! Snap out of it and wipe that horrible frown off your face!'*

▶ *Perhaps anger was expressed in physical violence or verbal aggression. This can cause fear and dread when angry feelings arise: 'Now, you two, just stop fighting or I'll confiscate that computer!' (thinks: 'I must stop them fighting or I'll lose control and knock their heads together! Why do I always want to cry when I'm angry?')*

▶ *Or it could be that anger was just seen as pointless: 'What's the use of getting angry? It won't change anything. No one ever listens to us.'*

▶ *If one person in the family had violent angry outbursts, others might have been too scared to respond in kind. They might have expressed their anger in cold resentment or sarcastic comments: 'I suppose you'll be too busy watching TV to help with this washing up' (thinks: 'What's the point of asking? I don't want to be shouted at.')*

Think about the messages you received and how they have affected you. Do you agree with them? How do you feel about your current pattern of responding to these messages? You may like to talk this over with someone who understands you. If you're working through this book with a friend, you could compare notes. Just being aware of the patterns you have received from the past gives you the freedom to make changes if you wish to. You are in charge of how you respond in the present.

Insight

I have realized that there was a gender difference in how anger was expressed in my family. My brother was rather admired for having a 'temper', but the girls were criticized or teased for showing anger and tended to end up in tears. – *Doro*

RECOGNIZING THE RED FLAG

The adrenalin surge which accompanies anger would be useful were you being chased by a crocodile or threatened by a mugger, but when you are faced with your child's defiant 'No!' you might wish you didn't have those hormones raging around urging you to lash out or escape. At moments like this, you may not consciously be aware of the physical sensations which accompany your feelings, but when heeded, they are like a red flag preventing a train hurtling towards a head-on collision. They can warn you to:

ACT rather than **REACT** (see Chapter 1).

In Chapter 5, you identified physical sensations relating to different emotions. Now you can use this skill as a preventative tool in potentially explosive situations. When you feel you're becoming emotionally flooded, take a deep breath, let it out and become aware of what is going on in your body.

How do you feel when you are angry? Hot? Cold? Clenched? Prickly? Tense?

You might like to write your own sensations in the places where you feel them on the diagram on the next page. Other members of your family can also draw some bodies and do the same exercise. You may be surprised to discover how different or similar your feelings can be. Just opening up the subject in this visual, non-judgmental way can also be surprisingly liberating. Talking about anger in calm moments can take much of the heat and fear out of it. This will make it easier to address frustrations at an early stage so your home will become a more peaceful place.

THE TIP OF THE ICEBERG

There are occasions when anger may come upon you or your child quite unexpectedly, and you can't quite understand why. It is helpful to see that anger can be a complex emotion which takes time to unravel.

A parent's story

After a long hard day, Ingrid snapped when her son knocked a vase onto the floor with his rucksack: 'Look what you've done, you idiot! You've knocked those flowers all over the floor! You're so clumsy! You could have broken the vase as well ... You always make such a mess! Look at your football kit all over the place! You never pick it up!'

Ingrid is very fortunate to have a husband who listens, and that evening she was able to confide in him about how ashamed she felt about having laid in to Eric like that. When she had a chance to talk it over, she could see that the anger she'd vented on him was just the tip of the iceberg. There was so much else going on underneath it. She'd been to see her mother in hospital that

afternoon and was really afraid she might die. It was very sad to see her so frail and helpless, and Ingrid was furious with the nurses because they were not feeding her properly. Afterwards she'd got stuck in a traffic jam and was anxious that Eric would be worried when she didn't turn up at school on time. On top of all this, she hadn't been sleeping too well of late and was feeling exhausted, and so the irritation she felt with Eric was quite out of proportion.

The biggest part of an iceberg is submerged beneath the water. Anger is the peak which shows above the water level, with other powerful feelings remaining hidden below the surface. For Ingrid, the iceberg might look like this:

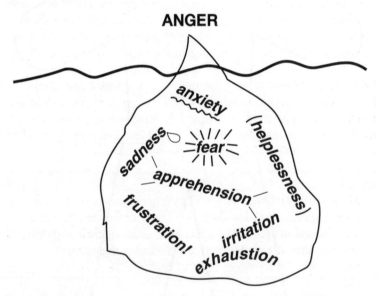

Figure 7.3 Emotional iceberg.

When you or other family members are angry, remember there may be far more to 'the iceberg' than meets the eye. Be prepared to look beneath the surface of the water. This is not always easy, but it really does help to identify hidden needs and anxieties.

FINDING HELPFUL WAYS TO EXPRESS ANGER

While it is easy to sympathize with Ingrid's feelings when Eric knocked over the vase after her long hard day, you can also imagine how he felt when showered with criticism and abuse. In the short time it took Ingrid to explode, she used the word 'you' seven times, called him an 'idiot' and 'clumsy', and exaggerated by using words like 'never' and 'always'.

As explained at the beginning of this chapter, the hormones associated with anger can trigger the 'fight impulse', which is why so many people respond aggressively when they are angry. The communication would have been very different if Ingrid had owned her feelings instead of dumping them on her son. She could have said: 'I've had a terrible time today, Eric, so I'm feeling very angry about the flowers all over the floor. I want you to help me by clearing them up right now. You can use the mop in the kitchen for the water.'

Eric would understand why his mother was so upset and would know exactly how to remedy his careless movement. He would not feel blamed or criticized, and would therefore be far more willing to clear up the mess. The exchange would encourage understanding and closeness rather than alienation and resentment.

Insight

Many parents tell me that for all their good intentions they do sometimes shout at their children in anger or frustration. Some are reluctant to apologize for fear of diminishing their authority, but they have already lost authority by losing their temper. Saying 'Sorry' is a powerful way of healing rifts. – *Glenda*

ASSERTIVE VERSUS AGGRESSIVE

What you do when you are angry has a profound effect on how others respond to you, and also how they feel about themselves. Aggressive expressions of anger tend to contain many 'you' statements and also labels such as 'naughty', 'silly', 'selfish' or 'stupid'. Two other favourites for hectoring mode are 'always' and 'never', as in: 'You never listen to me!' or 'You always make such a mess!' Others are unlikely to want to co-operate when spoken to like this!

Assertive communications, on the other hand, will contain more 'I' statements and will focus on your own feelings and needs, as you saw in the last chapter, rather than dumping them on someone else. Using the **A** part of **ACT** (see Chapter 1) will help you when you feel the impulse to go on the attack. When you manage to notice the red warning flag and **stop** to take a deep breath and ask yourself 'How am I feeling? What do I need right now?', you are less likely to 'pounce' on the person whose action has been 'the last straw'. This is not easy to do. It can take a lifetime of practice! This exercise gives you some ideas for changing your patterns.

Exercise: Expressing anger assertively

Change these aggressive expressions of anger into assertive 'I' statements:

For example:

'You two are so lazy! You always leave your plates on the table! I suppose you think I'm a slave!'

becomes:

'I feel angry when I see all those plates left on the table! I'd appreciate some help clearing them up.'

'You silly girl! You've left a wet towel on the floor yet again. How many times do I have to tell you to put it on the rail!'

'

'

'Look what you've done! You've got muddy footprints all over the carpet! Why don't you ever remember to take your shoes off before you come in?'

'   ,

'You're always taking my scissors without asking. I can't ever find them when I need them. Why are you so selfish?'

'   ,

Now run through a situation in your own home which makes you angry and formulate an assertive 'I' statement.

Speaking directly about yourself using the 'I' word:

- ▶ *helps you become more aware of your own feelings and needs*
- ▶ *helps others to understand you and know what you want without blame, or criticism*
- ▶ *is clear and direct*
- ▶ *sets an example for your children in how to communicate.*

Cutting out blame and criticism is a starting point in assertive communication. You will learn further ways to bring about changes in irritating behaviour in Chapters 8 and 11.

FORCEFUL YET NON-VIOLENT

One of the benefits of anger is the force it adds to the expression of your feelings.

Rather than allowing this powerful emotion to cause damage, you can turn your anger into something useful, like converting rushing water into electricity. When you make an assertive 'I' statement, it is useful to sound and look as if you mean business.

Insight
It's amazing how much more my children would listen when I took on the deadly serious tone I mustered when I was really angry about something. – *Glenda*

Children are expert at reading body language and will not take limp requests seriously.

For instance, if you smile apologetically while asking your child to stop catapulting peas across the room, she will probably go on doing it! At the same time, it is important not to cross the line and become aggressive, which could frighten her and make her resentful. Getting the right balance is what you are aiming for if you want to have a good relationship with your child. Being angry 'to the right degree', as Aristotle said; or in terms of the parenting styles in Chapter 2, being both firm and loving.

Top tips for helpful expression of anger
▶ *Be aware of physical sensations warning you of rising anger.*
▶ *Think about what frustrated need is underlying your angry feelings, and say what you want to happen rather than harping on about what you don't want.*
▶ *Remember that anger is often the tip of the iceberg, with other feelings lying under the surface.*
▶ *'Own' your anger rather than blaming others by starting sentences with 'I' rather than 'you'.*
▶ *Be clear and forceful without being intimidating.*

Parents' relationships

Many parents who have practised the skills of assertive communication have noticed they are useful in other areas of their lives. You may well find that 'I' statements bring rewards when talking to your own father or mother, or perhaps your partner or a brother or sister.

Children are so much happier when their parents get on well that it is worth remembering to own your feelings instead of 'dumping' them when you are about to have a go at your partner! It's not easy, but if you manage to apply these lessons to the other adults in your family as well as your children, you will have a more peaceful and happy atmosphere in your home.

To sum up, expressing anger in a helpful way:

▶ *benefits relationships and self-esteem*
▶ *allows fuller and richer communication and closeness*
▶ *defuses tensions before they reach explosion point*
▶ *helps to keep people healthy, both physically and emotionally.*

Prevention is better than cure

Although anger is a useful warning signal, it is of course better to look after your needs and those of your children before you start to feel angry. Many have found the following strategies helpful.

TAKING CARE OF YOURSELF

Look back to the 'oxygen mask' and the 'full cup' in Chapter 2. Remember what you read about nurturing yourself in order to be able to look after others. Are you treating yourself to anything on your list of ten things you enjoy doing? Most parents say they lose their temper more readily when their own batteries need recharging. Remember that doing something which makes you feel good is your first step to avoid getting on the cumulative anger ladder. You owe it to yourself and the rest of your family.

TRIGGERS AND HOW TO AVOID THEM

Consider what kinds of situations trigger your anger. You might like to compare notes with your learning companion or your partner. Think – what is a *better* way of dealing with that situation? It could be avoiding the scenario in the first place.

If you and your children get into quarrels when they come to the supermarket, perhaps you could arrange things differently. You might devise a way to make it interesting for them, or else go when there is someone else to look after them or when they are at school.

One mother found that whenever she drove the children home from school they would start fighting and she would get angry with them, whereas when they walked they were much calmer. Now she always takes the footpath home. If it's raining she just takes umbrellas and gumboots – and the children enjoy splashing in the puddles!

Exercise: Anger triggers and finding a better way

Think of what triggers anger in you. What do you do at the moment? What other ideas could you try? Write them down here.

Trigger	What I do now	A better way
e.g. being rushed in the morning	I get tense and shout at Abby when she dawdles	Get everything ready the night before
_____	_____	_____
_____	_____	_____

_____   _____   _____

_____   _____   _____

_____   _____   _____

_____   _____   _____

_____   _____   _____

_____   _____   _____

_____   _____   _____

_____   _____   _____

_____   _____   _____

After a few days, evaluate your 'better ways'. If they haven't
worked, try something else.

It can help, in a calm moment, to tell your children what triggers
your anger and ask them for possible solutions. They can be
surprisingly inventive when asked for their views.

> *The gift of anger is to go for what I want instead of fighting
> what I don't want.*

CHANGING THE ENVIRONMENT

Sometimes relatively small changes in the environment remove
triggers and rid you of a daily hassle.

If your children generally throw their jackets on the floor, a row of
hooks at their level could make all the difference. Or, if the remote

control for your TV has a habit of disappearing, you could keep it in a special box. It is worth developing your lateral thinking and imagination to find ways of avoiding the regular pitched battles which grind down your patience.

MANAGING EXPECTATIONS

An underlying message of angry people is that 'things ought to go my way!' If you expect your child to do a painting and remain clean you will be disappointed. On the other hand, if you recognize that young children are likely to get messy, you will accept that the price of creativity is a lot of clearing up! If you expect peace and harmony to reign at all times in your home, your hopes may be dashed when your children fight and you may get angry. If, however, you realize that part of growing up and learning negotiation skills will involve some fights, you may feel more relaxed about this and less irritated. There may be times when you see fights as an opportunity to teach your children how to generate solutions (see Chapters 8 and 12).

Insight
We remember one father who realized he was often irritable with his daughter for being 'clumsy'. In fact when he stopped to think about it he saw that his expectations were too high – children develop hand to eye co-ordination at different times, and learn through practice.

SEEING THINGS FROM THE OTHER SIDE – USING THE C OF ACT

A man is happily driving along the motorway when a sleek black car whizzes past him. He says to himself: 'So he thinks he's better than me, does he? I'll show him!' He puts his foot down on the accelerator. As it happens, the driver of the black car is a woman, and she's late for an important appointment. All she wants is to get there on time.

This scenario is typical of the false assumptions which underlie many incidents of anger. A very useful strategy if you want to prevent your hackles rising unnecessarily is to see things from the other person's point of view – the C of **ACT** (in Chapter 1).

It does mean you have to pause for a moment – the yellow traffic light – and think: 'What might be going on for him?' or 'What might she be thinking?' and 'What might be the needs behind this behaviour?'

A parent's story

The other day, Daniel got very angry with his daughter, Naomi. She was running up the stairs and her friend Sophie was ahead of her. When they were nearly at the top, Naomi pulled Sophie and Daniel had a flash moment of fear that they would both come tumbling down.

He said, 'I was about to shout at her, but somehow I remembered not to **REACT**. Instead of saying "You're a very naughty girl for pulling Sophie like that," I asked Naomi why she had pulled her friend.' Naomi told her father she'd wanted to run up together with Sophie. He then understood that it was not out of maliciousness that she was pulling her friend, so he just said: 'I was really worried that you were both going to fall down the stairs and hurt yourselves. Be very careful on stairs.'

The simple act of finding out what his daughter was thinking avoided an ugly scene of blame and resentment. Daniel understood Naomi better, and she knew that he cared about her and wanted her friend and herself to be safe on the stairs.

Top tips for preventing anger
▶ *Look after yourself; make sure you have enough fun and satisfaction in your life.*
▶ *Analyse the triggers for your anger, and work out ways to avoid them.*
▶ *Re-organize your surroundings to prevent ongoing causes of irritation.*
▶ *Be realistic about what can be expected of your children.*
▶ *Try to put yourself in your children's shoes. Imagine what is going on for them, or simply ask them.*

First aid

There may be times when you're simply too stressed to use any of these strategies, and just want to find some way to prevent yourself from 'losing it' altogether. When asked what they do to calm down, parents come up with many solutions; what works for some doesn't work for others. Remember everyone is different, and it is important that you find a way that helps **you** calm down when you need to. Here are some ideas:

- ▶ *take a long, deep breath and let it out very slowly*
- ▶ *acknowledge your own feelings. Say to yourself: 'I'm feeling very angry right now'*
- ▶ *go for a walk*
- ▶ *go to the gym*
- ▶ *go into another room and yell*
- ▶ *do the hoovering*
- ▶ *drop your shoulders*
- ▶ *say your phone number backwards. If you catch yourself quickly enough, doing a mental task can put your 'thinking brain' back in charge.*

Make a list of what helps **you** to calm down when you're really angry. Ask your friends what helps them: it's good to get as many ideas as possible. Stick it up somewhere as a reminder.

Penny, mother of Mia and Abby:

'When I feel I might lose control, I walk slowly down to the end of the garden and back, breathing in the air. By then I've usually regained my composure.'

Julie, mother of Anna and Jake:

'Believe it or not, cleaning the oven is the most therapeutic thing I can do when I'm feeling really angry. It must be something to do with the scrubbing movement!'

It can be useful to have a 'script' to fall back on:

You could say:

'I'm so angry that anything I say now won't do either of us any good. I'll be back when I've calmed down.'

Then, as long as your children are safe, leave the room.

For more ideas, there are some organizations listed at the end of this book.

What to do when your children are angry

Everything you have read so far in this chapter will have given you a better understanding of your child's anger as well as your own. Just as you picked up messages about this emotion from your parents, so your own attitude will affect how your children perceive their angry feelings. Remember: anger is a useful signal about unmet needs, even if you don't accept the way your children are expressing it.

REDUCING THE FLOODING

How can you help your children when they are besieged by such powerful feelings?

When they are feeling upset or angry, your children are likely to be flooded with emotion and therefore unable to think clearly, just as you saw in the illustration on page 110.

So your first priority is to help to ebb away the flood. You need to find a conduit for the high emotions to escape safely. One of the most effective ways of doing this is to acknowledge your child's feelings, however unpleasant they may be.

A parent's story

One day Gloria found her daughter Jasmine was in a horrible mood after school. On the way home, she was calling her sister nasty names, and later on she lost her temper with a puzzle and threw it all over the floor. Then she shouted at her little brother and stamped out of the room slamming the door. Gloria's instinct was to follow Jasmine and give her a good telling off, but she'd recently learned about the power of acknowledging feelings. So, finding her on the stairs, she took a few deep breaths and said: 'It looks like you're really angry about something.'

Gloria listened while her daughter told her what had been going on that day, and eventually Jasmine said: 'I had to walk back from swimming on my own. Everyone else had a partner except me!'

Clearly the tip of the iceberg had been the puzzle Jasmine couldn't do, but beneath that were many other emotions. Perhaps the most important one was feeling friendless on the way back from swimming. If Gloria had just told her off for behaving so badly, Jasmine would have felt even more rejected. At that moment, her need was for acceptance, and once her feelings had been heard she calmed down and felt – and behaved – much better for the rest of the evening.

WHY CHILDREN GET ANGRY

Children often get angry and fight after school, much to their parents' annoyance.

Children have to put up with a lot over the school day. The teacher may have told them off; perhaps they couldn't keep up with some work; or they may have grazed a knee and been told not to cry; perhaps someone called them a nasty name or their favourite friend wouldn't play with them at lunchtime. All these things can result in them coming home overflowing with unspoken feelings which may well spill over in anger.

The way in which parents react to an angry child can have a dramatic effect. If you feel defensive and blame the child, you are likely to inflame the situation. However, as you saw in Chapter 6, if you listen and acknowledge how your child feels, it can help to calm things down. Just feeling 'heard' and understood is like a cool balm on an angry wound. This may sound easy, but in fact listening can be extremely difficult. Chapter 9 is dedicated to developing your skills in this area. Try working out a helpful response to an angry child in the following exercise.

Exercise: Helping an angry child

In these two examples, write down how you think the child might feel after hearing the parents' replies:

1   Child: 'It's not fair! You said we could go to the park!'
    Parent: 'It's not my fault. You're the one that's late.'
    Child feels: _____

2   Child: 'Hey! He's got more than me!'
    Parent: 'Don't be silly. You've had the same as everyone else.'
    Child feels: _____

(Contd)

This time the parents manage to resist the temptation of denying the angry emotions and instead help to identify what the child might be feeling:

1 Child: 'It's not fair! You said we could go to the park!'
   Parent: 'You're disappointed aren't you. You really love going to the park.'
   Child feels: _____

2 Child: 'Hey! He's got more than me!'
   Parent: 'It's really important to you that everyone is treated fairly.'
   Child feels: _____

Now write down a response that would acknowledge the feelings of this child.

Child: 'Abby's left all the lids off my felt tips and ruined them. I'll kill her when I see her!'
Parent: _____

Helping your child identify feelings before they reach boiling point
Children can feel frustrated when they have a multitude of emotions simmering away and cannot identify the feelings because they don't know the words for them. As covered in Chapter 5, giving children a vocabulary of feeling words helps them to become familiar with their inner world. When you sense your child is out of sorts, you could sit down together and look back at the feeling faces on pages 78–9 and point to all the ones you each feel 'right now'. Remember that opposite feelings can co-exist.

You can be happy and sad or angry and joyful at the same time; there are many different parts to everyone's life.

Some parents have found it helpful to make a photocopy of the feelings faces pages and stick it up where they and their children can easily refer to it.

Looking for the needs and addressing them
In Chapter 3, you explored the relationship between feelings, needs and behaviour. You discovered that angry feelings emanate from needs which have not been met. Here is a succinct list of needs which is easy to remember.

The four 'A's children need:

▶ *Attention*
▶ *Acceptance*
▶ *Appreciation*
▶ *Autonomy*.

Children are often fighting to get these needs met when they are angry.

For each of the **A**s think of ways in which you can help to meet the needs in your children and reduce angry outbursts.

Insight
We find that some children really feel strongly about autonomy – starting from shouting 'ME do it' as a toddler. If you can give choice and responsibility to these children they tend to relax and are easier to be around.

Helping children handle their angry feelings
When your child is acting out her anger, it's tempting as a parent to stop the behaviour by getting angry in return. In doing this, you will miss a golden opportunity to help your child manage her feelings. The role of a parent is to bring up a child, which means raising her from the instinctive angry fight response to an emotionally intelligent way of dealing with her strong feelings. This means learning that how she acts will influence how others respond. This learning is a life-long journey; there will be many ups and downs on the road, and you will need plenty of patience and forgiveness along the way.

If a child is in the grip of angry feelings, she will be emotionally flooded and unable to learn anything. When you listen to her, you help her calm down enough to be able to think. Naming feelings and needs will help your child to understand rather than be driven by them. You can talk things through with her when she has calmed down using a simple formula: 'How were you feeling? What did you need? What could you do differently next time?'

Your child may find it hard to suggest acceptable ways of managing the situation differently, particularly if she's still angry. If this is the case, acknowledge how she feels and wait until later. Then ask for other ideas, if necessary guiding her towards a more satisfactory solution.

You will find a fuller exploration of putting a stop to unacceptable behaviour in the 'thinking time' section of Chapter 11.

Exploring safe ways to let off steam

A child who is helped in these ways will gradually internalize the process; however, just as parents need 'first aid' techniques for the times when they're too furious to think, so children need to learn ways of letting off steam without kicking, biting, scratching, bullying, breaking or any of the other activities favoured by children in angry mode.

When you and your child are both feeling calm, talk about what could help when she is angry. Get her own views because every person is different, and what helps one may be of no use to another. You can open up some possibilities by saying what you find helpful when you want to release anger; this will have the added benefit of showing your child that adults take responsibility for discharging their anger safely.

Write down her ideas. If you have more than one child, they can all contribute, and again, the very fact of talking about such strong feelings will enhance understanding and closeness.

What will help me when I'm angry?

What can I do to calm down without hurting myself, or anyone/anything else?

Here are some safe ways other children have released their anger:

▶ *writing it down (if they're old enough)*
▶ *saying it with words*
▶ *drawing a picture of their angry feelings*
▶ *having a cushion to punch*
▶ *jumping up and down or doing star jumps*
▶ *doing something active like running round the garden*
▶ *playing a video game*
▶ *pulling up weeds in the garden (important that parent shows them which ones to pull!)*

Dave, father of Grace and Adam:

'It was after reading *Where the Wild Things Are* that Adam started to draw his anger. Often it's just a scribble, but it really does help him to calm down. It's as if drawing can tap into a much deeper place in him than words can.'

Responding when you're on the receiving end of anger
When faced with a barrage of angry words or actions, it is completely natural to feel angry and defensive, and hard not to respond in kind. Left to your natural impulses, that's what you would do. But if you want to avoid World War Three, remind yourself that you are the adult, and that your child's behaviour

spills out from feelings, which in turn spring from deep-seated needs (see the Needs Fountain on page 36).

There is a time and a place for everything. You will know when it is appropriate to acknowledge your child's feelings to calm her down and when it's important to give her a reality check. If your child says 'I hate you, you're really mean' when she doesn't get her way, you can judge how to respond. If you suspect she is deeply upset about something,

you could say:

'My goodness! You must be really upset to say that!'

If not, **you could say:**

'When you call me names, I just don't want to help. In fact I don't even want to listen!'

Then your child will learn that venting in this way has a negative outcome, and she will watch what she says and how she says it – both very important lessons for life.

> *I will listen to my anger and I will take charge of it: I won't let it be my boss.*

Preventing anger in the first place

Although there are sometimes deep-seated causes of anger, much of your children's irritation can be avoided by careful planning. Observe the times when your children get heated. What happened just before? What time of day was it? Were they hungry?

If they are very tetchy on the way back from school, perhaps their blood sugar is low and a little bite to eat might help? Or when they often fight in the back of the car, would it be possible to put something between them like a large teddy? The triggers exercise you used for yourself is equally valid for your children.

Exercise: Avoiding children's anger triggers

Make a list of some of your children's anger triggers. Write next to each one way of avoiding it.

Trigger	How can we avoid this?
_____	_____
_____	_____
_____	_____
_____	_____
_____	_____
_____	_____
_____	_____
_____	_____
_____	_____
_____	_____
_____	_____

And when the trigger is unavoidable, make full use of the other strategies explored in this chapter.

> ## Top tips for handling your child's anger
> ▶ *Acknowledge your child's feelings and use skilled listening to help her express what is really going on.*
> ▶ *Help your child to identify her own feelings and needs, and to work out how she could meet these needs in a better way.*
> ▶ *Try not to confront her anger with your anger.*
> ▶ *Discuss ways to let out angry feelings without damage.*
> ▶ *Work out ways to avoid situations where anger is triggered.*

Tantrums

Tantrums can come out of the blue or they can build up slowly. Although mainly found in small children, they can also occur in adults. Remember the last time you really lost it. How were you feeling? When asked this question some parents said they had felt extremely frustrated, powerless and out of control. Look back at the emotional flooding diagram on page 110, where the feelings are so high that there is little room for thinking. Tantrums are even more extreme: the emotions are so powerful that they push out the thinking part of the brain completely. It can be a very frightening state, and if your child is prone to tantrums it is important that you remain calm and provide the firm anchor that she needs to stop her blowing away in the storm.

Occasionally a child will discover that the power she wields when having a tantrum can get her what she wants, and will then use tantrums for all they're worth! So never give in to a tantrum.

> ## Insight
> I remember hearing the screams of a child resonating round a big hall in the Science Museum. Her Dad obviously thought it best to turn a deaf ear to her behaviour, but no one else could possibly ignore the tantrum as it grew to ear-splitting

proportions. I just wished her father would take her out! It
would have taught her that it's ok to feel very angry, but it's
better to vent it in a way which will not disturb others. – *Glenda*

The following two stories illustrate the difference between a
'genuine' and a 'manipulative' tantrum, as well as their solutions.

Parents' stories

Amina had been on a very long flight and there was an endless wait
at passport control. In front of her was a family with several children.
The youngest, a little girl of about two, was tired and whiny. She
kept tugging at her mother's dress and asking to be picked up. The
mother was struggling with bags and was clearly on a short fuse, so
she angrily told her daughter to stop pulling her. Amina said: 'I was
longing for someone just to pick her up.' The little girl started crying
and her father ordered her to keep quiet, whereupon she threw
herself on the floor and let out ear-splitting screeches while pounding
the floor with hands and feet. All the family were exhausted, and
at the end of their tether, but finally another adult in the party
scooped the child up to her own eye level and said: 'You must be
very tired and very, very fed up!' As if by magic, the little girl stopped
crying. Someone had cared enough to understand what she was
feeling, and that was enough to calm her down.

* * *

Celia has three children, with quite a big age gap between the
last two. The youngest has been a little tyrant for quite a while
now. His tantrums are so terrible that everyone has been walking
around on eggshells trying to avoid them. It's hard to believe that
such a small person can wield so much power over the rest of
the family. But something recently changed for Celia. She says:
'The other day I was talking to a friend about Finlay's tantrums,
and she unexpectedly said: "You're afraid of him, aren't you?"
That really hit home. I'd never thought of it like that before, but
it was true. Something inside me suddenly clicked and I thought

(Contd)

to myself: "You're the parent. He's only a small boy." I can't quite explain it, but my bearing or tone of voice must have changed because the tantrums have stopped. They say that children are good at picking up underlying feelings, so perhaps he's sensed that I've decided that I'm in charge now.'

All the skills you have learned in this chapter will help you to handle a genuine tantrum. In the first story it was acknowledging the feelings of the child which brought her out of her frenzy. In the case of the manipulative tantrum, when Celia woke up to the fact that she was indeed the adult, it gave her clarity about her role and an inner firmness, which Finlay picked up. You will learn more about having 'spine' in Chapter 11 on boundaries.

TEN TANTRUM TACTICS

Here are some additional tips for dealing with tantrums:

1 **Keep calm.** *If you get heated, so will your child.*

2 **Take deep breaths** *to stay calm.*

3 **Acknowledge your child's feelings.** *For example, 'It's been a long, hot journey, and you're really fed up!'. If you can do this in time, you may prevent the tantrum before it starts.*

4 **Remember you are the parent** *and you need to provide boundaries. For example, 'It's alright to feel angry, but it's not safe to throw bricks.'*

5 **Take your child to a quiet place to calm down** *if they are causing disruption to others or damage (your car will do if it's nearby).*

6 **Provide comfort** *if the tantrum is from distress. For example, 'I can see you're really upset, let's see what we can do about it.' Sometimes it helps to hold a child firmly (from behind, if*

their arms and legs are flailing) to give them a sense that their strong feelings are safely contained.

7 **After acknowledging the feeling, it can work to ignore the tantrum** *and let children work it out on their own, but only if they are not in danger or causing disruption to others.*

8 **Offer ways to take anger out safely,** *such as punching a pillow or jumping up and down. Doing a drawing of angry feelings can help too.*

9 **Separation.** *With an older child, tell them to stay in their room until they have calmed down. This gives them the control rather than setting a time limit.*

10 **Praise for regaining control.** *Offer a hug to reassure them that they are still loved after outbursts.*

Important: **Never give in to tantrums!**

If children find that tantrums 'work', they will use them to get their own way. And a final word on anger – when all is said and done, there are times when laughter is the best medicine.

Little Johnny was practising the violin in the living room while his father was trying to read. The family dog was in there too, and, on hearing the screeching sounds, began to howl. Johnny's father listened to the dog and the violin for as long as he could bear it. Finally he jumped up, slammed his newspaper on the floor and yelled: 'For God's sake, can't you play something the dog doesn't know?'

PARENTS' COMMENTS

Laura, mother of Rory and Owen:

'Since we drew our feelings into the body outlines we all feel closer, and somehow the air is less charged.'

Celia, mother of Grace, Adam and Finlay:

'Adam is a boy who likes to know what is going to happen in advance, and I've finally put two and two together. I've realized that he got angry because I sprang things on him ... So I'm planning ahead more and letting him know what to expect, and we're all a lot calmer.'

Things which have struck me in this chapter

Something I am going to try out

HAVE SOME FUN

Making bread

Making bread is enjoyable and therapeutic. If anyone is feeling angry, kneading the dough will be just the job for getting it out of their system. Frayed feelings will be soothed as the wonderful smell of baking permeates the air; and a sense of peace and harmony will descend on the house as everyone looks forward to having a taste of the warm loaf. You can take it in turns to knead.

All you have to do is buy some bread flour and follow the instructions on the packet. Some brands even contain the yeast already.

10 THINGS TO REMEMBER

1 Anger is common in families, paradoxically because the home is where we feel safe to let out strong emotions; but it can hurt feelings and damage relationships, so it is important to channel it constructively.

2 Anger produces physical changes in our bodies which prepare us for 'fight or flight' and prevent us from thinking clearly.

3 Be aware of physical feelings which herald anger before it takes hold of you.

4 Think of anger as a useful warning signal telling you when you need to address something.

5 When you are angry, remember to start your sentence with 'I' not 'You' to avoid blaming and stirring up anger in response.

6 Be realistic about what you can expect of your children; they will be messy and forget things, because they are children.

7 Help your children become more aware of their feelings and find words for them so they don't burst out as anger.

8 Give your children safe outlets for their anger so they can slowly calm down.

9 Find ways to avoid 'trigger' situations.

10 Learn to discern the difference between genuine and manipulative tantrums and treat them accordingly.

8

Encouraging co-operation and positive feelings

In this chapter you will learn:
- *creative ways to change behaviour*
- *how to 'reframe' your language to go for the positive*
- *how to describe behaviour and give choices*
- *ways to avoid nagging and encourage responsibility.*

A parent's story

Sarah is seeking help with an ongoing difficulty.

'Every morning I have a battle of wills with my daughter Martha. She likes to play on the computer before school and that makes us late. I tell her to stop playing and get ready. She says "Yes", but then just goes on playing. Then I lose patience, storm in and switch the computer off. But while I'm feeding the little ones, she goes back to her game, and the battle starts all over again. I'd love to find a way of making her co-operate, but I have no idea where to start. We seem to be locked into a power struggle and she's got the upper hand.'

How often parents complain that their children are disobedient, don't listen, or that they have daily clashes over things that need doing! Struggles over cleaning teeth, homework, bath time, feeding the pet, going to bed, or meal times can be very wearing when all you want is for your children to do as they are told.

This chapter will offer you ways to avoid the conflicts and gain co-operation.

Do you have any persistent battles with your children? If so, you might like to write them down here so you can refer back to them:

Persistent battles

_____

_____

_____

_____

_____

Children would love to do exactly what they want whenever they want. However, as they grow up, they have to learn how to fit in with other people and the outside world. At times, they will learn from their own experiences, and often they will need guidance and correction. This is why parents have to 'raise them'. Some children take instructions easily, while others react strongly against being told what to do, or seem not to take on board what you tell them. This can be a struggle if, like Sarah, you are pitting your power against that of your child. The truth is that Sarah cannot **make** her daughter co-operate; she can only **gain** her co-operation. Coercion is about one person winning and the other losing (the severe parenting style in Chapter 2), and co-operation is about both people freely pursuing a common goal – where both win.

When you and your children are on the same team rather than on opposing squads, when you face the world together, with all its challenges, side by side, the ground is laid for gaining their co-operation. As you practise the attitudes and skills you have read about in previous chapters, you will find that you become closer to your children and understand each other better. Taking care of yourself so you have more patience with your children; thinking of your children's feelings and needs as well as your own, and how these affect behaviour; listening to your children; helping them deal with strong emotions and find solutions to their difficulties; showing them how to manage their anger while avoiding dumping your own frustrations on them – all these things will make them more willing to help you.

If you think of your child's development as different qualities growing like seedlings, then you – the gardener – can feed and water those qualities, and provide the conditions for the sun to reach them. In this chapter, you will learn more ways to grow co-operation and a positive attitude in your children.

The value of play and playfulness

> *Man is most nearly himself when he achieves the seriousness of a child at play.*
>
> Heraclitus, 535–475 BC

It is all too easy for family life to become a series of dos and don'ts, of shoulds and shouldn'ts, and for fun to trail so far behind that it almost disappears over the horizon. In the midst of their busy lives, parents often need to be reminded to have fun.

Children need little prompting. Their primary activity is play, and this is the way they learn about the world and relationships. Indeed, play is common to all young mammals. Ask an adult what made them happy in their childhood and they will often come up with examples of childhood games and adventures.

Playing games with your children – whether imaginary ones, board games, cards, sports or computer games – creates an atmosphere of fun and co-operation. There's a radiance to parents and children when they come in after kicking a ball around together or playing some other sport, which brings positive energy back into the home. It's also valuable to let children play on their own, uninterrupted by parents. The world of their own imagination is an important place. There are studies which show that some children's lives are filled with so many after-school activities that there is little time left for free play. Television and internet use is another consumer of the time that used to be spent in play.

The UK research company Childwise has found that, while TV watching has reduced, time online and playing computer games has more than replaced it. The average 'screen time' for five- to 16-year-olds is an incredible five hours and 20 minutes a day, and two thirds of five- to eight-year-olds have their own TV. So the screen takes away from family time as well as play time. To give more time for play, it is vital to find ways of rationing 'screen time' which work for you and your family (more about this in Chapter 11).

The unstructured time when children just make up their own games may seem like a waste to some, but it offers many benefits. From playing, children learn to:

- ▶ *take turns*
- ▶ *count*
- ▶ *develop their imagination*
- ▶ *relate to others*
- ▶ *express their feelings*
- ▶ *share*
- ▶ *assert themselves and make their needs known*
- ▶ *create and respect rules*
- ▶ *be good losers, not gloat as winners, and much more.*

They also develop creativity, co-ordination, balance and numerous physical skills as well as the parts of their brain which relate to all these. What's more, it is through play that children can process difficult or painful circumstances in their lives.

Even if playing often involves fights between your children, these quarrels help them learn to find creative solutions to differing needs and wishes. There is more on conflict resolution later in this chapter and in Chapter 12.

PLAYFUL WAYS TO GAIN CO-OPERATION

Since children make sense of the world through the 'language' of play, this can bring great results when you want to engage your children's co-operation. Parents have ordered, cajoled, nagged and shouted to get something done – without success. Then, to their surprise and relief, they have found that their children will happily co-operate as soon as an element of fun is injected into the situation.

Gloria, mother of Jasmine, Chantal and Nathan:

'I've been having so much trouble getting Chantal to hold on to the pushchair when we cross the road. A friend suggested I try to turn it into a game, so I asked Chantal if she'd like to skip, jump or hop across the road. Last time she chose to jump 'like a frog'. She didn't object to holding the pushchair because her mind was on something she enjoyed.'

Exercise: Playful solutions

Think of times when your child baulks at doing something you've asked him to do. It could be putting toys away, hanging up coats, practising a musical instrument, or clearing away his plate. Write down one example here:

What could you do, using the 'language' of play, to encourage your child?

Suresh, father of Asha and Hari:

'Asha's music teacher found a great way of getting her to practise the violin. She made a list of six things to work on and numbered them. Then Asha threw a dice and practised whichever number came up. If the same number appeared more than twice, she could throw again until every task had been done. It was brilliant. It turned it all into a game, which made practice so much more fun!'

As an adult, you also know how much easier it is to approach a task if you are in a good mood. If you tell yourself that cleaning the car is going to be entertaining – using those muscles, listening to the birdsong, seeing the passers-by, and having the satisfaction of a shiny clean car – it will be a very different experience from saying to yourself 'I suppose I'd better clean the car now. What a bore!'

Insight

My children's primary school headmaster used to illustrate this approach in assembly by shaving in front of them, describing how he played a game to make something he had to do every morning more interesting: seeing how few strokes of his razor he could use each day! They still remember this lesson years later. – *Doro*

Cultivate the fun approach in your family and see how everyone's mood improves.

The power of language

CREATING A POSITIVE ATMOSPHERE

Try this little experiment:

'Don't think about spilling the orange juice!'

What picture came into your mind? Most people report seeing orange juice in their mind's eye – and it's spilt.

Now imagine your child is holding a large carton of orange juice and is about to pour it into a glass. You nervously say: 'Don't spill it!' What picture will come into his head? He will get the idea that he might spill it, and consequently may well do so.

Don't is possibly one of the most common words in the parents' lexicon, and it is certainly not the most helpful one. In a statement like: 'Don't spill the orange juice', a complicated mental process is triggered by the 'don't':

1 *The child pictures the orange juice spilling.*
2 *He has to cancel the image planted in his imagination, telling himself **not** to do that thing.*
3 *He will then try to work out what he must do instead.*
4 *Someone has expressed the belief that he's going to get it wrong – a lot of negatives!*

How much easier it will be if you tell him what you **want** him to do. If you calmly say: 'Pour the juice very carefully.'

1 *He pictures the juice being poured slowly and accurately.*
2 *He doesn't need to cancel anything in his imagination.*
3 *He knows what he needs to do.*
4 *He feels you trust him to get it right.*

Every time you say '**Don't**', you put into your child's head the very thing you want him to avoid. To be more positive, and to engender confidence in your child:

Top tip
Go for what you want.

So, instead of saying: 'Don't make a noise when I'm on the phone'

you could say:

'Be nice and quiet while I'm on the phone.'

This does not mean that your child will always magically do what you ask, but at least he knows what you want and is more likely to co-operate.

Exercise: Changing negatives into positives

Change all the following 'Don'ts' into positive statements, indicating what you want to happen. For example, 'Don't hurt the baby!' becomes: 'Touch the baby very gently.'

'Don't be rude.'

'Don't forget your swimming things.'

'Don't knock down Adam's castle.'

'Don't pull Anna's hair.'

(Suggestions at the end of the chapter.)

Add your most common 'Don'ts' here, and think how to say what you do want instead of talking about what you don't want.

Don't

Don't

Don't

If your child is about to run out in front of a bus you will, of course, say whatever first comes into your head to save him, and rightly so. At the same time, with practice, it will become more automatic for you to put things positively. Think about the picture you plant in your child's mind if you say 'Don't run into the road!' It is far more effective to yell 'STOP!'

SAYING 'NO'

The family is not a democracy. Parents need to set limits and say 'No'. Children need to learn to accept that. It is fundamental for all human beings to accept they are not omnipotent; that there are things which are out of bounds, occasions when their needs cannot be met immediately, and other considerations which may take precedence over their wishes. When a child comes up against an obstacle to his desires in the form of a 'No', he learns to find other ways to meet his needs; he also learns to manage the inevitable disappointments which life will deal him.

A parent's story

Penny's daughters and their friends were especially looking forward to a picnic they had planned for some time, but she had to put it off because she had some urgent work to do. They pleaded with her in vain – it was a definite 'No'. She felt really bad about disappointing them, but was amazed to see that half an hour later, they had made a tent in the garden, and were having their own picnic. She was impressed with their inventiveness.

Although 'No' is a word children must come to terms with, it is also possible to over-use it. This can bring out an obstinate or rebellious streak in them. Try keeping a note of the number of times you say 'No' on a typical day.

All too often, when children ask if they can do something, a parent's default position is 'No'. Imagine your child wants to go and play with a friend after school. Do you sometimes find yourself saying

'No' because of other plans and later regret your hastiness on thinking the matter through? A number one rule before saying 'No' is:

Give yourself time to think.

In the above scenario, when your child springs a request on you,

you could say:

'Well, let's see ... Let me think about it for a minute ...'

In that time, you, he, his friend, or his friend's parent could come up with a viable solution.

> **Insight**
> We've come to realize that children learn much more from what we *do* than what we say. If they see us taking a moment to turn things over in our minds before coming to a decision they will learn to do the same.

AVOIDING CONFRONTATION

As you have seen, your child needs to understand and accept that he cannot always have his way. A blunt 'No' can be like a red rag to a bull, and he may charge at you with a 'Why not?' or simply disobey you. So if you don't want to give in and say 'Yes' to everything like the indulgent parent type in Chapter 2; if you don't wish to produce a tyrant who ignores the needs of everyone else and cannot co-operate with the people around him – what can you do?

Here are some ways you can set limits without inviting a confrontation.

▶ **Inform**

'Mum ... Can I go over to Andy's now?'
Rather than: 'No you can't',

you could say: 'Granny's about to arrive for lunch.'

Your child will realize that he will have to wait, with no need for a long explanation.

▶ **Describe the difficulty**

'Can we go skating this afternoon?'
Rather than: 'No, you'll have to wait for another time',

you could say: 'I'm waiting for a parcel delivery.'
Your child will realize it's a 'No' without your having to say so.

▶ **Acknowledge feelings**

When it's time to leave the playground and your child wants to stay, rather than: 'No, you can't stay! We have to collect Zach',

you could say: 'You'd like to stay here all evening, you're having such a great time (picking up the bucket and spade). It's hard to tear yourself away when you're enjoying yourself so much!'
It's easier to co-operate when someone understands how you feel.

▶ **'Yes' instead of 'No'**

Strange though it may seem, a 'No' can be a 'Yes' at another time. Make use of this for engaging co-operation:
'Can we have a story?'
Rather than: 'No. You must have your bath first',

you could say: 'Yes! When you've had your bath.'

Very simple language adjustments such as these can transform the atmosphere in your home.

DESCRIBE RATHER THAN LABEL

Another way to generate harmony in your home and a positive attitude in your children is to avoid the use of labels. This exercise may help to bring back memories of how you felt when people talked about you.

Exercise: Labels remembered

Think back to your childhood and remember any words which were used to describe you, such as: 'selfish', 'lazy', 'thoughtless', 'clumsy', or any others.

Think of just one word which was applied to you and remember:

How did this make you feel about yourself?

How did you feel about the person who described you?

Amina, mother of Hussein and Noor:

'I remember an aunt who used to call me "thoughtless". I never knew quite what she meant, but I reckoned there must be something wrong with me. I felt bad about myself but had no idea how to put things right. I didn't like that aunt; in fact, I used to keep out of her way when she came to stay.'

Penny, mother of Mia and Abby:

'When I didn't want to mix in a crowd of strangers, my mother would explain it by saying: "She's shy you know." I got an image of what a shy person looked like – rather small, pale and weak. So I was shy, whatever that meant, until my twenties, when I left home and realized I didn't have to be that way. I feel that I missed out on a lot in my teens as a result of that label.'

The dangers of labelling

Negative and often repeated language can have a 'hypnotic effect' on children. If you tell children something often enough, they will believe it and internalize it. This in turn creates adults with negative beliefs about themselves which are hard to change.

When you think about Penny being called shy, you can see how the label defined her.

▶ *A label coloured the parent's view of the child.*
▶ *The child saw herself as being shy.*
▶ *It became a self-fulfilling prophecy.*
▶ *It was hard for the child to act differently – she was in a box.*

Insight

When we talk about the effects of labels with groups of parents, they can feel guilty about the names they have called their children – words such as 'stupid', 'silly', 'naughty', 'careless' or 'selfish'. It is important to accept that we do the best we can with the knowledge we have at the time, and that it is never too late to change.

How you speak to your children is influenced by the kind of language which was used about you by parents, teachers, friends, and relatives, probably with the best of intentions, thinking it would improve you.

If you have a tendency to be hard on yourself, it is more encouraging to ask: 'What can I do differently? What will be more helpful?' This is a useful phrase to say any time you're not happy about something you've done. It reminds you that you can always choose how to behave. Remember – children don't arrive with an instruction manual. You learn on the job, and you will go on learning for the rest of your life, like all other parents.

DESCRIBING BEHAVIOUR

The drawback of words like 'naughty', 'silly', 'forgetful', 'clumsy' and other labels is that they don't give any useful information for the child to act upon. If Amina's aunt had said: 'You've left the basket behind at the shop', the child would have remembered what she had to do rather than feeling criticized. And if Penny's mother had said: 'You don't seem to like joining in when there are a lot of people', Penny might have told her mother that she didn't know what to say. Then they could have talked it over and come up with some helpful ideas.

Separate the doer from the deed.

Describing is much more effective than labelling if you want behaviour to change. Where a label limits, a description empowers someone to take charge of the situation.

Exercise: Converting labels into descriptions

Try changing these labels into descriptions:

Example: Mia orders her friends around.

Label: 'You're always so bossy.'
Description: 'You often tell your friends what to do.'

Note – Avoid saying 'always', as there may well be occasions when Mia goes along with her friends' ideas.

Logan likes to see how things work, and in the process sometimes breaks them.

Label: 'You're so destructive!'
Description:

Grace took some biscuits from the cupboard without asking.

Label: 'You're a naughty girl!'
Description:

Now think of some labels you apply to your children, then describe their behaviour instead.

Label:
Description:

Label:
Description:

In Chapter 11, you will see how a description can lead on to a request for change when the behaviour is unacceptable.

Not surprisingly, children also tend to label each other and even themselves, and the words they use can stick well into adult life. Listen to children's conversation in the playground, and you will hear how much labelling goes on. If, then, you find your children calling each other names, ask them to describe the deed instead.

Adam: 'Grace is so horrible.'
Parent: 'What has she done?'
Adam: 'She won't let me have a go on the computer.'

Once the behaviour has been defined, it is easier to take appropriate action.

POSITIVE LABELS

It may surprise you that even positive labels can be less valuable than describing behaviour. Some adults recount that being called 'clever' or 'good' felt like being cast in a role which was hard to live up to. If you were called 'clever' for example, you may have worried about what would happen if you didn't do well in an exam. Saying 'Good girl' gives very little information. Instead,

you could say:

'I noticed you let Adam have a go on the computer and that stopped you having a fight. I'm so pleased!'

From the description, your child learns that her kindness has not gone unnoticed, that it has had a positive effect, and that you're happy as a result.

Top tips for avoiding labels

▶ *Separate the doer from the deed by describing the behaviour rather than labelling the child.*
▶ *Be specific and use neutral rather than blaming language.*
▶ *Ask your children to describe what someone is doing rather than using labels themselves.*
▶ *Remember to describe positive behaviour in detail rather than using general positive words like 'clever boy'.*

Giving choices

Somewhere between 18 months and two years old, it seems that human beings discover they have free will. How often you can spot that determined 'You try and make me' look crossing the face of a toddler! Parents can feel completely powerless when faced with a battle of wills, however tiny their opponent! What can you do, when your child refuses to do as he's told? Firstly, think for a moment: how do you feel if someone orders you to do something? Are you more likely to want to comply if you freely choose to do so?

Insight

We have asked mothers and fathers how they feel now if their own parents try to tell them what to do. They tell us they often react against their parents' advice – even if it's eminently sensible!

A parent's story

Teresa is trying to set off for lunch at her father's place, but her two younger boys are holding things up: they're in the middle of a game and don't want to leave. As she impatiently hustles them along, Sean says that it's not fair – they hate it at Grandad's! It's so boring! At this, Teresa feels very upset, because she loves her father and wants her children to enjoy seeing him. She's starting to panic as she senses a battle coming on. She says: 'I'm sorry, there's no choice in the matter. He'll have cooked lunch for us and we can't disappoint him now. Come right now or you won't have any sweets this week!' The battle continues, and she's about to drag them struggling into the car when she pauses for a minute. Surely there must be a better way of handling this situation. She walks down to the end of the garden breathing deeply. Perhaps the boys might need to have some control in this situation rather than feeling forced into something they don't want to do. When she returns, she has a clearer idea of what to say.

Teresa: 'I can see it's annoying to leave when you're in the middle of a game'.
(acknowledges their feelings = first step in gaining co-operation)

'Would you like to take the game with you or come back to it later?'
(offers a choice = second step)

(Contd)

Sean: 'We can't take the game, all the pieces will get moved!'

Teresa: 'OK, so would you like to take something else or climb Grandad's oak tree?'
(continues to throw the ball back into their court = another step in gaining co-operation)

Logan: 'Let's climb the tree. We can always watch TV if we get bored.'
(end result = the children are happy to co-operate)

If you try to understand their behaviour by seeking the underlying needs (see the 'Needs Fountain' in Chapter 3), it is clear that the boys dig in their heels because they feel forced. Their needs for respect, autonomy and independence are not considered.

While in the garden, Teresa took the time to think (**ACT**), and the tools she used were to acknowledge their feelings and offer some choice – taking their needs into consideration. She kept sight of her own needs too. She did not offer them the choice to go or not to go to Grandad's. That was not an option. Instead, she offered them *limited* choices which gave them the freedom to find a way to enjoy their time at her father's house. This is an example of how the 'loving and firm' style works (see Chapter 2).

SOME MORE EXAMPLES OF LIMITED CHOICES

You could say:

'Would you like to do your homework before or after tea?'

'Shall I help you wash your hair or do you want to do it yourself? You choose.'

'Do you want to pick up the toys or shall we do it together?'

Make sure that either option offered is acceptable to you. If you only give one option, you may well get a 'No' – for example 'Do you want to pick up your toys now?'

164

GENERATING SOLUTIONS

As your children grow, you will want to encourage their independence and autonomy, and a good way to do this is to involve them in generating solutions, rather as Teresa did with her boys. It is surprising how much easier it is to resolve ongoing battles when you invite your children to join in the peace process. At the beginning of this chapter, you read about Sarah's battle with her daughter over using the computer before school – a battle which was repeated almost daily: order – ignore – angry intervention – disobedience – retaliation – frustration – and bad feelings all round. Here is what happened next:

A parent's story – continued

With the help of a friend, Sarah thought over her difficulty and decided on a different tactic. She waited for a calm moment after tea, well away from the battlefield, and said:

'Martha, you know in the mornings we often have fights about the computer? Well, I hate that, and I've been wondering if we can change things so we can have a nice peaceful start to the day, and you can get to school on time ... Any ideas?'

'Well, you could just leave me alone.'

'Yes. That's one idea. And for me to feel calm in the morning I need to know you'll be ready to leave the house at 8.30. How can we make that happen?'

'I suppose I could get dressed first.'

'OK. Good idea. Now tell me exactly what's going to happen tomorrow morning.'

'Tomorrow morning I'll get up and put my clothes on before I switch on the computer.'

'Right. I won't nag you, and you'll get dressed before playing on the computer. And we'll have a much happier morning!'

You will have noticed that Sarah coaxed the solutions from Martha rather than telling her what to do. She also ensured that her own need for punctuality was not neglected in the process. Martha is likely to go along with the new plan because she came up with the ideas herself. Note that Sarah asked her daughter to say specifically what she was going to do in her own words; this gave Martha a mental picture of what was going to happen and made it more real.

Remember, it's important to evaluate any new plan after a few days. If it's not working, go back to the drawing board and generate new solutions.

For more on problem solving, see the 'negotiation model' in Chapter 12.

Giving responsibility gives confidence

When you were a child, were you given any jobs to do? If so, how did that make you feel? Important? Capable? Proud of yourself? Valued? Respected? Responsible? Anything else?

When children are given responsibilities, it builds their self-esteem, and when children feel good about themselves they want to co-operate with others.

Mike, father of Eric:

'When we were kids, my Mum only allowed us to have pet mice on condition that we were entirely responsible for them. We learned a lot from that: we cleaned their cage, fed them, and let them out for runs. Two mice turned into 24, and we regularly had to find homes for the babies. It taught us quite a few life skills, and I suppose that gave us confidence.'

In some cultures, children still play a crucial part in the household, but it is increasingly common for parents to do virtually everything for their children. This can mean a child no longer feels they have an important role to play in the family. Doing things for themselves and others gives children a sense of value and teaches them that the world does not revolve around them. Try this exercise for some ideas.

Exercise: Giving responsibility

Look at the following tasks and consider which ones you could encourage your children to do for themselves. It can be helpful to think about levels of responsibility, depending on their ages and stages.

Level 1: Doing it with you

Level 2: Needing to be reminded

Level 3: Fully responsible

Put a child's initials and their level next to anything they are capable of doing.

▶ *Get dressed*
▶ *Make their bed*
▶ *Tidy their room*
▶ *Choose their clothes and lay them out for the next day*
▶ *Make their breakfast/school lunch/family meal*
▶ *Sort and put clean clothes away*
▶ *Tidy toys/put games away*
▶ *Bath/brush teeth/brush hair/wash hair*
▶ *Hoovering/dusting/sweeping/dishes*
▶ *Mowing the lawn/gardening*
▶ *Emptying the bins/collecting rubbish around the house for recycling*
▶ *Laundry/ironing/mending clothes*
▶ *Homework*
▶ *Choose and buy clothes/presents*

(Contd)

- *Make decisions about their routines/their friends/their lifestyle*
- *Help younger children*
- *Shopping (corner shop/online orders/putting away)*
- *Help washing, peeling and chopping fruit and vegetables*
- *Help grandparents or other friends and relatives*
- *DIY/home decoration*
- *Growing vegetables/herbs*
- *Clean the car*
- *Practising a musical instrument/dance routine/ gymnastics, etc.*
- *Care for pets.*

Is there one area of responsibility you could introduce your children to during the next week?

Make a specific plan:

What task? _____

Who will do it? _____

When? _____

What is the first step? _____.

You could also ask your children for ideas; see if there are other things they would add to the list. To engage co-operation, your attitude and words are very important. Which of the following is more likely to succeed?

- *Now you're older you've got to help with the dishes.*

Or:

- *I think you might be ready to learn a new life skill.*

Remember, every child is unique. They develop at different rates, have diverse abilities, and take pleasure in different activities. One child may enjoy gardening while another may prefer sweeping the kitchen floor; so go with the flow wherever possible, and allow people to do things which suit their temperaments.

Bear in mind that children will learn many of these jobs by doing them with you. Working on things together can be great fun and an opportunity for conversation.

Gloria, mother of Jasmine, Chantal and Nathan:

'Every week, I give each of my children a 'special job'. It could be emptying the rubbish bin, polishing the brass doorknob, dusting the piano, or taking the compost out into the garden. I've been quite surprised really that just calling them 'special' has made the jobs so appealing to the children. The little ones even get excited when I tell them what their special job will be each week. It's amazing how the language we use can make such a difference!'

Insight

We always remind parents that, while encouraging children to do things for themselves, they also need to be prepared for them to regress at times. A child who was dressing himself quite happily until a new baby was born might start asking for help; and a child who is unwell may cling and want more comfort. Loving parents don't criticize in these situations, but know that their children will bounce back eventually.

Nag busters

'If you just did as you were told, I wouldn't have to keep going on about it!' is a familiar parental moan. Many complain that their children don't seem to hear, let alone listen. This 'deafness' appears to be selective, since their children's hearing is perfect the minute a treat is mentioned! Why might this be the case?

REASONS CHILDREN DON'T HEAR

- ▶ *They are completely absorbed in an activity.*
- ▶ *What the parent is saying is not seen as important, particularly if not followed through.*
- ▶ *It's boring.*
- ▶ *It's something the child does not want to do, so he switches off.*
- ▶ *The tone of voice is not firm enough.*
- ▶ *The child may have a physical hearing problem.*

Having ruled out the last of these, by medical tests if necessary, you can address the other reasons your child may not listen to you. It is true that much of what parents say to their children is humdrum. 'Get dressed, wash your hands, remember your books, have you done your practice?' must all be very boring to hear! No wonder children switch off.

Nagging is also tedious for parents. When you are tired and stressed, and your children don't listen to you, it's not surprising you sound and look disgruntled – you certainly feel it! All this is hardly a recipe for co-operation. As well as making life easier at home, learning to listen and follow instructions is very important for children's success at school. So what can you do to get their attention and avoid repeating yourself ad nauseam?

KEEP IT SIMPLE

Small children (and children with ADD) find it very hard to remember more than one instruction at a time, so avoid giving lengthy requests. 'Boots in the porch' will be much easier to remember than 'Hey, don't come into the kitchen with your boots on, they'll be all muddy. Take them off, and leave them in the porch, and then ... Oh yes ... Find your slippers ... I think they're upstairs ... Have you done your homework yet? Well, you'd better hurry up and do it before supper. And what about the goldfish? Has he been fed?'

REMEMBER – CHILDREN FORGET

Children become deeply absorbed in their own worlds and may genuinely forget when you've asked them to do something. Reminding is positive – you are giving them a suggestion, a cue or a prompt. On the other hand, nagging comes with a critical and scolding tone. How much nicer to hear: 'Sally, remember the goldfish!' rather than: 'Why do I always have to tell you to feed the goldfish? Can't you remember anything for yourself? We never should have got it!' When you remind, you give the child the credit for having a mind, and at the same time help them to focus on what needs to be done.

SINGING, MUSIC AND GESTURES

Just as drawing pictures can help your children express their unspoken emotions (see Chapters 6 and 7), so music accesses parts of the brain that words alone cannot reach. When a child ignores or rebuffs your request, singing can bring a whole new dimension to the interaction. Try 'Time to go upstairs now' to the tune of 'Ring-a-ring-a-roses' or any other melody you like, and you may get a better result than with spoken words alone. Indeed, doing anything unexpected can move a child along when they've dug their heels in.

Some parents find that playing some suitable music encourages their children to do the required task. It could be something purposeful for tidying the toys away, or a dreamy piece for calming down before going to bed.

Miming and gestures can provide an interesting alternative when you've said the same thing over and over again with little success. To relieve the boredom of nagging, you could hold your finger to your lips instead of saying: 'Be quiet', or you could point to the towel on the floor rather than irritably demanding your child pick it up for the hundredth time.

ADVANCE WARNING

Much pestering can be avoided if you tell your children in advance what you expect them to do. Look at these two possible ways of getting help at supper time.

Ingrid: 'Can you help me at supper time?'
Eric: 'Yeah!'

Two minutes before supper:
Ingrid: 'Why haven't you come to lay the table? You said you'd help!'
Eric: 'Well, I didn't know it was ready, did I?'

A more effective exchange could be to say, on returning home from school:
Ingrid: 'Tonight I'd like some help laying the table for supper. I'll let you know ten minutes before supper's ready.'
Eric: 'OK.'

Fifteen minutes before supper, reminding of the previous conversation:
Ingrid: 'In five minutes' time I'd like help with the table.'

Ten minutes before supper:
Ingrid: 'Time to lay the table! Supper will be ready in ten minutes.'
Eric: 'OK.'
Ingrid: 'Thanks for coming so promptly. I like everything to be ready, so the supper doesn't get cold.'

Giving advance notice, so they know what to expect, helps children prepare mentally for what is to come.

For example, **you could say:**

'It may be a long wait at the doctor's surgery. What would you like to take so the time passes more quickly?'

LISTS AND NOTES

One father grew tired of endlessly reminding his son of all the things he had to take to school with him. So they wrote a checklist together, and stuck it up by the front door. The son looked at it before he set off for school, and reminded himself what was needed: a very simple cure for the nagging which had poisoned their departure before. How about doing the same thing for bedtime? The list could include putting clothes away neatly, bathing, leaving the towels on the towel rail, cleaning teeth and whatever else forms part of your child's bedtime routine. A picture of a book could be added at the end as an incentive.

Suppose you have a rule that school work is done before watching TV. Instead of nagging your children to switch it off, you could, in advance, stick a large piece of paper over the screen with the words 'Have you done your homework?' in bold felt tip pen. If the hamster's cage is getting smelly, instead of doing the usual thing of nagging your children to clean it out, try a note on the cage with 'I don't like my home smelling. Please help me.' And sign it off with the name of the hamster.

SUMMON ATTENTION

When your child acts as if he hasn't heard you, move into his line of vision, kneel down to his level, and make eye contact to ensure he is listening. Ask him: 'Would you tell me what I've just said?', in a firm and enquiring tone rather than a scolding one. If your child manages to repeat back what you said, you can reply: 'Fine. Now I know you've heard me, I won't need to mention it again.' If he is concentrating on something else and has zoned out, you can repeat your words, clearly and informatively. Give him time to process the instruction, and then follow through if necessary.

Forcing eye contact can distress children with Autistic Spectrum Disorder. However, they need to see what you are signing or showing them, so getting them to face you is fine.

_____

Positive attention

To conclude, children learn more from encouragement than criticism. Their good qualities grow best when their parents stop paying so much attention to mistakes and misdemeanours, and instead give them plenty of positive attention. Perhaps your best teachers were the ones who pointed out when you did something well and were sparing and tactful with their corrections?

Exercise: Encouragement

Quality of the week

Try this with your children.

1 *Choose the three qualities you most want your child to have. They could include kindness to others, patience, gentleness, co-operation, independence, creativity.*
2 *Pick **one** of these qualities as your goal for the week.*
3 *Notice every time your child shows this quality. Comment on how he has demonstrated this, describing rather than labelling. Other times simply take note. Make no negative comments at all – this might require a good deal of self-control!*

By the end of the week, you can be sure the quality will be on the increase. You could also let your child choose a quality and notice it together through the week.

Point out only when he **does** show the quality. If a whole week is too hard, practise it for a day, and gradually increase the time. You can also use this method to help you notice and develop your own good qualities.

(Adapted from *More Secrets of Happy Children* by Steve Biddulph)

An easy way to monitor your 'positive vs. negative' ratio is to put ten paperclips in each of your side pockets. Every time you give a positive description of what your child has done, put a paperclip from the left pocket into the right one, and every time you come out with something negative, put a paperclip from the right pocket into the left one. Count which pocket has the most paperclips at the end of the day! You could also use pennies or other small objects like buttons.

This chapter has explored a range of ways you can encourage your children to co-operate and take responsibility. See these as a selection of tools in your workshop. When fixing something in the house, you sometimes choose a screwdriver for a job and then realize that you need a spanner. It's much the same with life – what might work at one time may not work with a different person or at a different time. This is where **ACT** is so helpful. You can stop and think: 'What is going on for me? How do I feel? What do I need to happen?' Then you turn your thoughts to your child and stand in his shoes: 'How does he feel at the moment? What might he need right now?' And now you have a range of tools to choose from: 'What can I say or do which will help us both?'

PARENTS' COMMENTS

Celia, mother of Grace, Adam and Finlay:

'Thinking about labels has been a real eye opener for me. I realized that I think of Adam as 'the naughty one' and Grace as 'the responsible one'. Now when those words come into my mind, I try to describe something the children do instead. I realize there are times when Adam does behave responsibly. It's been incredibly liberating. I see them as whole people with all their rich diversity instead of type casting them.'

Travis, father of Jasmine, Chantal and Nathan:

'I've really found the paperclip idea helpful. At first I was shocked to see how negative I was with my children. Now I'm really thinking carefully before coming out with a criticism or a "don't". Of course, I often forget; but that's all part of the learning process. And the important thing is how much better I'm getting on with my children since being more positive.'

Things which have struck me in this chapter

Something I am going to try out

HAVE SOME FUN

Tell a story

Whether at bedtime, on a car journey or snuggled up on the sofa when it's raining, telling stories can be great fun. You may be a natural storyteller, but if not, use things which happened to you, the grandparents or others in the family: the time you got into trouble with the science teacher and how you felt about it; or when Granny ran up and down all the local hills to prepare for a charity race and to her surprise beat all the men! Events from life can be fascinating for your children. You can also pass on family history in story form. Let your imagination run riot and use pure fantasy or build stories around your children's favourite toys, like Paddington Bear or Buzz Lightyear.

Possible answers to the exercise on page 154
Changing negatives into positives – some suggestions:

'Don't be rude.'
'Talk using nice words.' *or* 'Speak politely.'

'Don't forget your swimming things.'
'Remember your swimming things.'

'Don't knock down Adam's castle.'
'Be careful of Adam's castle. Keep away from it.'

'Don't pull Anna's hair.'
'Either touch Anna's hair softly, or leave it alone.'

10 THINGS TO REMEMBER

1 A playful approach will often help to avoid confrontations.

2 Replace negative commands with positive instructions.

3 Children need to be able to accept a 'No', but when you can find ways to avoid using the word your children will be more co-operative.

4 Labelling a child can define him, and make it harder for him to change his behaviour.

5 Separate the doer from the deed by describing behaviour rather than using labels about a child.

6 Give limited choices to avoid being bossy and to gain co-operation.

7 Asking your child to generate a solution works better than nagging.

8 Giving tasks to your children breeds confidence and responsibility.

9 To avoid nagging keep the message simple, give advance warning, write notes, summon their attention, mime or sing.

10 For improved behaviour, notice what your child does well and tell him so.

Skilled listening

In this chapter you will learn:
- *how to 'be someone to tell'*
- *the importance of non-verbal communication*
- *how to listen with your heart and mind*
- *when to listen and when not to listen.*

In Chapter 8, you looked at ways to make family life run more smoothly. The next two chapters are about being an effective helper when your child is upset or struggling to work something out. A child with a problem seldom presents it in a way that is easy for a parent to understand and be supportive. Although parents may not be trained counsellors or life coaches, they do usually want to help their children deal with practical and emotional issues and assist them to find solutions when they are in trouble.

A parent's story

Celia's daughter Grace looks miserable as she sorts out her school bag for the next day.

Sob – 'Mum, I don't want to go to school tomorrow.'

'Darling, why not?'

'I just don't, I hate school, everyone there is horrible to me, I don't have any friends.'

'I'm sure that's not true, what about Tiffany, she's your best friend.'

Sobs – **'She is not!'**

'What do you mean she isn't? Have you fallen out with her? Did she pick a fight with you? Shall I ring her Mum?'

'NO, you **don't understand!**'

'Well, I won't understand if you don't *tell* me anything, it's no good getting hysterical, calm down!'

'I hate you! Just leave me alone!'

Grace went to her room, slamming the door behind her. Celia felt frustrated that her efforts to help had been thrown back at her and she really didn't know what to do next.

Insight

We notice that parents are often upset that their well-meaning attempts to help backfire on them. It is all too easy to escalate things rather than helping the child to calm down and think.

How can you be helpful to your child when she is hurt, puzzled, frightened or frustrated?

The skilled listening described in this chapter takes you one step further than simply acknowledging feelings. In **ACT**, this is the **C** for working out what the child feels and needs.

Being someone to tell

First of all, consider what kind of person you would choose to confide in or to approach for help if you had a problem or something you wanted to talk over.

Exercise: Who would you choose?

Who would you choose to tell first if you imagine that:

▶ *You are upset about a disagreement with your mother.*

▶ *You are worried about money.*

▶ *You are concerned that one of your children has become very clinging.*

▶ *You are dissatisfied with your job and want a change.*

▶ *You have started to write a novel.*

Did you choose to tell different people about different things? What was it about the person or people you chose that made them someone you would tell?

When you think of people you would definitely not tell, what is it about them that makes you reject them?

Julie, mother of Anna and Jake:

'I might choose different people for different things I think. The one about a child's clinginess I would probably talk over with my sister. I might even phone a helpline or join in an email discussion. I wouldn't want to tell my mother as she would get too worried and worked up herself.'

Patrick, father of Callum, Sean and Logan:

'As a man, I would definitely talk to my wife first. I wouldn't talk to my friends unless I wanted specific information from them.'

What are the qualities which make you more likely to confide worries, problems, hopes and dreams? Here are five elements of good listening which spell out the word **ADULT**.

ACCEPTANCE — they will allow you to tell your story without judging you.

DISCRETION — they will not tell others about your concerns unless you give them permission to do so.

UNDERSTANDING — they will try to understand what you are saying from your point of view.

LEVEL-HEADEDNESS — you know that they care, and at the same time that they will not be overwhelmed by what you tell them.

TRUST — they have confidence in your abilities and communicate that trust.

GENDER DIFFERENCES

As you can see from the quotes above, there can be a gender difference in the way people prefer to access and offer help. Men are often problem solvers and work out solutions, while women may find it helpful to talk things through without necessarily looking for a definitive answer or next step. Men tend to find hard information more helpful than talking about how they feel.

Recent research has proposed that the fight or flight response to danger is more male than female. From an evolutionary and a biological point of view, women with children can't fight or flee, and do better if they support each other against outside threats. Indeed, researchers found that female baboons who were more sociable had more offspring who survived. So perhaps when a woman is stressed she is more likely to call on her social networks – to 'phone a friend.

Blocks to confiding

Would you be likely to talk about a difficult subject if you thought
someone would:

▶ *tease or embarrass you*
▶ *be shocked by what you admitted to them*
▶ *gossip about you to other people*
▶ *lecture you and give advice which doesn't 'fit'*
▶ *over-react so that you ended up comforting them*
▶ *try to reassure you by minimizing the problem*
▶ *or make matters worse by intervening in a way you didn't want?*

If you think about these possible reactions, you can understand
that children are often right to feel that the grown-ups in their
lives will not respond to them as an ADULT – with acceptance,
discretion, understanding, level-headedness and trust. Indeed,
grown-ups often respond to their upsets in a way that is unhelpful,
even if this is done with good intentions. Typical reactions include:

Criticizing: 'You never leave yourself enough time for your
homework.'

Judging: 'You don't deserve to get a good mark for this.'

Prophesying: 'You'll never pass the entrance exam at this rate.'

Blaming: 'It's entirely your own fault for not getting down
to it sooner.'

Interrogating: 'So why didn't you remember your homework
diary?'

Parents who use these approaches are certainly intending to be helpful. They may hope that they can pass on the benefit of their experience and ensure that their child will not make the same mistakes again. However, if you imagine yourself in a similar situation, at work perhaps, or being told what to do by your own mother, you might recognize that these kinds of responses would not make you likely to open up to them in future.

Being a helper

There are times when your children need a 'good listening to' rather than a 'good talking to'. These are times when they are upset, when something has happened to them, and their needs really have to be met before yours do.

If you are to be a helper to your child in these situations, you must be feeling grounded and not be pulled into the problem yourself. It is like being on the bank of a river: if you are going to throw a rope to someone, you must be firmly on the bank. If you dive in, you may be swept away yourself. Of course, this is not always easy. Sometimes you may have to take a break and calm yourself down in whatever way works for you – deep breathing, talking it over with a partner or friend, acknowledging your own feelings to yourself (see the 'self-talk' section in Chapter 6). The important thing is to engage the thinking part of your brain.

As you remember from Chapter 7 about dealing with anger, if you and your child are flooded with emotion, feelings crowd out thinking. If you are to be an effective helper, you must be able to handle your own emotions and to focus on supporting your child to handle theirs. This may be more difficult if the situation is one which reminds you of past hurts you have suffered. If you find you are over-reacting, it may be useful to ask: 'What does this remind me of?' (the **A** in **ACT**).

A parent's story

Teresa said that she felt really upset when her ten-year-old son Sean came back from a school trip complaining that he had hated it and had a horrible time. It brought back memories of her own schooldays when she had felt excluded and lonely. She rang up a friend who had been on the same parenting course and let it all flood out. She felt sad and worried that he would never make friends, and at the same time angry with the school for not handling things better, and irritated with Sean for not making more of the opportunity (which had been an expensive option for the family). After talking about her feelings, she was able to listen to Sean more calmly and learned that, in fact, the trip had not been all bad. He had enjoyed some of it, and had even won the prize for being the bravest abseiler.

SHOWING YOU ARE LISTENING

Once you are feeling level-headed enough to focus on your child's problem, how does she know that you are really listening? At least 80 per cent of communication is non-verbal, so it is really important to get that bit right. However, children rarely bring up a problem at a convenient moment, and you will more often than not be cooking or sorting out bills or dealing with another child when you realize all is not well.

The first step is to show attention. Depending on how upset and how old the child is, you may want to fix a time to talk later. Sometimes a hug and an acknowledgement will help put it on hold until there is a convenient time to talk. At other times, you may have to stop what you are doing, sit down and put other things out of your head. It is important to be on the same eye level as your child if you can, so sit together, or work out some other way that they are not craning their neck to talk to you.

Although eye contact is great for some children, others find it easier to talk, especially about shaming or embarrassing topics, if they are not face to face.

Remember that tone of voice communicates as much or even more than words do.

Insight

I've noticed that when I pick up the phone to a family member or close friend, I can tell how they are almost immediately just by the way they say 'Hello!' – *Doro*

Your child is likely to be expert at reading your body language and expressions – after all they have been watching you closely since birth. If you are really not fully present and listening, they will pick it up and you will not get the full story. Attending with your whole body gives them the message that you are really listening and not just waiting to get your point across.

Empathy: listening with heart and mind

Empathy is the word that encapsulates listening with both heart and mind. It is the ability to identify with and understand another's feelings and difficulties. When you are being empathic, you sense what the other person is feeling.

Neuroscientists have found areas of the brain that light up both when you are feeling the emotional aspects of pain (fear, distress) and also when you see others experiencing pain. The more important the other person is to you, the more strongly these parts of the brain react.

These brain areas are not activated just by negative emotions; strong positive emotions also cause a reaction. So it looks as if empathy is 'hard wired' into the human condition. Indeed, even young babies will cry at a recording of other babies' cries – they recognize and react to the pain of others (amazingly, they do not cry at their own recorded cries).

The 'mind' dimension of empathy understands what is going on and puts it into words. To be a good listener, you need both dimensions – to be able to sense deep feelings in the other person and to use the thinking part of the brain to process what is going on.

ACKNOWLEDGING FEELINGS

Once you are in the right state to listen, the first step is to acknowledge feelings. Chapters 6 and 7 covered this in detail. To summarize:

Top tips for acknowledging feelings

- ▶ *Give a name to what you think your child is feeling.*
- ▶ *Remember feelings can be mixed, even opposite to each other.*
- ▶ *Match the intensity of the feeling in tone and words.*
- ▶ *You can notice and comment on feelings which are expressed through body language.*

THE POWER OF SILENCE

When your child has a problem, your instinct is to try to solve it and make it better. Your own anxiety often leads to questioning, reassuring and advising before you even know exactly what the problem is. As long as you are showing full attention, the less you say the better – as your grandmother may have said (though probably in a different context!): 'You have two ears and one mouth for a reason!'.

Silence gives you and your child a chance to calm down and think about what is going on. In fact, the ability to be relaxed with someone in silence is a real mark of intimacy – it shows that you can be yourself without putting on an act.

DOOR OPENERS

Some children will pour out what they are feeling and the full background to it, others will need some encouragement to let you in on their innermost emotions and concerns, especially if they are not used to receiving an empathic response in a busy family.

Here are some approaches which can help:

Notice non-verbal signals
You can notice signs of worry even if they have not been put into words. As long as you do it without sounding accusing, it can be a good way of showing that you are ready to listen.

You could say:

'Your eyes look sad this evening.'

'I noticed you were frowning over your homework.'

'Your voice sounds rather low and flat.'

An invitation to talk
This needs to be an invitation rather than a third degree interrogation. Remember to avoid communicating one thing with words and another with your body, for example by carrying on sorting the washing or unloading the dishwasher.

You could say:

'Do you want to tell me what happened?'

'I'm ready to listen if you want to talk.'

'Would it help to talk it over?'

'When you're ready to talk, just let me know.'

Encouragement

You are giving the message that you are really listening and want to hear more. If you watch someone talking on the telephone, you can see them giving signals that they are listening to the other person – saying 'mmm' or 'yes'. In fact, they do the non-verbal signals of nodding and facial expression too, even though they can't be seen. Short responses such as 'Right', 'OK' or 'I see' keep the momentum going.

You could say:

'Do you want to tell me more about it?'

'So what happened then?'

'It looks as if something else is worrying you as well?'

Another way to show attention and encouragement is to repeat one significant word or phrase that they have said – for example: 'unfair' or 'mean' or 'left out'.

Skilled listening

Once your child is talking, there is a way of responding which helps her work out what is really going on and calms things down so that she can engage the thinking part of her brain.

Because the child is in an emotional state, she sends an unclear message to the parent who is listening. The parent returns a clearer version of what the child has said, clarifying the underlying feeling and meaning.

Insight
We sometimes illustrate this by saying it is a bit like gently batting a balloon back. You are capturing the significance and sending it back in a way that can be accepted and heard.

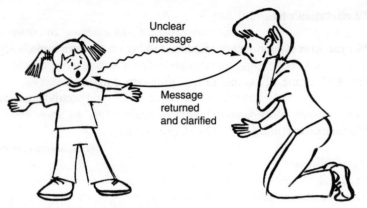

Figure 9.1 *Skilled listening.*

When you have heard the full story, you can summarize it in a neutral way.

You can see how this works in another version of Celia's conversation with Grace at the beginning of the chapter:

A parent's story – a helpful version

Sob ... 'Mum, I don't want to go to school tomorrow.'

'Darling, you sound really upset.'   **(naming the feeling)**

More sobs from Grace.

'It looks as if you need a hug.'   **(calming with touch)**

'Something's happened to upset you. Do you want to tell me
about it?'   **(door opener)**

'Nooo!'

'OK, when you want to talk, I'm ready to listen.'   **(door opener)**

'Well, I didn't mean it!'

'So you said something you didn't mean.'   (**return and clarify**)

'NOOO, not that, I wouldn't let Tiffany do skipping.'
                                             (**child corrects**)

'So you kept Tiffany out of the skipping circle.'
                                             (**return and clarify**)

'Yes and it's not *fair*, now everyone says I'm horrible and won't talk to me!'

'Not fair.'   (**repeating stressed word**)

'Yes it's not fair, *she* started it.'

'So you and Tiffany had a row. That must have been hurtful.'
                                             (**clarify and name the feeling**)

'Yes ... We were both crying.'   (**allow silence**)

'You sound sorry about it ...'   (**name feeling and silence**)

'I wish it hadn't happened.'

'So you and Tiffany argued and it turned into a bigger thing than you had intended and now you wish you could start today again.'
                                             (**summarize**)

Sigh. 'Yes ... I'm going to ring Tiffany and say "sorry, let's make up".'

In this version, Celia stays on the bank of the river of emotions and Grace works out the next step for herself. Naming feelings, soothing touch and allowing silence helps the thinking part of the brain to gain ascendancy. Even when Celia returns a wrong phrase, Grace easily corrects her. Returning what her daughter says in a slightly different form helps Grace to understand what is going on, and the summary moves her on to take action.

Insight

We suggest that you look out for a sigh, which often indicates that emotions are shifting.

Sometimes a child will need some more help to move on. This is discussed in the next chapter. However, it is surprising how often just listening is enough. The 'return and clarify' method makes sense of confusion. Children in the grip of strong feelings find it hard to express themselves clearly. Words may mean something different to them than to you, and they can often start talking about one thing when the real problem is something quite different. Also, you as the listener may well have pre-conceived ideas about what has happened. Returning and clarifying messages helps you to focus on what the child is saying and its underlying meaning.

When your children are older and start using this technique back on you, you will know that you have been successful!

Top tips for skilled listening

▶ *Give a name to underlying feelings.*
▶ *Open the door by inviting and encouraging talk.*
▶ *Return and clarify what your child says.*
▶ *Be comfortable with silence.*
▶ *Summarize the gist of the problem.*

Exercise: Skilled listening in real life

Practise skilled listening this week whenever you have an opportunity. This could be with a friend or your learning companion, or with one of your children.

Each time, ask yourself:

'How did it go?'

'What skills did I use from the list of tips above?'

'How did I feel?'

'How did the person I was listening to react?'

A parent's story

Shanti was rushing to go out for her evening class. Her husband Suresh was running late, so her neighbour was coming in to look after the children until he got home.

Her youngest, Hari, was not happy about being left:

'Why do you have to go out? I'm going to stay up until you get home.'

Shanti remembered to try skilled listening. Instead of using logic and reassurance ('My class is important for me to get a better job, you really like Auntie Sita'), she asked herself 'What is going on for Hari?', and responded:

'You truly don't want me to go out and you don't like being put to bed by anyone else.'

The conversation continued:

'Yes! I want you to stay in and read me a story.'

(Contd)

Shanti 'returned and clarified' what Hari said:

'I think you wish I would cancel my class and we could read your new book.'

Hari relaxed at being understood, even though he knew his mother would have to go out. He thought for a bit and came up with his own solution:

'No, I want my old book again ... Maybe Daddy could read to me when he gets home.'

Shanti was amazed when Hari settled down with the neighbour with no further fuss.

DIFFICULTIES WITH LISTENING

Perhaps the most difficult thing about skilled listening is to remember to do it! More often than not, children present their problems in a way that engages their parents' emotions – you feel their pain, or you are irritated by their behaviour, and before you know it, you are swimming around in the river with them. This is not to say that parents should or even can cut off their feelings when dealing with their children's upsets. But if you are too flooded with emotion, you will not be able to react skilfully and constructively.

It is very natural to react from your own position rather than trying to imagine what your child feels when emotions are running high. Parents often fear that naming feelings and clarifying what is really going on will cause more upset. They may be reluctant to get into an argument which will take up time and energy. The temptation is to start by giving a lecture, saying something like: 'That's no way to talk about your teacher. Show some respect!', or to give reasons: 'I have to go to work today, you know that'. When a child is wound up, they won't accept logical reasons. Skilled listening usually resolves an upset much more quickly than reasoning and lecturing does.

Skilled listening responses put the ball back into the child's court, and they can start thinking about what they could do to feel better.

This approach does not start an argument by denying what is going on for the child; neither does it signal that the parent will give in and make things better in the way that the child wants, as in Shanti's warm but firm response to Hari. Once he felt he had been properly heard, he calmed down and was able to use the thinking part of his brain.

Insight

We know that parents often feel false and unnatural using skilled listening. It can feel like speaking in a foreign language, and they worry that their children will notice and mock this novel approach. This can be the case if your child is *not* emotionally flooded. However if her feelings are running high she will 'go with the flow'. With practice, skilled listening will become part of your normal repertoire.

Repairing after a rift

Using listening skills is more difficult when your child sees you as the problem. A natural reaction when a parent is criticized or accused by a child is to reprimand or to justify actions, which usually only escalates the conflict. It requires a high level of self-control to give a skilled listening response and acknowledge feelings when you are under attack. You may need to play for time, and agree to discuss things when you are both calmer. Using listening skills to make up and repair a rift after a row is very important too.

A parent's story

Laura and Peter had a long-standing invitation to an out-of-town family reunion with Peter's cousins from overseas. The date clashed with a school disco. When their son Owen discovered this he was furious: 'It will be so boring, why do you always make me go and meet my stupid family?' Peter told him not to be so rude, and that he would do what he was told. The row went on until Owen was sent to his room. Later that evening, when Peter discussed the confrontation with Laura, he realized how important the disco was for Owen. He found Owen and said: 'I think I was a bit harsh on you this evening. I do understand how much you want to be at the disco, and I am really sorry about the clash of dates.' They went on

(Contd)

talking, and Owen in turn admitted that some of the things he had said had been out of order. They both felt that they understood each other's point of view, and Owen accepted that he would have to fit in with the family this time.

Using skilled listening to apologize and mend the damage done by an argument shows that you can process and learn from what happened. Next time, you both have a better chance of working things out without losing your temper.

When skilled listening is not appropriate

There are times when skilled listening is not going to work, and you have to use other 'tools'.

WHEN YOU ARE STRESSED

It will be clear by now that skilled listening is not something that you can do if you are feeling stressed yourself, as the focus has to be on the needs of the child. If you are tired and hungry yourself, or you have other strong needs, you are not going to be able to listen with heart and mind. In these circumstances, you will have to put off this kind of communicating until you are feeling calmer.

WHEN YOU ARE OVER-INVOLVED

When you are not separated enough from your child's problem, you may have to find help, or look after yourself in some way before you can listen to her. Perhaps you can phone a friend, take a bath, listen to your favourite music – anything to make you feel more resourceful and rational. Remember the sections on 'the oxygen mask' and 'filling your cup' in Chapter 2 – to be a good enough parent you need to nurture yourself.

WHEN YOU HAVE YOUR OWN AGENDA

If you have your own agenda – for example, when you want your child to go over to a friend's house so you can get some work done – your child is very likely to pick this up, and sense that you are not genuinely giving him space to explore feelings and options. In these circumstances it is better to state up front what your needs are and maybe negotiate or do a deal.

You could say:

'I really need to go to the library to finish my report. I know you get bored at Rufus' house, and I promise if you go there, you can choose between swimming and the cinema on Sunday afternoon.'

WHEN THERE IS NOT ENOUGH TIME

In busy families there is not much leeway for things to go wrong, and there may just not be time to listen when other children have needs too. When this is the case, it is better to acknowledge the feelings, set a limit on behaviour if necessary and promise to talk things over at an agreed time. If you are often too rushed to listen to your child, it may be that you and your partner need to look at your family life and commitments. Ask yourselves how you can make more space for unrushed 'downtime'.

Insight

The period when our children are young seems never ending at the time, but with hindsight we can see that in the span of our lives it is relatively short! It is a phase which we will never get back, and it is important to remember that the most loving thing we can give our children is time. Even a little more time, especially one-to-one time with a child, can make a big difference.

PARENTS' COMMENTS

John, father of Finlay and stepfather of Grace and Adam:

'I catch myself going in to lecture mode so easily. I hear a certain tone in my voice which gives the message: "You have messed up again!" No wonder the kids switch off. Now I am aware of what I am doing and that is the first step.'

Penny, mother of Mia and Abby:

'I was really proud of myself for staying calm in the shoe shop with Abby. I said "You are so fed up that they don't have those shoes you love in your size." She said "Yes", that her best friend had them and she wanted to be the same. I bit my tongue about telling her to show some originality and just returned: "So you want to be like Rosie" and the tears stopped. We've had so many tantrums in shoe shops over the years!'

Things which have struck me in this chapter

Something I am going to try out

HAVE SOME FUN

The 'UM' game
Some children find it hard to express themselves in words. Here is a game which produces lots of laughs and gives practice in talking and listening.

Like the radio panel game, draw some topics out of a hat and talk for just a minute (or half a minute) without saying 'um'.

Possible topics: My favourite TV character; going to the moon; what I want to be when I grow up; the last match my team won; my favourite teacher; my least favourite teacher.

10 THINGS TO REMEMBER

1 A child with a problem rarely presents it in a way that is easy for parents to understand and help.

2 'Being someone to tell' requires **ADULT** qualities: **A**cceptance, **D**iscretion, **U**nderstanding, **L**evel-headedness and **T**rust.

3 Parents with the best of intentions often respond to children's problems with criticism, judging and interrogation.

4 To be a helper to your child, you must be feeling secure and grounded yourself. Make sure you are not over-reacting because of past hurts.

5 Check that your body language tells your child that you are really listening. While this generally means making eye contact, remember that some children, especially boys, prefer to avoid eye contact when they are confiding in you, and may feel at ease chatting while doing a job together.

6 Empathy means using heart and mind – the heart to sense underlying feelings and the mind to understand and put those feelings into words.

7 Encourage children to talk by noticing non-verbal signs, inviting them to tell you what is going on and tolerating silence.

8 Skilled listening helps children to work out what they want to do by returning, clarifying and summarizing what they say.

9 When your child sees you as their problem, skilled listening is hard, but pays dividends. Repairing a relationship after a row is a really important way to use skilled listening.

10 It is best not to use skilled listening when you are stressed, over-involved or have your own agenda.

10

Problem solving

In this chapter you will learn:
- *a model for supporting children to work through a problem*
- *how to ask questions which help*
- *when you have to be more proactive.*

In the last chapter, you learned to approach upsets in a way that helps children find their own solutions and strengthens relationships through empathic, skilled listening. However, there are times when listening, however skilled, is not enough.

If your child has an intractable problem and needs help to work it out; if he gets stuck in the negative and cannot extricate himself, you may need to build on listening skills to help him work out strategies or offer some ways forward.

A parent's story

Peter hears crashing upstairs and goes to check on Owen, who is supposed to be doing his homework. The exchange then goes like this:

'This maths homework is stupid!', *throwing the book at the wall.*

'Hey! What did you do that for? You could damage things!'

'It's *stupid*!'

(Contd)

'Why is it stupid?'

'It just is!'

'Why didn't you ask your teacher to explain it?'

'She doesn't care, she just gave it out.'

'Well, haven't you got any notes about it?'

'No, it's stupid!'

'Why don't you let me have a look?'

'No, I'm just thick at maths, I'll never understand it.'

'Of course you're not thick, why don't you just get down to it?'

'I *am* thick and you're being horrible to me!'

Peter gets more and more irritated as his advice is spurned, and Owen gets angry with his Dad instead of thinking about his homework.

Problem solving is an approach to be used with caution. It is natural to feel anxious when your child is suffering, and to want to make things better as quickly as possible.

Insight

Think about the last time you were given advice that you hadn't asked for. Did you think, 'What a great suggestion!' or did it feel more like a criticism of you?

You may be tempted to give answers rather than helping a child to find his own way through what is happening.

In the long run, you are trying to give independence and practice in making sensible decisions. If you take over too much, he will learn more slowly. Happiness comes from being able to cope with life's ups and downs, to feel that you can handle what life brings.

Of course there are some situations – to do with safety, the law, bullying or learning difficulties – in which you as the adult must take the lead and your child needs to be supported and protected. Even then, you must take care not to make a child feel even more disempowered.

A model for problem solving

A useful approach for helping your child with a problem involves three steps, which can easily be remembered as **AIM**:

A – Acknowledge feelings
I – Identify underlying needs
M – Move on.

ACKNOWLEDGE FEELINGS

As covered in detail in preceding chapters, the first step is to name and validate feelings.

> **Reminder: Top tips for acknowledging feelings**
> ▶ *Give a name to what you think your child is feeling.*
> ▶ *Remember, feelings can be mixed, even opposite to each other.*
> ▶ *Match the intensity of the feeling in tone and words.*
> ▶ *You can notice and comment on feelings which are expressed through body language.*

Remember also that, to be a helper, you need to be on the bank of the river, not flailing around in the water with your son or daughter. If your feelings are running high, find a way to calm down beforehand so you can focus.

The best attitude might be described as one of sympathy and interest – what is really going on for them?

So in response to: 'This maths homework is stupid!',

You could say:

'You sound really fed up with it at the moment!'

'It looks like you're finding your maths very frustrating this evening!'

Note that describing a feeling in terms of a time – by saying 'at the moment' or 'this evening' – gives the message that the state of frustration is not permanent, that it can feel different at another point. This is important for children who live in the moment and find it hard to remember that their feelings can change dramatically in minutes.

You may have to set a limit on actions. Remember all feelings are acceptable, but not all actions are.

You could say:

'Throwing things at the wall is not OK, it might make a mark. If you have to throw your book, do it onto the bed.'

A limit needs to be set with kindness and understanding in situations when a child is overwhelmed by feelings. You are trying to calm down anger and fear, not redirect these emotions onto you.

Sometimes it can be useful to have a change of scene, some physical exercise or a snack before attempting to problem solve. The brain needs oxygen and sugar to function effectively. Remember also that a hug or a shoulder rub can make an impossible situation seem less daunting.

IDENTIFY UNDERLYING NEEDS

You are helping your son or daughter to work out what is wrong for themselves. After feelings have been acknowledged, you can use skilled listening to shed light on the difficulty.

Reminder: Top tips for skilled listening
▶ *Open the door by inviting and encouraging talk.*
▶ *Return and clarify what your child says.*
▶ *Be comfortable with silence.*
▶ *Summarize the gist of the problem.*

Open questions
When a child (or an adult) is too distressed to think straight, contrary to what one might expect, questions can be a distraction. Very often, the questioner is following their own line of thought, and questions are 'leading' in the direction of a solution of their own. Rather than trying to identify a child's needs, questions often have a hidden statement in them – there is an assumption already which may or may not be true. Their underlying message is one of blame or 'I know better than you'. This kind of questioning may take a confused or distressed child completely off the track of what is really going on.

Questions which contribute to the flow of the conversation are ones which are known as 'open'. Open questions cannot be answered with a 'Yes' or a 'No' and therefore invite a longer and hopefully more thoughtful response. Invitations and encouragement to speak are open questions.

You could say:

'Looks like you're finding your maths very frustrating this evening, what's the problem?'

rather than:

'Haven't you got any notes about it?'

which invites the answer 'Yes' or 'No' and has an underlying statement which could be:

'You should have paid more attention in class.'

Here are some more examples of open and closed questions:

'Did the teacher tell you off?'   **(closed, 'Yes' or 'No' answer)**

'You seem upset about something at school, what happened?'
                                             (open)

'Was it Alan who hit you?'   **(closed, making assumptions)**

'So someone hit you, what was going on?'   **(open)**

'Did you have a good day?'   **(closed, 'Yes' or 'No' answer)**

'How was your day? What was a good thing that happened today? A bad thing?'   **(open)**

'Why' questions

Somehow children rarely respond clearly to questions which start with a 'why'. The answers to 'why' questions can be too abstract, children may be having to admit to impulses which make them feel guilty, or they may be having to guess at the motivation of another person. Questions starting with 'what' are easier to grapple with, and the answers will be more concrete.

MOVING ON

Once you and your child have been able to identify the need, he can work out what he wants to do about it. You can help by asking the right questions and offering practical help without taking over.

Moving on questions such as: 'What might help?' and 'What would make you feel better?' help the child to say what he wants. Moving on questions need to be as specific as possible and usually start with 'what' or 'how'. Sometimes it is good to have more than one suggestion for a solution.

You could say:

'What is another idea?'

'How else could you get to what you want?'

An example of AIM in practice
A different version of the exchange between Peter and Owen at the beginning of the chapter might be as shown below.

You may have to go back and forth between **A**, **I** and **M**. The child is not ready to move on until the real need underlying the emotion has been expressed. In this case, Owen needs respect and to feel competent. If you are not careful, you could be trying to solve the wrong problem, or even make things worse, and your child will just get more and more negative.

'This maths homework is stupid!', *throwing the book at the wall.*

'You sound really fed up with it at the moment!'
                              (**acknowledge feeling as not permanent**)

'Yes, I just can't understand it!'

(Contd)

'And throwing things at the wall is not OK, it might make a mark. If you have to throw your book, do it onto the bed ... So what's the problem with the maths?' **(limit behaviour and identify need)**

'I'm just thick at maths, it's too hard!'

'You sound really discouraged with this worksheet.'

(name feeling)

'Yeah, it's decimals, what's the *use* of decimals?'

'You can't see the purpose of working with numbers in this way.'
(return and clarify)

'I really can't do it!'

'It sounds like you're feeling stuck. Decimals are definitely hard to understand at first, what do you think might help?'
(moving on question)

'Nothing will help. I'm just thick at maths!'

'Hmm, so you really don't think you can do it?'
(return and clarify)

'No, the teacher told me off for daydreaming, but I wasn't!'

'So you felt picked on, it must have been embarrassing.'
(name the feeling)

'Yes, and people laughed.'

'No wonder you are feeling bad about your maths! What would make you feel better?'
(acknowledge feeling and ask a moving on question)

'Getting them all right would show her!' **(need is identified)**

'Right, what could be a first step towards that?'

(moving on question)

'Maybe you could work through the first one with me, I've got a revision book with the rules in it.'

Insight

Parents sometimes object, saying that they don't have time to use this approach, especially when there are several children needing attention. When they try it out, however, they report back that it does in fact save time and emotional energy.

Challenging limiting beliefs

When your child seems trapped in the negative, here are some questions based on NLP (neuro-linguistic programming) which can challenge 'unconstructive' thinking and help your child find a different viewpoint.

▶ **Never say never!**
   'I never do well in exams.'
   – 'Never? Can you think of a time when you did do well?'

   'I always panic and forget things.'
   – 'Always? Do you remember when … ?'

▶ **Can't do this, it's impossible.**
   'I can't finish this.'
   – 'What's stopping you?' or 'What prevents you?' or 'What would help?'

▶ **Must, should, have to**
   'I have to be Jenny's partner every time.'
   – 'Who says so?' or 'What would happen if you didn't?'

▶ **Blocks – 'I could never ...'**
  'I could never ask my teacher to help me with this.'
  – 'What would happen if you did?'

These questions can be really effective, but they should be used with care. If a child does not feel that you are really entering into his feelings, they can sound patronizing and accusing.

When the child has worked out what he wants to achieve, the task needs to be broken down so that it doesn't feel too overwhelming.

You could say:

'What could be a first step towards that?'

'What do you need to get started?'

'How can you tackle this a bit at a time?'

> **Insight**
> We really like the method recommended by researcher and author John Gottman. He calls it 'scaffolding' – the parent acts as a coach, 'chunking' the task into stages and giving specific feedback and praise at each point.

You could say:

'Good thinking to remember about your revision book.'

'How about starting off by explaining to me what the rule is for decimal points and multiplication?'

'Let's have a look at the first sum.'

'You certainly know your times tables by heart now!'

'You realized you made a mistake and corrected it, that's good.'

'Try the next section and give me a shout if you need me.'

Top tips for problem solving

▶ *Name feelings and put a limit on behaviour.*
▶ *Imagine a transparent shield so you don't get buffeted by your child's strong feelings.*
▶ *Use skilled listening and open questions to identify the needs.*
▶ *Start moving on questions with 'What' or 'How'.*
▶ *Use 'scaffolding' – break up a task into chunks and praise small achievements.*

Problems without a solution

Of course, some problems do not have a solution. If a best friend is moving schools, a pet has died or a grandparent is gravely ill, your child has to accept that he will feel sad, that it is not his fault and that he can find ways to be comforted.

If you jump in with 'helpful' suggestions too quickly, or try to shield your children from sad situations, you can dismiss painful emotions and make things worse. Parents have a tendency to do this when they are suffering themselves and they are worried about showing their strong emotions. Even though they are unable to make things better immediately they can listen and accept their children's feelings.

Sarah, mother of Zach, Martha, Naomi and Ben:

'Our old cat had to be put to sleep. I just couldn't bear to talk about it in advance, so I didn't tell the children until afterwards. They were devastated and very angry with me. I realized that I had deprived them of being able to say goodbye to him because I didn't want to cry in front of them. In retrospect, I really regret how I handled it.'

There is more on talking about various forms of loss in Chapter 13.

Problems which need adult intervention

There are times when a parent needs to step in and take a more active role in working on a problem. Bullying is one example of such a problem. In some cases, you may have to go beyond problem solving, do some research and get involved yourself.

Insight

Parents have told us that even when they needed to take action, it worked better to use skilled listening first to find out what was going on under the surface. When this was clear they could make a plan together about what to do next.

A parent's story

Penny's daughter Mia was crying. She'd received a horrible text message and didn't know who had sent it. Penny was very upset herself, and was at a loss over what to do. She rang Parentline that night, and the call-taker helped her work out how to talk to Mia and what to tell the school the next day.

She showed Mia a website where it said that nearly a quarter of schoolchildren had been 'cyber-bullied' in the last few months, to prove to her that she wasn't the only one. She also let her know that sending abusive messages through the phone system was actually illegal, so the school would have to know and the police could be involved if it went on.

Mia was impressed that adults took these things so seriously, but she didn't want anyone else to read the text, and she definitely didn't want to change her phone number. Penny asked her how she would like to handle it. Mia agreed that her mother should tell the head teacher, but ask him not to say that it was Mia who had been bullied in this way to anyone else. Mia also decided to turn off the message function of her phone for a week (the phone company helped with this) and for her voice mail message to be spoken by an adult for a time too.

Penny said: 'I think the really horrible thing was not knowing which of her friends had been copied in to the text, or been involved in the whole thing. It really knocked her confidence. I told her that Parentline had been really helpful for me and gave her the option of ringing Childline to talk it through some more.'

In some situations, children need to have information about how things work in the adult world, for example that cyber-bullying is against the law. However, it is still important to listen to their feelings and opinions about what to do next. Penny asked Mia how she would like to handle things, and between them they came up with a sensible plan. For older children, there are lots of good websites giving advice on issues like bullying – advice which may come better from an outside source than from you.

PARENTS' COMMENTS

Shanti, mother of Asha and Hari:

'Asha suddenly started saying that she didn't want to go to her dance class. Asking her why got me nowhere, but when I said: 'I see that you don't find dancing fun anymore, what is it about the class that is different now?', she told me that her best friend had been put in a different group to her. And when I asked her what she wanted to do about it, she said that she would ask the teacher if she could move groups. I was so impressed that she wanted to handle it herself!'

Celia, mother of Grace, Adam and Finlay:

'Adam was playing up at school a lot and he didn't seem to be making progress with reading like some of his friends. I got him assessed, and this showed that he did have a problem with reading, though his IQ was high. We discussed the options together, and he preferred to have help outside school rather than in class. We found a specialist tutor and it has really helped.'

Things which have struck me in this chapter

Something I am going to try out

HAVE SOME FUN

Fortunately/unfortunately game
This is a game which calls for creative problem solving! One
person starts a story with the word 'fortunately' and the next
person carries on, starting with 'unfortunately'. For example:
'Fortunately the lion was asleep when we drove past him in the
safari park; unfortunately someone honked their horn and woke
him up; fortunately all the doors and windows were closed;
unfortunately the car ran out of petrol ...' and so on.

10 THINGS TO REMEMBER

1   *Sometimes children need help to solve a problem. However, you must take care to avoid making them feel disempowered – unasked-for advice can be interpreted as criticism.*

2   *The model for problem solving is **AIM** – **A**cknowledge feelings, **I**dentify underlying needs, and **M**ove on.*

3   *Imagine a transparent shield between you and your child to prevent yourself being pulled into their strong feelings. Try changing a mood through exercise or a healthy snack.*

4   *Identify the underlying need through using skilled listening.*

5   *Use open questions, which cannot be answered with a 'Yes' or a 'No', to keep your child talking.*

6   *Avoid using questions starting with 'Why?'. They only make an upset child feel more pressurized.*

7   *Once the problem is clear, use 'moving on' questions starting with 'what' or 'how' to ask your child what they want to do about it.*

8   *Use 'scaffolding' to break down a problem into small steps, giving encouragement at each stage.*

9   *Some problems have no solution, and a child needs help to accept this and find comfort.*

10 *Adults need to intervene when problems are too big for a child to handle. Even then it is best to allow the child to have some say over what action to take if at all possible.*

11

Boundaries and freedom

In this chapter you will learn:
- *the meaning of boundaries and why they are important*
- *how to come up with family rules based on your values*
- *what discipline means*
- *approaches for keeping boundaries*
- *how to be firm when necessary.*

'Why a chapter on boundaries so late in the book?', you may wonder. Setting rules and being able to enforce them is of course an essential part of being a parent, because children are much happier when they have the security of knowing where the limits lie. They can get on better at school and survive in society at large once they know what is expected of them and have the self-discipline to respect the frameworks within which they have to operate. While all this is true, it has been consistently shown that children accept and internalize rules and guidelines far more easily once parents have developed the empathy, trust and understanding that you have been working on in earlier chapters. Children may well obey if they are frightened of harsh punishment, but obeying out of fear does not foster self-discipline. In fact, severe parenting leads to more problem behaviour in the long run. Once children realize you are on their side, firmness can be reassuring rather than frightening.

This chapter will explore the meaning and importance of boundaries, and also the role of discipline in enforcing them.

Just as much as warmth, you need firmness and some rules to give structure to your family life. You will see how discipline can be a way of teaching your children rather than a rod of iron – something you do with them for everyone's benefit.

> **Insight**
>
> We find parents these days are more interested in helping children to develop a moral sense rather than just seeking obedience, due perhaps to the history of the twentieth century where unquestioning obedience led to so many horrors.

What are boundaries and why are they important?

Perhaps the easiest way to approach this question is to look at a completely familiar area – the physical world. Everywhere you go there are boundaries which are perfectly visible: fences, signs, walls, hedges. Boundaries often give the message: 'This is where my territory begins'. While telling you where to stop to avoid trespassing on another's property, they also protect your own space and guard you from outside dangers. Boundaries are important for your children for exactly the same reasons. They help them to feel safe and be safe.

PERSONAL BOUNDARIES

Personal boundaries are just as real as fences and walls, even if they are harder to see. They define who you are – what is you and what is not you. For children, this sense of self is developed in many ways. When they are valued for the unique person they are (as you saw in Chapter 4), when they are not compared to their siblings or friends and when their parents accept that they are not mini-versions of themselves, children begin to gain a sense of their own identity. It is equally important to let them know where **your** boundaries lie – what you will and will not tolerate; and to teach them to consider and respect others.

THE BODY

The most basic boundary which defines you is your skin. It protects the blood, flesh, bones, and keeps germs out. Perhaps the first way a child learns that she is separate from others and the outside world is through the sense of touch. It is no coincidence that when someone infringes personal boundaries people will say: 'He gets under my skin!'.

From an early age, a respectful parent will be sensitive to a child's physical boundaries. When you bounce a baby on your knee, you notice when the ecstatic smile turns into a frown and a grizzle, and then you know she has had enough. Or when a father plays rough and tumble games with his son, there will be a point when the boy may shout: 'Ouch, that hurts. Stop!', and the father will recognize the boundary between pleasure and pain. Conversely, the boy will learn just how far he can go when his Dad says: 'Hey! You kicked too hard that time!' Knowing where the limits lie is crucial for learning how to get on with other children and adults.

As children grow, their parents will also teach them which parts of the body are private, and when and where such boundaries apply. Thus you may feel it is perfectly natural for your small child to run around the house or garden naked, while you may not think it appropriate in public. Similarly, there comes a time in most families when parents and children no longer want to dress and undress in front of each other, and it is advisable to be sensitive to your child's messages about privacy. At a certain stage, it feels more comfortable to knock before entering a child's room, and if you prefer her not to barge in to your bedroom or bathroom, you only need to let her know your wishes in a pleasant way.

WORDS

As you can see from the examples above, words are crucial for indicating your limits to others. 'No' is the most basic boundary-setting word there is. As children become aware of their own identity and free will, they become almost addicted to this word. Toddlers will sometimes say 'No' even to their favourite things, so important is it for them to make their own choices and not be the 'puppet' of anyone else.

This can be infuriating for parents. However, it is important to respect your child's early attempts at boundary-setting, so it's worth saving your insistence for the essential things, and giving your child a bit of leeway in unimportant matters.

Although there are many times when obedience is called for both towards parents and teachers, it is important for your son or daughter to know that your love does not depend on their agreeing with everything you say. This independence of character lays the foundations for their being able to say 'I don't agree' when their peers want them to do something which goes against their beliefs. It gives them the boldness to say 'No' if anyone attempts to infringe their physical boundaries.

Words let others know where you stand and what you need. They are the 'boundary edges' that help identify who you are. For example, when you say: 'I don't like it when you shout at me' you give others a clear message about how you conduct relationships and what you consider acceptable. As a parent, you need to be sure of what you will and won't tolerate. This gives you inner authority, a quality which good teachers have.

Insight

The same primary school headmaster who shaved in assembly (see page 152) never raised his voice and yet was always in charge! If you know someone with this inner authority it is worth watching them carefully and trying to learn from them. – *Doro*

More on standing firm will come later in the chapter.

Family values and rules

If boundaries are vital in preserving everyone's mental and physical space as well as defining their individuality, they are also crucial for the successful functioning of a social group. This is especially true of the family, where relationships are so complex. Some think of the family as a team in which everyone has their part to play; and these parts change over time. Others picture the family as the crew of a boat, where children gradually learn that 'rocking the boat' affects everyone else. Both metaphors suggest the importance of rules.

Most families have implicit rules, which are not expressed out loud. But in order to live together more easily, it helps to make them explicit so they can be owned by everyone.

But how do you decide which boundaries need rules to back them up, and how do you enforce them?

Your best starting point is to look at your values – what is important to you. When your children are young, you, as parents, will be the main 'navigators' in the family boat, setting boundaries and instilling values in your children. As you come from different families, your views and your partner's may sometimes be poles apart, so in order to 'navigate' in the same direction, you can work together on the following exercise before involving your children in the discussion. You may well find that there are some values that you share and others on which you agree to differ. For these, you will have to find a compromise! Bear in mind also that your children may well question your values when they reach their teenage years; that is an important part of growing up!

Once you have taken some time to mull this over together, ask your children how they might answer these questions (don't feel you have to finish this in one session).

▶ **Values about relationships**
How should we treat each other? How can we cherish each other, organize ourselves, communicate, resolve conflicts, make decisions, and look after each other?

▶ **Values about learning**
How do we learn? How important is education? How can we develop and respect our knowledge, skills, talents, wisdom and experience?

▶ **Social values**
What part do extended family, friends, sports, clubs and groups, school and charities play in our lives?

▶ **Values about enjoyment**
How do we relax and have fun? How important is play and humour in our family? How can we be creative and enjoy others' creations, like the arts?

▶ **Values about health and the environment**
How do we look after our own body and health and enjoy physical activity? In what ways do we care for our home, the environment, the planet?

▶ **Spiritual values**
What part do our beliefs, morals, traditions and religion play in our lives?

(Contd)

Teresa, mother of Callum, Sean and Logan:

'Looking at our values, Patrick and I realized that, although we felt it was important to spend time as a family, in fact we very rarely ate together, or even watched TV together. Nowadays, computers seemed to take over everyone's leisure time. When we discussed it with the children, we came up with a 'family cinema' evening on a Friday when we all watch a DVD together with pizza and popcorn.'

To communicate their values, parents need to spend time with their children. If children spend too much time with an 'electronic babysitter', their values will be influenced by large commercial enterprises which are trying to sell them things!

Insight

We recently read research which showed that, on average, children spend twice as long in front of a screen (including internet, games and TV) as they do in class, and one and a half times more than with their parents. Children as young as seven are being recruited to promote products to their friends and family.

Family mission statements

Organizations spend millions on creating 'mission statements' to build team spirit.

How about producing a 'family mission statement' which will give you direction and a shared way of operating? Here is an example which comes from Steve Covey, author of *The Seven Habits of Highly Effective Families*.

'The mission of our family is to create a nurturing place of faith, order, truth, love, happiness, and relaxation and to provide opportunity for each individual to become responsibly independent and effectively interdependent, in order to serve worthy purposes in society.'

For younger children, you would no doubt use simpler language, but everyone can join in with their thoughts about what to include in your own family mission statement. You can draw on the ideas you all had about values.

SETTING RULES

Looking back at the values in the earlier exercise, you may find it interesting to see how they are inextricably linked with the basic human needs discussed in Chapter 3.

For instance, safety is an important need for everyone in the family, as are kindness and love. If a value is a fundamental principle enshrining a need, a rule will help to make sure it is respected and put into practice. For example:

Principle = Kindness ...   Rule = No hitting
Principle = Appreciation ...   Rule = Say 'Thank you'
Principle = Respect for others ... Rule = Listen without interrupting

A rule can be seen far more positively when you recognize that it protects your needs.

Although rules are the adults' responsibility, if your children take part in setting them they will understand what the rules are and why they are needed. Looking back at your values, make a list of the boundaries or fundamental principles you would like to see in your family. How do these translate into rules?

Writing the rules down – perhaps in colourful marker pens – and putting them up somewhere prominent is a good reminder for everyone. Children can also decorate the 'poster' so the rules will look attractive and fun rather than regimental.

At the same time as setting rules, talk about what the consequences for breaking them will be. The stress should be on making up for any damage, hurt or worry caused. Could someone lend a favourite toy, offer their mother a foot massage or a cup of tea, clean out the car, or sacrifice pocket money to pay for something broken?

Psychologists have discovered that children have a moral sense at a surprisingly early age. By three years old, many children can distinguish 'right and wrong' rules from mere manners.

At quite a young age, for example, a child comes to realize that name-calling is wrong because it causes distress, as does hitting, biting or stealing. On the other hand, they understand that table manners are just a polite convention. When you talk these things over with your children, it provides an opportunity to share your values with them and develop their moral awareness.

The fewer the rules, the easier to remember. 'No hitting' or 'No name-calling' are effective reminders, but wherever possible, use positive rather than negative language. When you start a rule with 'We', it emphasizes that you are all 'in the same boat'. For example: 'We sit down to eat' or 'We ask before borrowing things'.

Rules may be general – for example, 'No hurting' – or specific – for example 'Staying with friends is only permitted at weekends' or

'TV and games only after homework is finished'. Some will be set in stone, while others will change as your children grow up. Revise your list from time to time, to bring the most important principles to the forefront of everyone's minds.

Every family will have its own approach to rules. When your children are small, it can be very simple.

Julie, mother of Anna and Jake:

'The other day, I asked my two little ones to suggest a list of rules for our family. They came up with just three: "No hurting", "No pushing" and "Listen". They were very excited when I wrote them down and put them up on the kitchen wall. That very evening, Anna pointed at the rules when Jake was pushing her. He smiled sheepishly and stopped. Although he can't yet read, he'd taken the rule in, and I think he observed it because he'd been involved in choosing what went on the list.'

Top tips for setting rules

- ▶ *Rules grow out of your values. Agree with your partner what is really important to you and ask your children what they think too.*
- ▶ *Involve your children, even young ones, in making family rules.*
- ▶ *Keep rules simple and positive, and remember you have to follow them too!*
- ▶ *Be prepared to remind children about rules.*

Insight

Of course, however carefully we involve children in making rules, they do get broken. We often have to remind ourselves that it is not easy for children to remember rules and agreements at all times, especially if they are absorbed in their own world. We have to be prepared to explain and remind again and again. The challenge is to do this in a matter of fact way rather than nagging!

Keeping boundaries

Having explored various ways to generate rules which will safeguard everyone's boundaries and make family life easier, you may wonder how to go about enforcing them. How can you make all these nice ideas happen in reality?

HELPFUL DISCIPLINE

In order to be clear about your aims when enforcing rules in your home, it's worth stepping back and taking a look at your attitude to discipline generally. Mention this word to parents of any age, and you can expect a lively debate in no time. Some personalities (Chapter 4) may love spontaneity and hate being told what to do. Also, for many the word 'discipline' is inextricably linked with punishment or being told off, and these negative connotations can put parents off the whole idea. Parents who believe this may fall into the indulgent category (see Chapter 2 on parenting styles) who are reluctant to hold their children to rules but then snap when their behaviour becomes too infuriating.

Whatever the word means to you, it is interesting to know that 'discipline' used to refer to the systematic instruction given to a disciple or pupil. It comes from the Latin word *discere*, which means 'to learn'. Therefore, 'helpful discipline' means teaching your children all about the boundaries and values which will help them stay safe and healthy, fit in with society, have fulfilling relationships and operate happily in the world. It also means setting the rules and guidelines which give children a sense of security and predictability and let them know what is expected of them.

Insight
I find it helpful to think of discipline as something you do *with* your children rather than something you do *to* them – to help them learn. – *Glenda*

If a car drove into your wall, it would not be much use if it just fell down. You would prefer your wall to stand strong and the car to crumple. That way the driver would learn to be more careful another time! In the same way, the boundaries you establish in your family need to be strong enough to withstand 'unruly' behaviour – they need to be backed up or they are of no use. Much of what you have read in earlier chapters will have paved the way for a relationship of co-operation with your children. Nevertheless, there will still be times when you need to stop or change behaviour which is causing problems. In these cases, discipline can be seen as an *external* boundary which is designed to develop *internal* boundaries in your children.

The following pages will offer some strategies to add to your 'discipline toolbox'.

Challenging unacceptable behaviour

Before thinking about how to challenge difficult behaviour in your child, it is helpful to look at what worked or didn't work in your own childhood experience.

Exercise: How were you punished or told off as a child?

Think back to a time, if possible in your childhood or teens, when you were punished or told off by an adult for doing something they didn't like you doing.

1 *Describe what you were doing.*
  (If you don't remember what you were doing, move on to the next question.)

(Contd)

2   How did they tell you off? Describe the words they
    used, their tone of voice, their posture, etc. What, if
    any, was your punishment?

3   How did you react?

4   How did you feel about yourself when you were
    punished or told off?

5   How did you feel about the adult?

6   Did you want to change your behaviour as a result?

7   What, if anything, would have been more helpful?

Laura, mother of Rory and Owen:

'I remember I was punished by being left behind with an elderly
aunt when the rest of the family had a day out. I recall being really
angry, thinking it was unfair, and hating my Dad who had shouted
at me. But I really can't remember what I did wrong to earn the
punishment, so I actually couldn't say if I behaved differently
afterwards because of it!'

Mike, father of Eric:

'I remember my mother really blowing her top once when we came back late from our friends' house. She certainly wasn't prepared to listen to us, so we couldn't explain that we'd lost their dog and were looking for him. If only she'd let us have our say, we could have worked out what to do differently another time – like phoning her to let her know.'

It is surprising how often people cannot remember what they did wrong when they were punished as children. Their anger and fear flooded out any reflection about their misdeed.

When scolded they were often blamed or criticized, which made them resentful, particularly if they hadn't been the culprit! Their parents seldom waited to hear if they had anything to say on the matter. Others recall complying to rules out of fear, which didn't do much for their relationship with the adult concerned.

Often children do not really understand what they have done wrong because parents come out with confusing messages, like: 'What do you think you're doing?!' which certainly doesn't give any useful information. Following that, punishment won't show them what they need to do differently.

If a punishment or a good telling off is not the answer, how can you enforce the rules?

It will help to think what you are aiming for in challenging your child's behaviour.

It is important that:

- ▶ *they receive clear information about what behaviour you want them to change*
- ▶ *they understand the reason why you want them to behave differently*
- ▶ *the needs for respect are met on both sides*

> - *the relationship is strengthened, not damaged*
> - *the child is motivated to change their behaviour out of a desire to help rather than from fear.*

A strategy for challenging which has worked for many parents is a variation on the **ACT** model (you may like to remind yourself of how **ACT** works by revisiting Chapter 1).

Children are much more likely to do what you want if you show care and respect for their needs too. 'Connect before you correct' is a very useful motto. This is how the strategy works:

C = *Child*
A = *Adult*
T = *Tools.*

To understand this better, see how Teresa could use **CAT** to challenge her boys, Sean and Logan, about playing football indoors:

C = She connects before she corrects her children by thinking of what their feelings and needs are, and acknowledges them: 'It looks like you're really enjoying playing football in here, especially as it's cold outside.' (The boys are already listening because their Mum is seeing things from their point of view.)

A = She brings in her own point of view (Adult). In a firm voice she says: 'And ... I feel very tense because I'm worried something will get broken. That's why the rule is: "Football outdoors". I can't relax enough to get on with cooking supper.'

T = Tools. There are many possible 'tools' for this situation: a firm instruction to play outside; seeing if they'd like to do something else; asking them what would help resolve the problem; or any of the other tactics she might have up her sleeve. This time Teresa decides to offer them a limited choice: 'You can either play football outdoors or play something else inside – you choose.' The boys choose to go out in the garden, and Teresa can breathe a sigh of relief.

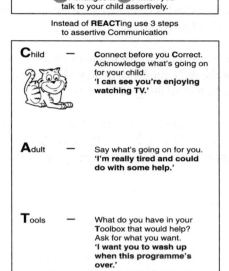

ACT changes to CAT when you
talk to your child assertively.

Instead of **REACT**ing use 3 steps
to assertive Communication

Child — Connect before you Correct.
Acknowledge what's going on
for your child.
**'I can see you're enjoying
watching TV.'**

Adult — Say what's going on for you.
**'I'm really tired and could
do with some help.'**

Tools — What do you have in your
Toolbox that would help?
Ask for what you want.
**'I want you to wash up
when this programme's
over.'**

Talking assertively helps sort
out problems together.

Figure 11.1 Challenging with CAT.

Trying something new is not always easy at first, so it will help if
you work through a few questions to establish what is best to do in
your own home.

Exercise: Challenging undesirable behaviour using CAT

Think of a situation in which you are finding your child's
behaviour problematic.

Describe what your child is doing (or not doing).

(Contd)

How do you feel and what do you need to happen?

What do you think your child feels in this situation? What need is she trying to meet?

Work out what you could say to challenge the behaviour using:
C (Child) = Acknowledge what's going on for your child.

A (Adult) = Say how you feel and what you need (start with 'And' rather than 'But').

T (Tools) = Say what you want to happen, or ask child to come up with an idea that will help you.

Practise it on your partner or learning companion and ask how it sounded to them. Otherwise rehearse it when you're on your own and then say it to your child.

CAT is particularly useful when **you** own the problem, in other words, when your needs are not being met. Remember to use the **A** stage of **CAT** for your challenge to have maximum effect. In the example above, playing football in the living room was not a problem at all for Sean and Logan – they were enjoying themselves. It was a problem for *Teresa*, because she didn't want anything to get broken. Later on, she said:

'Before I learned about CAT, I always used to blame the boys. As long as I kept saying "You, You, You" as in "You never listen!", it never really sunk in. Now I've told them that it's a real problem for *me*, that I mind if things get broken! I think the reason for playing outdoors has finally registered with them.'

In order to challenge successfully, it helps if you are clear in your own mind what you feel, and what those feelings are telling you – i.e., what you *need*. Parents are often so busy looking after everyone else's needs that they forget about their own completely. Remember, your own needs are as important if not more important than those of your children (see the section on the oxygen mask in Chapter 2). It helps to get the point across if you show how strongly you feel about the problem.

CAT is also effective if your child has damaged something or is disturbing other people.

This is discipline in the 'teaching' sense, as it shows your children very clearly how their behaviour impacts on other people.

A parent's story

Suresh was at his niece's graduation party, and his children got restless and started playing 'catch'. This was obviously disturbing the guests and he wanted to stop them rushing around without making a scene. He ran through some possible strategies in his mind and came up with CAT. He said: 'I can see you're enjoying running around, **and** this is a grown-up party. I'm afraid you will knock into people and bother them. Can you think of something you could both do sitting down?' They remembered their Mum had packed some cards in her handbag, and found a corner to play 'Snap'.

The discipline of consequences

One of the most important lessons children have to learn in life is that actions have consequences – both positive and negative. The world they inhabit is made that way: if Mia allows Abby to join in her game, Abby will smile and be happy; if Owen hits a cricket ball into a window, the glass will break and he will get into trouble; if Finlay touches the hot oven shelf, his fingers will get burnt.

> ### Insight
> Watching our children grow up, from early infancy through adolescence we've noticed how hard it can be for them to anticipate the consequences of their behaviour or indeed make a link between what they do and what might follow on from their actions. This is why it's so crucial to let them learn from experience as well as teaching them to think about cause and effect.

POSITIVE CONSEQUENCES

As most people learn more from experiencing something than from being told about it, positive consequences often work well for motivating children:

Grace, daughter of Celia and Dave:

'Mrs Green was very pleased when I played my piece today. She said I must have worked really hard to improve so much. I'm going to have a go at the new piece she set me today.'

As you saw in Chapter 8, showing you've noticed your child's good behaviour by smiling or describing its effect on you encourages her. She will see that her actions have a positive outcome. It also helps to reinforce self-discipline in your children when you point out the results of their behaviour.

You could say:

'It's great you've cleared up the Lego so quickly ... Now we have time for a story.'

or 'Cleaning your teeth so well helps them to stay healthy. You're brushing off all the nasty bacteria which cause damage.'

REWARDS

There are times when parents have to orchestrate a positive consequence to bring about a change in behaviour which is bothering them. For younger children, simple rewards can be enough to break a habit. One mother gave her daughter an animal sticker each time she slept in her own room all night and was amazed how quickly her daughter's sleep pattern improved. Another put a 'tick' on her four-year-old's hand in biro each time he remembered to hang up his coat.

Everyone knows that it is much easier to do a difficult job if you've got something to look forward to at the end: the holiday after exams; the cinema outing after finishing decorating a room. Rather than taking things away as a punishment, you can think about giving them as a reward. Punishments look back, rewards look forward. This can work particularly well with 'screen time' – TV, computer games, time on social networking sites – which nearly all children want to spend more time on than their parents will allow them! Rather than being seen as a right, 'screen time' can be a reward for completing homework and other tasks.

Peter, father of Owen and Rory:

'I was always confiscating the DS as a punishment. Now, on Saturday morning after Owen has finished his school work, brushed the dog and tidied his room, he gets it as a reward.'

NEGATIVE CONSEQUENCES

Adults are constantly learning from the results of their actions: when they have too much to drink, for example, or forget an appointment, or drive carelessly. The part of the brain which apprehends consequences is more developed in adults than in children, so parents often have to help their children see that one thing follows from another. When Logan accidentally hits his Dad on the head with his cricket bat, the father could say to himself: 'He's only young, he didn't mean to do it, so I won't create a fuss and make him feel guilty', but then Logan will not learn much. If his Dad says: 'I know you didn't mean to, but that cricket bat really hurt me! Be more careful in the future!', then Logan learns how much it can hurt someone when he doesn't look around before swinging his bat.

You reap what you sow.

This is a well-known saying, but only partially true. Sometimes people don't reap what they sow because someone else steps in and reaps it for them. Parents often 'rescue' their children from consequences because they don't want to see them suffer. Although well-meaning, they are depriving their children of useful learning.

A father might take over and complete a late running project for his daughter. He may even enjoy working on it and imparting his knowledge. However, this will not teach her anything about organizing her time and doing her own research. That is the object of the project, and his rescuing action won't help at all with that.

With all discipline, however, kindness is also essential. If your child feels demoralized and needs an extra leg-up or if she has been having a hard time at school, you may decide to go ahead and provide support when asked for help with homework. Ways to support without taking over are detailed in Chapter 10.

Thinking time

Penny, mother of Mia and Abby:

'I've tried all my repertoire of tactics with Abby, but nothing seems to stop her using my make-up when she's playing Princesses with her friend. I even tried hiding it away, but I realized they'd found it when I discovered my favourite lipstick under the sofa and broken.'

When a rule (e.g., 'We ask before borrowing things') has been repeatedly broken, it is time for a parent to display their 'warm and firm' style (see Chapter 2). For your children to acquire the clear framework they need, it is necessary for you to hold up an immovable boundary when you want them to stop whatever they're doing.

'Thinking time' is advocated by Steve Biddulph in his book *More Secrets of Happy Children*, where he calls it 'stand and think'. It is a more constructive approach than the 'naughty step' or 'time out', both of which are currently popular, but have a punitive flavour. Punishment looks back – the payment for wrongdoing. The discipline of 'thinking time' looks forward to the lessons you need to learn to avoid making the same mistake again. The idea is to give your child a better understanding of herself so she can handle things more thoughtfully in the future, and act less impulsively. This is how it works.

The advantage of '**Thinking time**' is that it shows in no uncertain terms that you will not tolerate the unacceptable behaviour, and you want your child to do things differently.

You acknowledge the feelings and needs behind the behaviour while at the same time helping your child use her thinking skills to come up with a better way of operating in the future.

Thinking time

- *Choose the thinking spot – a place or a seat in the same room as yourself.*
- *Tell your child: 'Stay there and think about what you did. As soon as you've worked it out, and I'm ready, I'll come and talk it over with you.'*

It is important to respond as soon as your child has shown signs of readiness to change her behaviour.

Dealing
This is where you help your child understand what drove her to behave in an unacceptable way, what she can do differently, and how to remedy the situation.

Ask your child:

- *'What did you do?' It's important for children to own up to their actions.*
- *'What were you feeling?'*
- *'What did you need?'*
- *'What can you do next time to meet your needs?'*
- *'Show me.'*

In some situations, it is possible for the child to do an 'action replay' using her new suggestion. Other times, when circumstances don't permit this, simply say:

- *'What can you do to make things better?'*

You may also say this when your child needs to make amends for some injury to feelings, body or property.

This is how it could sound in a dialogue between Penny and Abby:

Penny (very firmly):	'Abby, I'm not going to put up with your taking my make-up any longer. That's my favourite lipstick ruined. Stand here and think about what you did. As soon as you've worked it out, and I'm ready, I'll come and talk it over with you.'

Penny continues to wash up the pans; Abby looks glum, and after a few moments, starts to sidle away.

Penny:	'So you've thought it through.'
Abby:	'Yes.'
Penny:	'What did you do?'
Abby:	'Your lipstick got broken.'
Penny:	'Yes. What exactly did you do?'
Abby:	'I took the lipstick to make Jenny look like a princess.'
Penny:	'I see. How were you feeling?'
Abby:	'I wanted to make Jenny look pretty.'
Penny:	'Hold on a minute, let's just think about what you needed ...'
Abby:	'We just needed something to make us look like princesses.'
Penny:	'So what can you do next time to meet your needs?'
Abby:	'I dunno ...'
Penny:	'Think about it for a moment.'
Abby:	'I suppose I could get some face paints with my pocket money. I've seen some in "Jane's Toys".'
Penny:	'Yes, we could go there tomorrow. And what about my broken lipstick?'
Abby:	'I'm sorry Mummy. I can give you some of my pocket money for a new one.'

Children do not learn self-control overnight, so Penny may well need to use '**Thinking time**' a few times if Abby forgets about the 'Ask before you borrow' rule.

The important thing is that Abby knows that the behaviour is not OK, and that her mother will not allow it to go on.

Being firm

There are times when you are not prepared to negotiate with your child. Perhaps you feel strongly about something and you are not prepared to compromise on it; perhaps there is an external constraint of health, time, space or money; or it could be that your needs override those of your child at that moment. How do you get this message across without shouting and blaming? You can probably think of people in your life who seem to have natural authority – they don't need to raise their voices and children obey them without fussing. Experienced teachers often have this ability. It is worth breaking it down into its component parts to see how you can cultivate it yourself.

GENTLE CERTAINTY

If you are really sure of your ground, you can stand firm. The secret is to be soft on the inside, so you are telling yourself that you love your child and understand what she wants, while at the same time being firm on the outside. Steve Biddulph, the parenting writer and speaker, calls this a 'relaxed struggle' – you are relaxed while your child is struggling.

COMMUNICATING FIRMNESS

Drop your shoulders, breathe deeply and lower the pitch of your voice. A low voice has more authority. Try getting quieter rather than louder. Choose your words carefully; say, for example:

'I want you to' or 'I don't want you to' rather than 'Please could you ...' or 'Please could you not ...'. You are instructing rather than requesting. Make sure your child is looking at you, and keep your expression serious. Use 'and' instead of 'but'.

For example, **you could say:**

'I understand that you really want to stay up to watch "Vampire Special" AND it is time for bed'.

This kind of firmness works best when your child really believes that you have her best interests at heart. Acknowledging feelings, playful ways to get her to co-operate and skilled listening make up the *warm* part of being warm and firm. You also have to be able to do the *firm* part, in order to give your child the boundaries she needs.

THE SOFT 'NO'

Do you ever find yourself getting into a futile argument with your child which you know you can't win? Here is how you can avoid this. When you are sure of your position, you can explain it once, acknowledge your child's feelings, and then calmly say 'No'. The more heated your child gets, the cooler and calmer you become. Rather than raising your voice, drop it.

A parent's story

Nine-year-old Grace wanted a computer with internet access in her bedroom. Her mother Celia was uncomfortable about her daughter being able to use instant messaging and get onto social networking sites without supervision. She managed to discuss it with her ex, Grace's father, and they agreed on a united front. The next time Grace brought it up, Celia was prepared to stand firm:

'Mum, why can't I have a computer in my room, all my friends do, you're so mean!'

'I know you really want to have a computer in your room, AND your Dad and I have both decided we want the computer where we can see what's going on.'

'I'm the only one out of all my friends, I really hate you.'

(Contd)

'I can understand you are upset AND we have made up our minds.'

'Please! I would promise not to use it after bedtime.'

'No.' (very calm, rather quiet, you're not going to be drawn into an argument)

'Why can't I have one?'

'No.' (very quietly)

Eventually, Grace petered out. Celia was relieved that she had avoided losing her temper and had stuck to what she felt was right.

Soft certainty can be a 'No, you can't' or a 'Yes, you have to'. It is healthy for a child to see that there are times when you are not prepared to negotiate. Parents need to have spine, because children get out of control when their parents bend to their every whim. Indeed, they thrive on firm and reasonable limits.

Insight

I remember the first time I tried out the soft 'No' on one of my children who was expert at drawing me into an argument. He wanted to watch a film I considered unsuitable. I was amazed that my quietly repeating 'No' meant he soon gave up! – *Glenda*

Boundaries and the outside world

The world is full of rules and regulations, and it can be an unhappy place for the child who hasn't learned to observe them. If your child has not come to respect your 'No', she will have a hard time in school, and may well get in trouble with teachers. Even if you are educating your child at home, she will still need to fit in with the rules and boundaries of society at large. Therefore, when you put into practice the approaches outlined in this chapter, you will be helping your child to get on with others more happily.

Other families often have different ways, and all you can do as a parent is to help your children recognize which rules are constant and which are variable. In your house, for example, you may all sit down round the table to eat, while in Jen's house the children sit round the TV. Your children will go along with Jen's rules when at her house.

Another area for differing values can be around language. If your child has picked up language which offends you,

You could say:

'It's a funny thing about words. Some people are offended by certain words and others are not. Even though Tim's family don't mind it, most people don't want to hear that word, and I *certainly* do not. In this family we care about others' feelings, so from now on you know that we don't say X.'

If you make your point calmly, your child is less likely to use offensive language or swearing to get a rise out of you. You will also have to do your best to abide by the rule!

When you talk through your family values, it is helpful to discuss which of your principles applies everywhere, and which things can vary. This is where your job as a parent is crucial – raising happy children involves showing them how to recognize and respect the customs and limits of friends and the broader world of school and society, while remaining true to their own values.

PARENTS' COMMENTS

Jamal, father of Hussein and Noor:

'My children kept wanting me to buy ice creams from the van which was very conveniently parked outside their school. I came to dread the daily battle. Finally, I came up with a good solution. I said: "Although ice creams are delicious, they're not very good for you if you have them too often. How about you choose one day a week to be your 'ice cream day'?" So they chose Friday, and now if they ask to have one at other times, I just say: "What's your ice cream day?" Having the rule has taken all the arguing out of it, which is a great relief all round.'

Teresa, mother of Callum, Sean and Logan:

'Last week, we sat down as a family to talk about our values, and come up with a few rules based on them. Since then, Callum has been much better about letting me know if he's going to be coming home later than usual. He understands that it's all about safety and consideration for others.'

Things which have struck me in this chapter

Something I am going to try out

HAVE SOME FUN

Face painting

Buy some face paints and let everyone in the family paint each others' faces. There are plenty of websites and books with ideas for designs. Face painting is popular at many charity events, so your children may be developing a skill for raising money too!

10 THINGS TO REMEMBER

1 *Boundaries are necessary for children to be able to live happily alongside others and to develop self-discipline.*

2 *Children need to develop a sense of their own boundaries for their safety and to be themselves.*

3 *Considering what your values are – what is important to you in life – helps you to set priorities and rules and lets children know what you will and will not tolerate.*

4 *Involve your children in making family rules and in revising them as they grow older.*

5 *Discipline is about learning. Too often a punishment leads to anger, fear and resentment rather than learning and growth.*

6 **CAT** *stands for* **C**hild, **A**dult *and* **T**ools, *and is a way of acknowledging what is going on for the child, stating what the adult needs, then going on to use an appropriate 'tool' for changing behaviour.*

7 *Consequences, both positive and negative, help to teach children about the results of their actions (or inaction). Rewards can be a potent way to motivate.*

8 *'***Thinking time***' is a way of getting your child to reflect on what she did, what her need was and what she can do instead, and also to make amends.*

9 *You have to be firm at times when your needs and values override those of your child.*

10 *Communicate firmness by lowering your voice and repeating one good reason, or softly saying 'No'.*

12

Tackling sibling conflict

In this chapter you will learn:
- *about underlying causes of conflict between siblings*
- *how to avoid favouritism and comparisons*
- *how to respond helpfully when children fight*
- *a way to reach a win–win outcome.*

Gloria, mother of Jasmine, Chantal and Nathan:

'The decibel level in our house seems to be set so high. The two girls are always shouting: "Not fair!" They both gang up on Nathan, but he does provoke them. Their Dad and I get irritated and shout at them all and then at each other, doors get slammed, there are tears and rudeness. I find it so *exhausting*. Will they never get on?'

Arguments and disagreements are part of life – to experience conflict is to be human, but to be human we also have to learn to live with others; and the family is where we start learning to do this, for better or worse. A relationship in which there is never any conflict is probably not a very intimate one. Conflict makes us define ourselves – our needs, wants and values. On the other hand, ongoing bickering and fighting make the family atmosphere unpleasant for everyone.

> *Having one child makes you a parent. Having two or three makes you a referee.*
>
> David Frost

Physical tussles and verbal sparring between siblings are extremely common, and parents – especially ones who were themselves only children – tend to find this stressful. One piece of research found that three- to seven-year-olds fight on average 3.5 times an hour.

However, it is important to accept that sibling fights can convey some advantages: children learn skills such as how to handle rejection, work on disagreements and do deals, react coolly to teasing, and understand others' strengths and weaknesses. These skills are useful in the playground and beyond. Indeed, handling rejection from a game without fussing and being able to resolve disputes are both factors which help with popularity at school.

Nevertheless, parents wish that their children would get on with each other. After all, the sibling relationship is probably the longest one that they are likely to have, and if they are lucky, it will be a source of mutual support, fun and shared memories throughout their lives.

Insight

In our experience, half-brothers and -sisters as well as step-siblings who have experienced some shared upbringing have equally lasting bonds.

As a parent, you can have an effect on the quality of your children's relationships. This chapter will look at what you can avoid and what you can do to promote family harmony – or at least fair fighting!

It is worth looking at the way the adults in the family resolve their differences too, as this is a powerful model for children.

If parents can show that different views can at least be respected, even if not taken on, that a disagreement does not mean putting the other person down, or that one parent does not always give in to the other, children will be more confident in handling conflicts themselves.

Researchers in the US offered parents of pre-school children a group focused on their own relationship as a couple. Their children adapted better than others to starting kindergarten and were still doing better at school at nine years old.

Causes of conflict

The most obvious underlying cause of conflict is a clash of needs. Working out the need underlying feelings and behaviour is a first step in understanding all kinds of situations (as covered in Chapter 3). When you think about a child's need for closeness and love from a parent, it is clear why brothers and sisters often fight, and often fight more when parents are around. As well as the competition for love, having brothers and sisters means that there can be less to go round in the family, less space, less time on the computer. In a 'blended' family where children from different parents are having to share, these feelings of being diminished by the others can be even more acute.

The great white shark has a gestation period of ten months. Up to 40 embryos start to develop, and they gradually attack and eat each other in the womb until only one survives to be born. This is called intrauterine cannibalism – a very extreme form of sibling rivalry!

Competition for love, attention, resources and respect gives rise to the feeling that if one sibling has more, the other has less. This is the trigger for many of the fights between brothers and sisters, and parents can exacerbate or soothe this rivalry by the way they react. In contrast to seeing family relationships as competition for a finite 'cake', having the underlying attitude that more family members means more fun, interest, ideas and love, as well as more opportunity to care and nurture others, is an alternative and positive approach.

Right from the beginning, as well as acknowledging feelings of jealousy, parents can help their existing children to care for a new baby and to understand what the baby may be feeling too. They can be reminded that they themselves were also completely dependent once. Research shows that this approach does help strengthen sibling relationships.

Insight

I well remember the shriek of anguish of an older child on seeing a new baby being fed, and wish I'd had the skills then that I have now! – *Doro*

TAKING A STEP BACK

One thing is sure: when your children are fighting, if you get irritated and pulled into the conflict it won't improve things, indeed it may well make them worse. You can apply some of the skills you have learned in this book to analyse what is happening, keep your cool and intervene in a helpful way.

First of all, it can be useful to think about the situations where your children are in conflict.

Exercise: Analysing fights

At what times do conflicts arise between your children?

Take one specific incident and ask:
What was each of the children trying to achieve?

What were their feelings and needs?

How did this make me feel?

Sarah, mother of Zach, Martha, Naomi and Ben:

'Naomi picks on Ben when she gets back from school and teases him until he cries. I think she feels jealous that he has had more time with me during the afternoon and I feel guilty, but I don't know what to do about it.'

Amina, mother of Hussein and Noor:

'It's easier to think of the few times when they don't fight! And that's when I'm not around. When they are with my parents, apparently they play together in the garden for hours. As soon as I come back, they are fighting to get on my lap. I get really irritated.'

Battles for love and attention

Understanding the strong needs that children have for your love and approval makes it easier to **ACT** rather than react. Children who express these needs by attacking a sibling paradoxically make their parents less loving and approving. It seems contradictory, but acknowledging hostile feelings between brothers and sisters and bringing them out into the open is helpful. As covered in Chapter 6 on feelings and Chapter 9 on listening, all feelings can be accepted even while a limit is put on behaviour. Putting strong feelings into words makes them more manageable and engages the thinking part of the brain. Remember – you can name the feelings without agreeing with them!

Sometimes this is best done away from the other siblings.

A parent's story

Sarah decided to use skilled listening with Naomi about Ben.

Sarah: 'You seem to be really angry with Ben these days.'
Naomi: 'Yes I hate him, I wish he would disappear down a big hole and never come back.'
Sarah: 'You wish he wasn't around all the time.'
Naomi: 'Yeah.'
Sarah: 'Maybe you wish you could have an afternoon on your own with me like he does.'
Naomi: 'Yeah I do!'

Naomi visibly relaxed, and over the next days was kinder to her little brother.

It is worth noting that, though children often say that they wish their siblings did not exist, or would disappear, they do not on the whole mean it. Their feelings are usually mixed, and this can be acknowledged too.

Teresa, mother of Callum, Sean and Logan:

'When Sean went away on a school trip, the youngest one, Logan, who had been crowing about having toys to himself and so on, was quite subdued and really wanted to talk to his brother on the phone when he rang home. In the end I said: "Part of you likes having more time with us and Callum, and part of you misses Sean a lot."'

When it feels like there are too many battles for attention in your family, it is worth making a real effort to find individual time for each child. For children, time is the most evident marker of your love. Parents have come up with some creative ideas to carve out one-to-one time, and all say that it makes a difference to the atmosphere.

One very organized family with three children allocated a Saturday afternoon a month to each, alternating with mother and father. There was a budget, and within that the child could choose what he or she wanted to do. This was a particularly good system as it gave each parent time with each child.

Another mother arranged for her younger child to go to a friend once a week so she could collect the older one from his karate class and have a snack with him on the way home. Children in blended families may be visiting for a weekend and need time with their own parent as well as with the rest of the step-family, which can make for complicated timetabling but it is worth the effort. Families where there is a child with special needs may have to really think hard about how to give adult attention to the other siblings too.

These one-to-one occasions can be a chance to 'be someone to tell' and use skilled listening (see Chapter 9), as well as to simply hang out and have fun.

Top tips in battles for love and attention

▶ *Acknowledge feelings by putting them into words.*
▶ *Remember siblings usually have mixed feelings for each other.*
▶ *Find ways to spend some one-to-one time with each child.*

JEALOUSY

Being jealous is very often considered to be an unacceptable feeling. 'You're just jealous!' is often said in an accusing way – but jealousy is unlikely to go away if you scold a child for manifesting it. It is better to acknowledge how painful it is and try to see it as a signal of a need or a want. You cannot meet all your children's hankerings for material things, nor would that be appropriate, but it is important to take underlying needs seriously, and acknowledge the pain when they cannot be met. At its deepest level, a child's jealousy is probably rooted in feeling that someone else is more important to his parents or teachers than he is.

You could say:

'You feel jealous of Owen, you wish you were in the top football team like him.'

'You wish your godmother would give you presents like Grace's auntie Annette does.'

'You think I like Chantal best because she has been ill and I have spent so much time with her. I like spending time with you and hearing what's going on for you just as much.'

> ### Insight
> I have noticed that everyone coos over new babies and says how sweet they are, while the older child will be ignored. How natural for that child to feel ousted by the newcomer, and how important it is to make sure he gets plenty of attention too! I now make a point of always speaking to the older child first, before turning my attention to the baby. – *Glenda*

FAVOURITES

When you think back to your own family, could you say which one of you or your siblings was favoured by your mother or father? Though many parents will deny having a favourite, most children will recognize that one of them gets preferential treatment in subtle or not so subtle ways. One piece of research found that nearly two thirds of mothers and a higher proportion of fathers admitted to such favouritism, and that their children were well aware of it.

Favouritism brings up uncomfortable feelings in parents and children. Parents do not like to admit to themselves that they might feel differently about their different children. Children who feel unfairly treated (whether that is actually the case or not) will be more likely to take out their feelings on the child who is perceived to be the favoured one – look at the bible story of Joseph and his coat of many colours.

Insight

We have heard a saying in family therapy circles which is worth bearing in mind: 'A healthy family is one in which members take turns to be the problem.' If one child is consistently seen as the naughty one, for example, it is worth looking hard at what is really going on – what are the feelings and needs behind the behaviour?

It may happen that a parent is the same personality type as one child, understands how he 'ticks' with no problem and struggles to empathize with another.

Penny, mother of Mia and Abby:

'Yesterday I watched Abby go in to a new drama class where she didn't know many other children. I could see her sussing it all out, looking round and finding her friends but not rushing over to them straight away. It was just how I would approach a similar situation. Mia is short-sighted and so much more timid. She would look at the ground and take a long time to talk to anyone.'

It may be that a child reminds you of a relation who is loved or loathed, and you link him with that person without realizing it.

Amina, mother of Hussein and Noor:

'My son looks just like my husband's brother. It's uncanny, he even has the same walk. I have issues with my brother-in-law, as he is a terrible womanizer, and I have to catch myself for assuming that Hussein will be like that too!'

Parents often identify more strongly with a child in the same position in the family as they were. So a younger child being left out will gain more sympathy from a youngest child, and an older child who is being teased by a younger one may get more support from another first born.

Sarah, mother of Zach, Martha, Naomi and Ben:

'I was the youngest, always tagging along after my big sister and being told to go away. The other day, I *made* Martha let Naomi join in playing a board game with her friends, which in retrospect wasn't really fair.'

Rather than denying their feelings of partiality, parents will do better to admit how they feel to themselves and their partners, and to use that awareness to make sure that they open their eyes and hearts to the qualities of all their children.

Insight

We think that Adele Faber and Elaine Mazlish put it beautifully in their classic book *Siblings without Rivalry*: 'It is perhaps natural and normal to have different feelings towards different children. The only thing that is necessary is that we take another look at the less favoured child, seek out her specialness, and then reflect the wonder of it back to her'.

COMPARISONS

Comparing children in the same family is both natural and unavoidable, however much we try to value their uniqueness (see Chapter 4). From the moment of birth, we are looking at a second child and comparing him to his sibling – weight, appearance, sleep patterns, fussiness. Of course, same gender children are compared more than brothers and sisters. Children compare themselves to each other too, as part of finding their place in the family and working out their own identity.

But comparing can be dangerous. All too often, the implicit message from a parent who makes a comparison is: 'Why can't you be like that too?' Far from making a sibling try harder, this builds resentment and can even make them less likely to compete. Siblings compare themselves with and define themselves against each other without any encouragement to do so. There can be a 'sporty one', an 'arty one' and a 'musical one'. If parents are not careful, children will take themselves out of an area in which they feel they do not excel, limiting their choices.

Patrick, father of Callum, Sean and Logan:

'I was the sporty one, and my brother was the academic one. We were 40 before I did an Open University course and he took up skiing!'

Parents can challenge the stereotyping that children put on themselves and each other, thinking of ways to get them out of the boxes that they put themselves in. They can do their best not to compare children, but to praise or challenge them individually for their own actions, preferably out of earshot of their siblings.

Sarah, mother of Zach, Martha, Naomi and Ben:

'I found myself looking at three school reports at the kitchen table when they came home. There was a lot of "Nyeh nyeh nyeh" going on between them – "I got higher than you" for this or that. In the end I said, "Right, stop, we are going through these with Dad when he gets home, one by one, so each gets full attention".'

Top tips for avoiding favouring and comparisons

▶ *Be aware of your different feelings for different children. Ask your partner or another family member if they think you are being fair.*

▶ *Try to open your heart to understand the unique qualities of a less favoured child.*

▶ *Open up the boxes that children put themselves in, and avoid labelling them yourself.*

Status battles

Fighting for privileges as the oldest child and resisting them being given to the ones coming up behind is almost inevitable whatever the size of the age gap. The sense of injustice often lasts into adulthood. Sometimes the older one feels they fought all the battles to be allowed to do things and the younger one benefited from less strict parents. Even adult siblings often continue to treat each other as 'the oldest' or 'the baby'.

It is hard to get children to see things from another's point of view. Here is a way of making the pros and cons of position within the family more explicit.

Exercise: Family position

When all the family is together, ask:

▶ *What are three good things about being the eldest? And what are three bad things?*
▶ *What are three good things about being the middle child? And what are three bad things?*

And so on.

You can join in from your own perspective looking back at your childhood.

You could also ask:

▶ *What are the good things about being a girl or a boy?*

Opening up the discussion about birth order and gender can be instructive for you as well as for the children, and it might get some issues out in the open.

Penny, mother of Mia and Abby:

'Mia said: "Everyone thinks whatever Abby does is so cute". It made me think: she is only eight, if she were the youngest everyone would think she was cute!'

'SPILL-OVER'

All too often, conflicts happen in families which are actually the result of things that have happened elsewhere. Stress from school or the workplace is brought in through the front door, and it spills over into the home.

Problems at school can be at the root of persistent squabbling and taunting between siblings. Older children in particular can find it satisfying to demonstrate their power over a younger brother or sister when they have been made to feel small at school in some way. You need to find out what the real problem is as well as tackling the fights in the home.

HUNGER AND BOREDOM

It may seem obvious, but a low blood sugar level certainly makes children ratty and more likely to fight. Bringing a snack when you collect them after a long day may mean less bickering.

Another very common cause of conflict between brothers and sisters is boredom. Being in the car for a long journey, or even being at home on a wet afternoon, can trigger fights about nothing which bring stimulation and adult attention even if it is negative. Wailing things like: 'She's crossing her eyes at me again!' or 'He's licking me, that's yucky!' are ways to bring you in to the situation and raise the emotional temperature.

Rather than getting pulled into the rights and wrongs of the accusation, you could tackle the need for stimulation.

You could say:

'It sounds like you're bored, do you want to think of a game to play or shall I make some suggestions?'

BOUNDARIES AND POSSESSIONS

In families as in nations, boundaries and possessions are ongoing causes for war, especially when claims are disputed, or if one party feels that they are hard done by in some way.

It can be helpful to have some family rules about borrowing and sharing. Family rules are discussed in Chapter 11. These could include:

▶ *The owner can say if they want to share or lend something.*
▶ *If something borrowed is damaged, it must be repaired or replaced.*

This can help in clear-cut situations where possession is undeniable, but children will fight over the best chair, a stone they found on the beach, the right to sit in a certain place in the car, whose turn it is to feed the goldfish, and so on *ad infinitum*.

The next section looks at how parents can deal with this kind of squabbling.

Dealing with fights

How was conflict handled in your family when you were growing up? Being aware of your own patterns is the first step to doing something differently, and reflecting on your own experiences as a child can help you to understand what is going on for your children too.

Exercise: Memories of fights

Think of a row or a disagreement between you and a brother or sister which happened when you were a child.

What did your parents say or do?

Was what they did helpful or unhelpful?

How did you feel afterwards?

Peter, father of Rory and Owen:

'My brother and I had to share a room, and there were continuing battles, especially about music – it was never really resolved until he went to college. My parents just used to stay out of it, which I thought was unfair. He was bigger than me and usually won through sheer weight. I remember once he just threw all my CDs out of the window into the garden.'

Ignoring disputes and refusing to get involved may sometimes be appropriate, but not when one child is continually being victimized by another. In this case, the younger brother was left without any back-up, and feeling resentful of his bigger brother. Both siblings got the message that 'might is right'; definitely not a useful approach in future relationships.

Celia, mother of Grace, Adam and Finlay:

'Once I remember my father got so angry at my sister and me bickering that he actually purposely smashed a plate on the kitchen counter in front of us all. We were so scared we held hands under the table and didn't argue for days afterwards.'

Rebuking both parties does nothing to help children resolve disagreements. In this case, fear of the parent makes the children closer – but is it really worth jeopardizing one relationship to strengthen another?

Mike, father of Eric:

'I could set my older brother off just by implying that he was like a dog. I only had to put out my tongue and pant, or go 'woof' and he would go for me. My parents used to tell him off because I was the little one. It was worth the risk of being sat on to see him being punished!'

Many siblings will recognize this pattern – younger and smaller does not necessarily mean innocent! Parents will seldom be able to see the whole story and need to take care not to make assumptions.

Selective attention

If parents intervened in every single disagreement, they would probably go mad. Low-level bickering is best ignored. So just how and when should you get involved?

FIGHTS ABOUT COMMON PROPERTY/AREAS

Making children share may backfire. It will usually mean taking one child's part against another. Beware of the message this can give – does the favoured one feel that their parent feels sorry for them? The one who has had to give something up is likely to feel resentful and plot revenge.

Learning how to persuade and negotiate gives a skill for life. Young children may need to be given a few ideas.

You could say:

'Could you swap something?'

'Could you use the kitchen timer to take it in turns?'

There is a model for more complicated negotiations later in the chapter.

If you acknowledge the feelings of both children, and define the problem, then

You could say:

'I'm sure you can work out a deal that seems fair to both of you', and then leave them to it. If you hang around, the drama is likely to escalate.

Playing or hurting?

Rough and tumble play is something that all young mammals do. Playfulness is one of the basic mammalian feelings, as was mentioned in Chapter 5. Professor Jaak Panksepp, the researcher who wrote about these primordial feelings, argued that rough and tumble play is an important way for all young mammals to learn to socialize. He described it as a 'flurry of dynamic, carefree rambunctiousness', which causes joy and laughter.

Interestingly, his studies of young rats showed that, if one rat always ended up on top, the rat underneath would stop playing with him. To keep playing, the dominant rat had to handicap himself so that the other could win about 30 per cent of the time. Maybe the same proportion applies to siblings.

Play-fighting has to be mutual. If one child is playing and the other is consistently hurt and angry, a parent has to intervene.

You could say:

'Is this playing or are you hurting each other?'

What starts off as play may move into hurting. You may want to institute a rule that fighting ceases when one person shouts 'Stop!' It's important that children learn to respect each other's boundaries (see Chapter 11).

There will be times when play is not the motivation for a fight. If there is a likelihood of damage to people or property and feelings are running really high, obviously a cooling off period is necessary before any negotiating can be put into practice. When you are setting limits on physical contact, you can suggest creative ways for children to express their feelings (this is covered in Chapters 6 and 7 as well). Crayons, playdough or writing letters for older children are all possibilities.

INSULTS AND NICKNAMES

Verbal games and contests are like rough and tumble play, in that they give chances to learn and enjoy language. Learning to react calmly to teasing and finding ways of turning it back are extremely useful skills for the playground. However, teasing can easily tip over into abuse. There is a fine line between teasing and tormenting, and it can be difficult for parents to police that line. Siblings know each other so well that they can find weaknesses and embarrassments and really twist the knife.

A parent's story

Celia's son Adam kept calling his sister Grace a 'fatty'. She was going through that plump stage that many girls do before puberty and a growth spurt, and was feeling very sensitive about it. The media focus on obesity did not help either. Celia decided that she had to put a stop to Adam's cruel remarks. 'I talked to them both separately. I said to Adam that I knew he could be kind and supportive, and that name-calling was absolutely forbidden in our family. I showed my daughter a photo of myself at that age, a very similar shape, and helped her to think of a cool response to Adam.'

Different families will have different tolerance levels for rows and teasing, but if the tears and fury go too far, it is time to think hard if the antagonism is being fuelled by feelings of favouritism, or perhaps because of a spill-over of feelings from school.

Bullying in the family

There is much discussion about bullying in school, and all schools must now have a policy for dealing with it. Bullying in families between brothers and sisters is less discussed, but can be just as real a problem. Teasing is playful, bullying intends to hurt, is persistent and causes distress to the person in the position of less power.

As with play-fighting moving into real fighting, it can be hard to tell when teasing has moved into real bullying. Children bullied at home are at risk of both bullying and being bullied at school too, and bullying in the family can have lasting effects on a child's confidence, self-worth and happiness, so it is highly important to be aware of what is going on and take action.

If you are worried about ongoing verbal and physical cruelty, you need to use skilled listening and problem solving with both children involved, in privacy to begin with.

Reminder: Top tips for problem solving
- ▶ *Name feelings and keep naming them.*
- ▶ *Put a limit on behaviour.*
- ▶ *Imagine a transparent shield so you don't get pulled into strong feelings.*

(Contd)

Try to avoid labelling children as the 'bully' and the 'victim' – it can be hard to get out of 'boxes' like these. You can describe behaviour instead.

You could say:

'I heard you really shouting at Sean, what was all that about?'

'Your sister seems to have some of your favourite toys in her room, how did that happen?'

This is a way of focusing on the 'deed rather than the doer' and steering clear of stereotypes.

Remember that punishment of the bully is very likely to make things worse. You cannot be watching your children every minute of the day, and a child who feels hard done by may well take revenge. Rather than punishing, you can use 'thinking time' (see Chapter 11) to set a clear boundary – separate the child and ask him to say what he did, what he was feeling and needing, how he can act differently in future and make amends.

A bullying child may well be reacting to problems in some other context. It may be painful, but it is worth asking yourself if there is anything going on in the family which is making your children feel insecure, or even giving them examples of bullying?

Insight

We have observed that cruel behaviour can be like a 'hot potato' which is passed from one situation to the next.

You can teach the 'victim' some tools for asserting himself. Practise saying: 'Stop! That hurts, I don't like it' or 'That's mine, I don't want you to have it'. These are skills for life – in many contexts children and young people have to learn how to protect themselves and their boundaries. It helps if there are family rules about hurting and ownership, so that when you enforce them you are not taking sides.

Top tips for tackling bullying in the family

▶ *Use skilled listening with each child separately.*

▶ *Avoid labelling 'bullies' and 'victims' – describe behaviour instead.*

▶ *Try to see if the bullying behaviour is caused by other bullying, in or out of the family.*

▶ *Use problem solving:* **You could say:** *'What do you think would help prevent ...?'*

▶ *Make it clear that 'no hurting' and 'no name-calling' are family rules, and if bullying persists, use 'thinking time' to mark a clear boundary.*

▶ *Teach some assertiveness skills.*

Model for negotiation

There are times when children need some more tools and skills to be able to resolve their differences. You will need to intervene to teach them these skills, especially when there is a big disparity in age or verbal ability, when feelings are running too high, or when there is an ongoing feud.

Children can progress from suggestions for taking turns, or doing deals to a slightly more advanced model for negotiation. This is an extension of the **AIM** problem-solving method (Acknowledge, Identify underlying needs, Move on), and may be familiar to you from management and conflict resolution trainings.

You will need paper and pen for the exercise overleaf.

1 STOP.

Call a meeting of people concerned.

You could say: 'There is a real disagreement going on here. We need to work out what to do for the best.' There may need to be a 'cooling-off period', so that rage and fear can subside and people's thinking brains can be engaged. Remember to name feelings without blaming.

2 INVESTIGATE.

Each person involved takes a turn to say what the difficulty is without interruption. Start with the child who seems most upset.

You could say: 'What happened and how do you feel?'

You can use skilled listening to help less articulate children: return and clarify what they are saying. Rather than going over past rights and wrongs, it is best to define the difficulty as one which needs a solution in the future. Once the definition of the difficulty is agreed, you can go on to the next stage.

3 CREATE.

Ask the children to make suggestions to resolve the difficulty and write them down. They can be evaluated later.

You could say: 'There is your way and your brother's way, can we find another way?', 'What would Harry Potter do?' or 'Is there a deal you could do?'

4 EVALUATE.

The next stage is to evaluate the solutions and see which ones are acceptable. Remember that a way-out idea may have the kernel of a workable solution.

5 PLAN.

Work out who will do what to implement the decisions. You may need to do some physical re-arrangements, or ask for help from someone else.

6 RE-ASSESS.

Fix a time to check out whether the plan is working.

You can also apply this sequence in situations where you have a problem with your children's behaviour.

A parent's story

Daniel heard raised voices and crashing upstairs and went to find out what was going on. His two elder children, Zach and Martha, were shouting and tussling in Martha's doorway. He said: 'I can see you are really angry with each other, so take five minutes each in your rooms and then come down to the sitting room and tell me about it.' When they appeared, he allowed each to have their say without interruption and summarized: 'So Zach says that it is his turn to have Hammie hamster in his room this weekend, but that Martha blocked her door and said that Hammie liked her best. And Martha says that Zach doesn't feed Hammie or help clean his cage, so she has more right to him.'

He went on: 'It sounds like you both feel hard done by about playing and looking after Hammie, and there needs to be a way to share him that you both think is fair.'

The ideas that they came up with were:
▶ *Hammie would stay in Martha's room permanently.*
▶ *Magic another hamster.*
▶ *Write on the calendar which weekend Hammie would go where.*
▶ *Put Hammie's cage on the landing so all could play with him.*
▶ *Agree that whoever helped clean the cage had Hammie that weekend.*
▶ *Put a reminder to feed Hammie on Zach's computer.*
▶ *Martha would lend Zach her goldfish in return for an extra night with Hammie.*

They went on to the 'Evaluation' stage. Zach said 'No' to Hammie being in Martha's room permanently; Daniel said 'No' to another

(Contd)

hamster; but the idea of the calendar and the computer reminder were accepted by both children. Everyone agreed to putting Hammie on the landing during the week (as he was not allowed in bedrooms on school nights). Swapping for the goldfish was agreed if both wanted it.

Daniel moved a table onto the landing and Martha wrote on the calendar, while Zach worked out the computer reminder. They agreed to check how things were going in two weeks' time and wrote that on the calendar too.

Parents report that steps one and two – stopping, acknowledging feelings and working out what is really the matter – are enough to defuse many conflicts. In moving on, the key is to keep the focus on what will happen in the future rather than what has happened in the past.

LIMITS TO WHAT YOU CAN ACHIEVE

As parents, you can make rules that siblings should not hurt each other, you can teach ways for anger to be expressed safely and disputes to be resolved, you can value children's individuality and specialness and you can challenge stereotyping.

However, whatever you do, there will be times when your children fight. To some extent, it is a matter of luck whether siblings have the kind of temperaments that 'fit' together, and the exact age gap does not seem to make too much difference to this either. Bear in mind that siblings who fight a lot may also have a lot of fun together, and get on well in later life.

Insight

I have daughters who fought horribly through their teen years and are now happily sharing a flat! – *Doro*

PARENTS' COMMENTS

Gloria, mother of Jasmine, Chantal and Nathan:

'I thought a lot about how to give one-to-one time to each of my three kids. Something I came up with was to give each of them a day near the time of their birthday. They could choose what they wanted to do. It made me realize how often Nathan, the youngest one, was hustled to fit in with the older two's schedules. He took two hours to spend his birthday gift vouchers in the toy shop and it was good for me to slow down to his pace too.'

Teresa, mother of Callum, Sean and Logan:

'We tried the negotiation model for continuing arguments about whose turn it was to clear the table. I would yell: "In the time it has taken to argue this, you could have done it and be watching TV already!" They came up with the idea that each would have a coloured card with their name on it, put on a high shelf. Every time someone cleared the table, their card would go to the back. So far, it's worked!'

Things which have struck me in this chapter

Something I am going to try out

HAVE SOME FUN

One at a time
Choose a song that everyone knows. Then sing it through taking one word each, as fast as you can. For example, the first person sings 'Baa', and so does the second; the third sings 'black', the fourth 'sheep' and so on.

A variation of this game is to tell a story with each player contributing one word at a time.

10 THINGS TO REMEMBER

1 *Clashes of needs are at the base of most sibling conflicts, especially for the love and attention of parents.*

2 *Acknowledge feelings by putting them into words, and remember siblings usually have mixed feelings towards each other.*

3 *Find ways for both parents to spend one-to-one time with each child.*

4 *Be aware of how you think about and treat your children differently, and consciously open up your heart to the qualities of a less favoured child.*

5 *Challenge the boxes that children put themselves in and avoid comparisons.*

6 *Be open about the advantages and disadvantages of different positions in the family.*

7 *Family rules about name-calling, hurting and possessions are useful so you can apply the rule rather than take sides.*

8 *Play-fighting is healthy, but can turn into real fighting quite easily. Check: are all the children smiling? Ask them: 'Is this for play or for real?' Intervene and set limits if hurting is going on.*

9 *Bullying can happen within the family too. Intervene to set limits; avoid labelling; look for the need and feelings beneath the behaviour; teach assertiveness and problem-solving skills.*

10 *Use the negotiation model for family disputes. Remember to go for the underlying issue rather than the presenting problem, and focus on the future solution rather than who was right or wrong in the past.*

13

Time to talk about difficult issues

In this chapter you will learn:
- *how to talk sensitively about conflict, separation and divorce*
- *ways to help your child cope with death and bereavement*
- *how and when to start talking with your child about sex and relationships*
- *ways to approach the subject of drug and alcohol abuse.*

There are times when you know it is good to keep the communication channels open with your children, but it is far from easy to do it. This chapter looks at approaches and ways to handle issues which can be hard for parents to raise. Parents may be embarrassed, ashamed, overwhelmed themselves or simply uncertain how to start.

Life happens – your children will be lucky not to experience some kind of loss and change in family relationships. The support they receive in a time of crisis will make a huge difference to how they get through it and will mitigate its effects.

'Grown-up' subjects such as sex, drugs and alcohol are now being covered in primary schools, and parents also need to start opening lines of appropriate communication at an early age. The changes of puberty come sooner than they used to, and ignorance about physical developments can cause needless shame and distress. Starting secondary school means contact with older pupils, who may use drugs, alcohol and tobacco. Your children need to have both knowledge and strategies to deal with any undesirable approaches.

Conflict, separation and divorce

By current UK trends, two in every five marriages will end in divorce and of these half will involve children, most of them under the age of ten. By the age of 16, around a quarter of children in the UK will have experienced divorce within their family. Co-habiting couples are not included in these statistics, so the number of children experiencing family change will be even higher than this. Figures in the US are comparable. Children from separated families are at risk of leaving home and school earlier, of having children earlier, of being divorced themselves and being less happy in later life. However, not all children suffer in this way, and how parents relate to each other and to their sons and daughters during and after a break-up can be a very powerful protective factor.

PARENTS FIGHTING

Conflict between mothers and fathers is the most damaging element in a separation. It is almost inevitable that children will witness or overhear arguments in the run up to a divorce. Children may end up blaming themselves for what is going on.

Penny, mother of Mia and Abby:

'I remember that when Mia was only three, she used to say "Sorry, sorry" when we had a row. It was heartbreaking.'

Paradoxically, it can be even more difficult for children to understand and adjust to a separation if they have not witnessed any confrontations and cannot understand the reasons for the rift. If this is the case, you may have to think carefully about how to explain what has happened in a way that they can grasp. You may have to revisit the topic as they get older and are able to understand more, but children do not need to know what has happened in detail.

Peter, father of Rory and Owen:

'I always knew my parents loved each other, but they had such different life plans they couldn't live together. They separated when my younger brother was three. When he was 12, he and I were talking, and it came out that he really believed they broke up because we had been playing roughly with our little sister!'

Talking about conflict is difficult, but necessary. Most children will overhear shouting even if they don't observe it directly. If you can say or show that a conflict has been resolved, you are demonstrating that the inevitable disagreements in any relationship can be worked through. If not, you can say honestly that you cannot agree about some things, without going into details. It is frightening for children to see their parents out of control, and parents in the grip of fury with a partner are likely to ignore children and forget their needs.

Celia, mother of Grace, Adam and Finlay:

'I found to my horror that Adam was sitting on the stairs in his pyjamas crying and clutching his teddy while he listened to me and my ex shouting at each other. I don't know how long he was there and what he heard. I gave him a chance to talk about it the next day, and I told him that we said things we didn't really mean when we were very angry.'

Children should be kept out of fighting as much as possible, and certainly should not be allowed to act as peacemakers, mediators or go-betweens themselves.

TALKING ABOUT DIVORCE AND SEPARATION

Research shows children adjust better to divorce and separation if their parents have managed to listen and talk to them about what is going on and understand their feelings. Chapters 6, 7 and 9 on feelings, anger and listening can give you some ideas of how to approach this.

Remember that feelings can and often will be mixed. Some children will be relieved that day-to-day conflict is lessened after a separation, even while they are scared of the changes to come in their lives.

A study carried out by the University of Leeds in the UK interviewed children of separated couples and went back to talk to them four years later. It found that children wanted to be 'citizens of their families'; that is, they wanted to be consulted about where they would live, how often they would see the non-resident parent and other practicalities. This did not mean that they wanted the responsibility for making decisions, but that they wanted their views taken into account. One boy said: 'The children should get a say and the parents should be able to sort things out for everyone. They should be able to act like adults about it really.'

They defined their families in terms of quality of relationships, not necessarily living in the same house or linked by birth. One girl in the study put it like this: 'A family isn't like blood relatives. It's just people who love each other.' Where parents had moved on emotionally from the divorce, children too were more able to adjust.

WAYS TO BE HELPFUL

Some other points to bear in mind during a separation:

▶ *Make it clear to children they are not to blame in any way.*
▶ *Tell your children, over and over, that although you and your partner cannot live together any more you both still love them just as much as before.*

- ▶ *Remember that they may be trying to protect you from their strong feelings. Talking to other friends and family may be easier for them.*
- ▶ *As well as the family talking as a whole, individual children should have a chance to talk things over alone with you.*
- ▶ *Accept that they may wish you could get back together while being clear that it will not happen.*
- ▶ *Try to avoid bad-mouthing their other parent – after all, half your children's genes come from them.*

It is important to remember that different children will react differently when their parents split up. Anger and behavioural problems are common in the aftermath of separation, particularly among boys, but this does not mean that they will necessarily suffer ill effects in the long run. On the other hand, children who seem quiet and well-adjusted at the time of the divorce may have problems at a later stage.

It is most often the father who becomes the non-resident parent. A big survey of teenage boys found that those with an involved father figure were more likely to be self-confident and high achieving. Encouragingly, it did not matter whether the father figure was resident or not – the important thing was whether the boy felt he could talk to him.

Here is a last, optimistic quote from the University of Leeds study, from a 14-year-old boy: 'Providing parents act properly, divorce shouldn't be a problem.'

Acting 'properly' is not easy amid the rage, hurt and turmoil of a relationship breakdown, but it is the best way to protect children from the harmful effects of family splits.

Insight

We like the way one parent who joined in a Parentline Plus discussion put it: 'You have to love your children more than you hate each other'.

There are excellent websites with advice about divorce and separation for both parents and children – some are listed at the end of this book.

Death and bereavement

At a time of tragedy, adults often want to protect children by keeping silent about what has happened. In fact, grown-ups are usually more uncomfortable with talking about death than children are. Adults who are overwhelmed with grief themselves obviously find it difficult to deal with their children's sorrow as well as their own. However, children have some understanding of death from a very young age. They are able to cope better if their questions are answered clearly, without using euphemisms such as 'losing someone' or 'passed away' which can lead to real confusion.

If you possibly can, be honest with your children if someone close is very ill and likely to die. When they feel they have been lied to or things have been concealed from them, there can be a huge loss of trust. They will pick up your worry in any case. Secrets about death, such as a relative's suicide, can be damaging to children in the long run. They may feel betrayed when they find out what really happened, perhaps from someone outside the close family.

As in divorce, children may have a kind of primitive belief that they are to blame for a death, particularly if they have been playing up during a time of family stress. It is important to reassure them that it is not anyone's fault that someone has died. Acknowledging feelings – your own and your children's – is difficult, but necessary.

Insight

We have found it helpful to understand that children's strong feelings can sometimes come out in different ways: thinking back to layers of feelings, anger can be a 'top' feeling overlaying grief, for example, and a big row can lead to tears which would not come directly.

As well as talking, it can be helpful to find other creative ways of expressing feelings, for example:

- ▶ *writing letters or drawing*
- ▶ *making scrap books of photos and memories*
- ▶ *listening to the dead person's favourite music*
- ▶ *blowing bubbles and sending love on the wind.*

Young children will often be sad for short periods of time and then seem to be playing and joking as if nothing has happened. This can be upsetting for adults, but it's a natural way of coping for them. Don't be shocked at young children playing quite explicit games about death and funerals either.

Stephanie, mother of Jack:

'My son made up songs about his Dad. At first, I was rather disturbed by it, but then I realized it was his way of processing what was going on.'

Gloria, mother of Jasmine, Chantal and Nathan:

'After my sister died, Chantal and her best friend played funerals for weeks, climbing in and out of the toy box as if it was a coffin.'

Children can ask the same questions again and again. Disbelief is a completely natural reaction after bereavement, in adults as well as children. Children can have several contradictory beliefs at the same time – for example, that a good doctor can make someone better even if they are dead, and that dead people can still feel pain when the body is cremated. If they feel that they are being listened to and that you are not going to get annoyed with them, children will usually talk and ask questions about death without much inhibition, and it is important that you can help them to a way of understanding what has happened.

Stephanie, mother of Jack:

'The most difficult question was "Will you die too Mummy?"

I said that I was extremely healthy and didn't intend to die until I was a very old lady and that seemed to comfort him.'

Laura, mother of Rory and Owen:

'Owen asked me: "Do you think I will ever forget Grandad?"

We talked for a bit, and I said that in time he wouldn't feel so sad, but that memories of fun things he did with Grandad and how much he loved him would always be in his heart.'

Try to ask for help and accept all offers of support after a death in the family. Children can really suffer, not just from their own grief, but also from the natural deficit of attention that a bereaved parent can give.

Talking about sex and relationships

Research shows clearly that children whose parents have found ways to talk to them about sex and relationships benefit. One result is that they delay their first full sexual experience. Interviews with 16- to 24-year-olds found that a fifth of young men and more than four in ten young women felt that they had had sex too soon and regretted it. The younger they had been at their first experience, the more likely they were to wish they had not done it.

It may be hard to think about these matters when your child is still in primary school, but in modern western society sexualized images are everywhere: on TV, in posters, magazines, fashion and films. It is also true that many people are embarrassed to talk about their own experiences of sex. This can be a toxic brew for children, who get mixed messages about sexual images used in advertising, and, at the same time, that they should be ashamed of normal developments in their bodies.

Most parents have not had good experiences of being taught about sex, which makes it even more difficult to broach the subject.

Exercise: Sex education

How were you educated about sex?

Think about what you were not told as well as what you were told.

What would you have found more helpful?

Talk this over with your partner, learning companion or a friend. You will probably laugh a lot, in embarrassment as well as from genuine amusement at your younger self!

Laura, mother of Rory and Owen:

'My big sister was my main source of information. And magazines of course. I knew the biology, but I would have liked someone to talk about the difference between love, lust and liking; how the excitement of sexual attraction can befuddle your judgement about what someone is really like!'

Celia, mother of Grace, Adam and Finlay:

'I started my periods early, didn't know what was happening and was really ashamed and terrified. I have made sure Grace knows about menstruation. I got a book out of the library to bring up the subject. I've told her that when she starts, she and I will have a celebration, a grown-up meal.'

Travis, father of Jasmine, Chantal and Nathan:

'All the classes at my secondary school were about what could go wrong – STDs, AIDS, unwanted pregnancy – all about how sex could make you unhappy rather than happy. The most useful thing they could have told me would be always to carry a condom!'

TALKING ABOUT SEX

What are some ways of bringing up the subject of sex and relationships with young children?

> ▶ *Firstly, respond calmly when they ask questions. Ask them in return what their ideas are about the question to get an idea of what level and what detail to go into. Playground chat may be quite shocking when children don't really know what words mean. Try to be matter of fact and use accurate terms for parts of the body.*

'Gay' is a very common term of abuse in schools. But does your child really know what it means? The approximately one in 15 adolescents who are lesbian or homosexual are at greatly heightened risk for depression and suicide. Most say that they recognized their sexual orientation from an early age. Despite changes in the law and celebrity role models in many western countries, there remain fears and prejudices and indeed religious rulings against same-sex relationships. If you can talk calmly and openly about homosexuality, you will be giving an example of understanding which may help your child and school friends to avoid homophobic bullying.

> ▶ *Schools will usually tell you when they are covering the facts of life and the way they are covering subjects in personal, social and health education (PSHE). You can bring it up and ask children for their opinions about the lessons.*
> ▶ *TV and films give many story-lines about relationships, sexual or otherwise. You could ask if they think the characters*

are being fair to each other, if they love each other equally, whether one is taking advantage of another, if they are taking risks by not using contraception (something very seldom mentioned on screen!).

▶ *For younger children, explain the difference between secrecy and privacy. What you do in the privacy of your bedroom is private, but if an adult (even an adult you know well) does or suggests doing something that makes you feel uncomfortable and asks you to keep it secret, that is a sign that you must tell someone.*

In most western countries, young teenagers tend to have their first sexual experience (kissing and petting) at 13 or 14. If you do not find ways to talk to your children about sex and relationships before they reach puberty, you may regret not raising the subject sooner.

A parent's story

Sarah was horrified when her son Zach, 11, came to her very upset. He had been looking at porn sites on the internet and dreadful pictures kept popping up onto the screen, whenever he turned on the computer. Sarah said: 'I was shocked but also relieved that he had come to me. I said that I understood he wanted to look at naked women, but that some of these sites were violent and degrading, and *that* I didn't like. In the end, we agreed that he could put up pictures from magazines in his room. At least those images were easier to control.'

It will not be long before internet access via mobile phones will be cheap or even free. There are already instances of pornography received via mobiles and shared around the class at school. Do your children really need to access the internet on the phone?

> **Insight**
> Our children and their friends reached puberty at very different times. There were problems for those who grew early and were treated as more mature than they really were,

and for those who were late and left behind by their peers. One father, after seeing his son suddenly outstripped by his friends who were much taller, reassured him by remembering that he himself had grown a foot in the year he turned 15!

Giving your children a model of how to talk openly about sex and their feelings will help them in turn to be able to talk to boyfriends and girlfriends. This makes them more confident and less likely to be pressurized to do things before they are ready.

Again, there are good websites and resources (listed at the back of the book) to help parents talk about sex and relationships with their children, and also to give information to children. Some of them have quizzes which may test your knowledge too!

Alcohol, smoking and drugs

Parents are concerned about their children's exposure to illegal drugs in teen years; however, use of alcohol and tobacco is far more common at this age. By the age of 15, around 25 per cent of girls are regular smokers (but fewer boys), and in one study in England and Wales, 45 per cent of 15-year-olds reported drinking alcohol during the last week.

Smoking rates seem to have gone down slightly in recent years, but drinking has increased, especially among girls. Research published by the National Health Service in 2005 found that 27 per cent of 15-year-olds in England reported having used cannabis, and 34 per cent said that they had used an illegal substance. However, cannabis use has declined in recent years in the UK and in the US.

Of course, these figures show that the majority of young teenagers do not drink, smoke or use drugs. However, the proportions are high enough to worry parents and motivate them to do what they can to protect their children from the damage that mood-altering substances can do, even if some of them are legal for adults.

The bad news is that growing brains can be permanently damaged by drug and alcohol abuse, which can affect areas of the brain crucial to motivation, memory, learning, judgement and self-control. Clearly, none of this is good for school success. Early smokers are much more likely to become addicted in the long term. It is particularly worrying that so many young women smoke, since tobacco is very harmful to the developing foetus during pregnancy.

The good news is that, in a survey of 11- to 15-year-olds, over three quarters reported that they had received helpful information about smoking, alcohol and drugs from their parents. If you can find ways to talk about drugs and alcohol before they become hot topics in the early teenage years, you are helping to safeguard your children.

TALKING ABOUT ALCOHOL, SMOKING AND DRUGS

Here are some suggestions to bear in mind when you broach these subjects.

▶ *Do some research into the effects, risks and legalities of various substances. There are good websites and leaflets available and you need to know what you are talking about. If your child asks something and you do not know the answer, go and look it up together.*

▶ *Be explicit about your values – say what you approve of and disapprove of and why. Be aware of the messages you give which are not explicit too. Do you talk about getting drunk as a bit of a laugh? Do you sigh 'I could do with a drink' after a stressful day? Do you smoke yourself? Do you buy celebrity magazines which feature stars 'off their heads' in one way or another?*

▶ *Ask your children why they think people take drugs and alcohol. Is it for fun? To avoid difficult feelings? To try something new? To be part of their group? All these are understandable reasons. People in every culture have substances or ways of making themselves feel 'high', from magic mushrooms to whirling in circles. These substances and activities often help to build and cement social relationships. Why might some of these cause problems?*

▸ *Ask your children what they might say or do if they were offered an illegal substance by a friend. How could they react to keep themselves safe while remaining cool? What situations would make them more likely to be tempted?*

Insight

We have found it useful to ask 'What if' questions to help children prepare for difficult situations; for example 'What if you were the only one who said "No"?' or 'What if a friend seemed to be dangerously spaced out on something?'

Teresa, mother of Callum, Sean and Logan:

'My children all know that my brother's first wife died from inhaling her own vomit after being a heroin addict for years. I try to make sure that they don't see drugs as glamorous in any way.'

Sarah, mother of Zach, Martha, Naomi and Ben:

'Zach says if anyone offered him a joint he would say: "My Mum would kill me!", and all his friends would believe him!'

PREVENTION

Some children are natural risk-takers, whatever their family circumstances, but children who are unhappy are more likely to seek solace in drugs and alcohol to blot out their feelings. Keeping the lines of communication open is the best way to keep your children safe. Once they are teenagers, you will not be able to supervise their movements and friendships as you did when they were younger, so the mutual trust built up in pre-teen years will be a lifeline.

One factor which promotes self-confidence and reduces drug use is doing things as a family – things as simple as eating together or going for a walk. This is probably because meals and walks give chances for conversation with adults. Outside the family, sports and organized activities are protective factors. If children and young people can experience 'flow' – the feeling of losing themselves in a complex, pleasurable activity (see Chapter 4), they are less likely to try out other ways of getting 'high'.

PARENTS' COMMENTS

Penny, mother of Mia and Abby:

'When my ex and I split up, I said to my children that some things would stay the same and others would be different.

I showed them a kaleidoscope and then twisted it so the beads moved a little and made a new pattern. I said that the new pattern was also beautiful, but different, and that eventually we would all settle in to a new pattern, even though it felt so strange and difficult now.'

Laura, mother of Rory and Owen:

'I am an only daughter and I realized that my father had never talked to me at all about sex or relationships; if there was even a kiss on telly he would clear his throat and leave the room! I would have liked to be able to talk to him – not about sex, but about what boys thought of girls, for example.'

Patrick, father of Callum, Sean and Logan:

'I was really scared about Callum going to secondary school and getting offered drugs. But I didn't want to go on about it too much, as I was afraid it would make him more interested. When we were both relaxed I asked him what he thought about drugs and the law, and I was surprised what a mature conversation we had about it.'

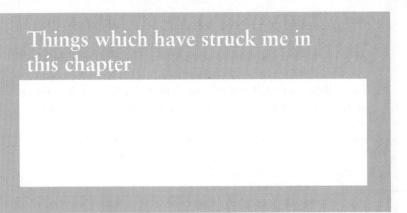

Things which have struck me in this chapter

Something I am going to try out

HAVE SOME FUN

Birds and bees quiz

For pre-teens, use books and websites and make up a quiz. They can ask you questions and you ask them questions about sex and contraception. See if they can catch you out. This is good for children who tell you they know it all already!

You could use the quiz format for other topics too, such as the effects of drugs or alcohol.

10 THINGS TO REMEMBER

1   A row between parents is frightening for children. Be aware
    that they are very likely to overhear it if they are in the house.
    Talk about it afterwards and acknowledge how they are
    feeling, but don't allow them to get involved in mediating.

2   Children are happier after a divorce or separation if their parents
    have told them what is happening and listened to their fears.

3   Reassure children that they are not to blame and that their
    parents still love them, even if they no longer love each other.

4   Tell children the truth about the illness and death of someone
    close. Allow them to ask questions and make sure they do not
    feel guilty.

5   Remember that children may try to come to terms with death
    through play and this is a healthy thing.

6   Answer questions about sex and relationships in a matter-of-
    fact way – check first what they already know by asking them
    what they think the answer is.

7   Use TV and films as a way in to talk about relationships,
    sexual or otherwise.

8   Research the effects and risks of mind-altering substances, both
    legal and illegal. Tell your children about the damage they can
    do to their brains through early use of drugs and alcohol and
    talk with them about why people might take drugs.

9   Say what you approve and disapprove of, and be aware of
    your unspoken messages about drink and drugs as well. Talk
    frankly about the pleasure and pain of getting high, but don't
    make it seem glamorous.

10 Help your child to find ways to resist peer pressure, and to
    experience 'highs' from sporting or creative activities.

14

Happiness

In this chapter you will learn:
- *about the elements of happiness*
- *when parental guidance is needed*
- *the value of satisfaction*
- *ways to promote pleasure and joy.*

Happiness has been the source of debate and speculation for thousands of years, and is currently receiving much attention from researchers, policy makers and the media.

In reading this book, you have delved into the conditions for creating the fertile ground in which happiness can flourish – not the happiness as it appears in holiday brochures, where the sun is always shining and everyone smiling, but more the happiness which endures through the ups and downs of real family life. You have explored ways of making your children feel valued, soothing frayed tempers, and offering an understanding ear when someone is sad, as well as having moments of pure fun together.

Happiness derived from meeting needs

As you saw in Chapter 3, happiness depends on meeting basic human needs. Anyone who has gulped down a huge glass of cold water after a long walk on a boiling day will know the pure bliss of quenching their thirst – meeting their need for re-hydration.

Sociologists, psychologists and philosophers who are currently studying happiness generally agree that it is composed of a number of ingredients, which is hardly surprising considering how many human needs there are: some of these are universal such as food, shelter, security and love, while others may vary from person to person.

For one person, the definition of happiness is mowing the lawn on a sunny day with the birds singing; for another it is a noisy gathering of friends. Perhaps you have a child who adores curling up with a book, while another never reads but loves Lego.

If you have a child with a degree of autism or with learning difficulties, being in a familiar and comfortable environment may bring the greatest happiness. Allowing your children to explore the different activities which bring each of them enjoyment is one way you can appreciate them for who they are and build on their strengths, both of which will bring enduring wellbeing.

Connectedness

> *All sentient beings developed through natural selection in such a way that pleasant sensations serve as their guide, especially the pleasure derived from sociability and loving our families.*
>
> Charles Darwin

A major ingredient of happiness is connectedness. Happy children have secure and loving relationships with their parents, get on with other children and have at least one good friend.

This book has therefore mainly focused on relationships and how they are strengthened and deepened through communication. Having empathy for the feelings of others, and the ability to communicate their own, will be invaluable for your children in order to relate to friends and wider society. This is sometimes described as emotional intelligence or EQ, which probably contributes to success in life more than IQ.

GIVE TIME

It takes time to connect. A recent survey by a major UK charity, the Children's Society, revealed that children would rather spend time baking or playing with their parents than receive the latest computer games for Christmas. This is backed up by research which suggests that children are more likely to cherish the memories of a treasure hunt, a family game, making decorations or listening to bedtime stories than playing with expensive toys. Contemporary parents' lives can be exceedingly busy, but it is worth remembering that time invested relaxing with your children pays rich dividends for your present happiness as well as your long-term relationship. Time with grandparents and other close relatives is also fondly mentioned in people's childhood reminiscences.

FRIENDSHIP

Encourage your children to invite their friends round to your house. Doing things with family friends often creates life-long bonds of affection so it is fun to include them when going on outings. You can be an 'uncle' or an 'aunt' figure to other children, and your friends can fill this role for your own children, whether as godparents or simply as people who take a special interest in them.

Insight

When my mother died some of my childhood friends told me how much it had meant to them that she had kept in touch with them all her life. – *Glenda*

CULTIVATING JOY AND HUMOUR

One definition of happiness is pleasure and the absence of displeasure.

Pleasure certainly contributes to happiness, and the word enjoyment comes to mind – the acquirement of joy. Laughter, playfulness and humour are part of what makes a happy family life. Laughter strengthens the immune system as well as social bonds.

It can help you all get through the harder times too, so this is one 'happiness ingredient' which is well worth cultivating whether through funny games, jokes, or watching humorous programmes on TV together.

> Young children laugh on average 300 times a day.
> Adults much less: around 17 times.

Parental guidance

Unfortunately for parents, one of their roles inevitably involves causing displeasure in aid of longer-term happiness. Children naturally follow their desires as and when they arise, and have little ability to delay their gratification, so there are many times as your child grows up when you have to step in and say 'No' or 'Yes ... later'.

> **Child thinks:** 'I want that cake now ... It looks yummy'.
> **Parent thinks:** 'If he eats the cake now, he won't have an appetite for the main course which is much healthier. Better if he eats it afterwards.'

It is essential for you as a parent to teach your child that it is possible to wait for things, however annoying he may find it. Impulse control is such a crucial lesson that you will frequently – and patiently – need to remind him when he needs to stop and think. This is particularly true of children with AD(H)D who find it harder than most to think before they act and remember what they've been told.

> **Insight**
> We knew one mother who got her child to imagine that he had a spotlight like a head-torch in his mind which he directed onto things he had to remember or focus on. This visual image helped him to concentrate.

Another important message to impart is that some things take time and hard work before you can fully enjoy them. Encouraging a child to practise an instrument, for example, will teach him how much pleasure will be gained when he can finally play that piece which he found so hard at first. Similarly, planting seeds and waiting for the first shoots to show will give a child the pleasure of anticipation and delayed gratification which is so crucial for successfully operating in the world. Seeing a father kicking a football around the park with his child or painstakingly throwing and catching a ball warms the heart. As well as strengthening the bond between them, he is also teaching skills which take time and patience to develop.

TELEVISION AND OTHER SCREENS

Children usually need no encouragement to play, but playtime can be restricted by one of their commonest pleasures, namely watching TV. In fact, sad to say, watching TV is linked with unhappiness: this may be because viewing is more of a solitary activity now that the internet and multiple sets have replaced the family 'box'. Children are also spending increasing time on social networking sites. It will be interesting to see the effect on friendship patterns, but they are unlikely to strengthen family life in which time together is already at a premium.

Frighteningly, the number of hours of television watched is directly correlated with levels of both obesity and aggression in children.

Shanti, mother of Asha and Hari:

'It's strange, but after my children have watched TV they're almost always in a bad mood; but when we've been to the playground they're happy.'

Children with TVs and computers in their rooms tend to multitask, doing homework while they flick between programmes and websites. This does them no favours, as research shows that they take 50 per cent longer to do their assignments and, unsurprisingly, make more mistakes. If they fall asleep with the TV on, they will sleep fewer hours and less deeply too. Even a mobile phone in the bedroom makes children sleep more lightly as youngsters wait for the beep to show that a text message has arrived. Children who have not slept enough are not happy, and neither are their parents!

> **Insight**
> A parent in one of our groups who felt very strongly about this used to make her children bring all their electronic 'goodies', phones, games consoles, laptops, etc. to her at bedtime and lock them away till they were dressed and ready to go in the morning.

The impact of advertising and other forms of marketing on children makes for unhappiness too: a US study found that the more children were exposed to the consumer culture the more likely they were to be depressed, anxious or have low self-esteem. Since the aim of brand promotion is to make you feel like a loser if you lack the latest product, this is entirely predictable. You can make your children more 'media savvy' by discussing what advertisements are trying to achieve and how.

Of course, television and computer games can bring information and interest, laughter and excitement. Children who do not watch certain popular programmes feel left out at school when they cannot join in playground chat. But families have to find some kind of balance between screen time and allowing space for children to play and experience all the things which actually do contribute to happiness.

The value of satisfaction and creativity

> *True happiness comes from the joy of deeds well done; the zest of creating things new.*
>
> Antoine de Saint-Exupéry, author of *Le Petit Prince*

Children have a natural desire to stretch themselves, whether by throwing a stone that little bit further into the sea, completing a difficult jigsaw puzzle, or building a taller tower of bricks than they've ever managed before. Doing something well brings as much satisfaction to children as it does to adults. You can bring a smile to your child's face by providing opportunities to learn new skills and master something appropriate to their age and abilities, whether it be one of the arts, a sport, or learning to garden or cook. *Raising Boys* author Steve Biddulph says that a child should be able to cook a family meal by the age of 11.

Children are wonderfully creative – put them by a stream and they will be building a dam, making mud pies or crafting boats; give them a few pots and pans, and they can create an orchestra; supply paper and paints, and pictures will emerge. Their creativity is so natural that a parent just needs to provide the openings for it to flourish. A large sheet and some chairs for a den; old formal clothes (and especially hats) kept in a dressing-up drawer; rolls of lining wallpaper for huge art works – there are endless possibilities for creativity, quite apart from formal classes. Happiness is not merely the satisfaction of desires, but rather more vital and dynamic: it often comes from 'doing'.

Sometimes, happiness can also come from doing nothing: daydreaming or watching a bee buzz from flower to flower on a lazy summer's day.

The other side of the coin

It is natural for you to feel pleasure when you see your children enjoying life. Similarly, children are much happier when their parents are cheerful; so looking after yourself is an important ingredient in your children's wellbeing.

Insight

As a child I remember being very impressed when my best friend's mother took up piano lessons at the age of 36. I realized that just because you were old didn't mean you couldn't go on learning things and having fun! – *Glenda*

However, no one can expect to have fun all of the time. As Carl Jung said: 'Even a happy life cannot be without a measure of darkness, and the word 'happy' would lose its meaning if it were not balanced by sadness.'

If you have bad childhood memories, you may want to move heaven and earth to ensure that your child is always cheerful. In fact this can be a burden for a child, as one mother said: 'Sometimes having to have the happy childhood my parents never had was just too much of a responsibility. I want my kids to know that they're entitled to be sad without their mother falling apart.'

Letting your children know you accept their feelings, whether joyful or painful, is the best way of showing you love them.

Resilience and optimism

Resilience is the ability to come through despite challenging circumstances, and children who learn to cope with life's setbacks and disappointments have a head-start for happiness. Our instinct is to protect our children from disappointment, but when it does happen, it can be seen as something which, with proper support, strengthens rather than weakens them.

> *A 'good' parent smoothes the road ahead for their kids, a great parent prepares their kids for the bumps.*

Some children appear to have a more pessimistic outlook by nature – they see the glass half empty rather than half full, which can mar their appreciation of life.

Fortunately, some studies suggest that optimism can be taught. Certainly the kind of 'moving on' questions in Chapter 10 can be used to challenge the notion that nothing can be done about a problem – for example, 'I can't do this' can be countered with: 'What's stopping you?', 'What prevents you?' or 'What would help?'

The suggestions for building confidence in Chapter 4 are also useful, such as recalling past successes: 'Remember when you managed to get the kitten down from the tree when we were about to call the fire brigade?'

What's more, praising your child for effort and trying things out rather than only focusing on success seems to be particularly effective in strengthening positive attitudes.

Thankfulness

Everyone knows the joy of an unexpected treat. Taking things for granted is a great enemy of happiness. Children who feel they are 'entitled' to what they get are less contented than those who have an attitude of thankfulness. As Leo Tolstoy said: 'Happiness does not depend on outward things, but on the way we see them.'

One recent study showed that people who wrote down five things they were grateful for once a week were measurably happier after a month – they even slept better and took more exercise! Teaching your children gratitude, therefore, will be an important ingredient in their wellbeing. How about thanking the person who has cooked the meal, and showing appreciation for the little acts people do for each other in the family, or at school? Children need prompting to understand this at times.

You could say:

'Miss Green must have worked very hard to prepare the outing you enjoyed so much today. I'm sure it would make her happy if you thanked her for it.'

You can ask children to say three things they are grateful for as part of your bedtime ritual. Some people keep a stone in their pocket as a reminder to count their blessings.

Giving and receiving

Children can be taught the pleasure of giving joy to others.

Happiness is not so much in having as sharing. We make a living by what we get, but we make a life by what we give.

Norman MacEwan

Picking flowers for Granny or baking some biscuits for an old friend can give enormous pleasure to both giver and recipient. Playing games can help build generosity of spirit too.

Insight

My son used to hate losing games, and then one day an old family friend pointed out that when you win you're pleased, and when someone else wins they're happy, and that's good too. – *Glenda*

Nature and walking

Children who are used to the stimulation of electronic entertainment can take some persuading to go out for a walk. But a wealth of excitement awaits them outdoors – climbing trees and turning over logs on a rainy day to find a multitude of creepy crawlies brings deep satisfaction to children. The word 'walk' can be a turn-off, but if you present it as an 'adventure' or say 'Let's go and see if we can find some good sticks for making bows and arrows', children may be much more enthusiastic. Flying kites is also a wonderful way of lifting the spirits. Over the centuries, the simple act of walking has been linked with happiness, and the sheer abundance and scale of the natural world tends to feed the spirit.

As the great environmentalist Rachel Carson said:

If a child is to keep his inborn sense of wonder, he needs the companionship of at least one adult who can share it, rediscovering with him the joy, excitement and mystery of the world we live in.

Moral and spiritual happiness

There is a happiness far deeper than mere pleasure, which is to be found when people live in tune with their values and moral principles. Gandhi and Martin Luther King Jr could hardly have enjoyed the beatings they received during their non-violent quest for freedom, but could they have been happy without acting on their convictions? Giving your children a moral dimension can bestow a deeper meaning and purpose to their lives. As the Dalai Lama said:

We begin from the recognition that all beings cherish happiness and do not want suffering. It then becomes both morally wrong and pragmatically unwise to pursue only one's own happiness oblivious to the feelings and aspirations of all others who surround us as members of the same human family. The wiser course is to think of others when pursuing our own happiness.

Interestingly, in this secular age, research shows that prayer, meditation and worship increase happiness. If you have religious faith, St Augustine's words will ring true: 'Thou hast created us for Thyself, and our heart is not quiet until it rests in Thee', and you will doubtless want to share this spiritual dimension with your children.

Whatever your beliefs, having loving rituals like lighting candles for birthdays, or quiet moments gazing at the intricacy of a tiny flower or the stars at night will endow your children with the wonder and beauty of existence, and their part in it – perhaps the deepest source of happiness.

Postscript

Only parents who care about their children take the trouble to buy a book on raising happy children. Some of the things you have read may seem obvious, while others may be new to you. Everything in these pages is about putting love into practice. There may be some ideas which have already made a tangible difference to your family, and some could take longer to sink in. Change takes time, and it is often a question of two steps forward and one step back. When you feel stuck and want to find encouragement, turn to the pages you found most helpful. We very much hope that this book will get to look creased, dog-eared and well worn.

Taking it further

Websites

GENERAL

www.parentlineplus.org.uk
24-hour helpline 0808 800 2222

The national organization offering support to parents. Call-takers are specially trained and are themselves parents. The website covers all ages and has a special section on bullying, forums for parent-to-parent discussion, an email service and video clips. You can access sessions of one-to-one telephone support via the helpline, and telephone groups via the website. There is a comprehensive list of links to specialist organizations on the website too.

www.mumsnet.com
Mumsnet offers a supportive online community in the UK. You can contact mothers in your area and beyond, and find out about local activities. They have an interesting archive of webchats with various parenting experts.

www.raisingchildren.net.au
Excellent site for parents of children up to eight years old funded by the Australian Government. Good on discipline and health issues, it is about to extend its age range.

www.familyeducation.com
A US site with commercial sponsors, covering the whole age range. Comprehensive and up to date, it features good articles on children and new technology. You can avoid some of the advertisements by clicking on 'go directly to your link'.

www.greatergood.berkeley.edu
This centre based at the University of Berkeley in California has a website for parents called Raising Happiness, covering the 'science of raising happy kids', with lots of accessible research based articles and a regular video discussion on related topics which is also posted on You Tube.

www.fabermazlish.com
Adele Faber and Elaine Mazlish, renowned authors of *How to Talk so Kids will Listen and Listen so Kids will Talk*, answer questions from their many thousands of readers around the world on this site.

www.partnershipforchildren.org.uk
An international charity which works to promote mental and emotional wellbeing in children. Their website has a section for parents covering bereavement, bullying and divorce and separation. It also gives ideas for activities for parents to do with children to support coping skills and has a guide, 'Good Books for Tough Times', about children's story books dealing with difficult issues.

FATHERS

www.fatherhoodinstitute.org
The 'think tank' about fathering in the UK has lots of information about research and policy and invitations to get involved.

www.dad.info
A commercial and interactive site with a comprehensive range.

www.Fathers.com
The National Center for Fathering is a US non-profit organization. They have good material on involvement with children's schooling.

IDEAS FOR FUN

www.kidsandcooking.co.uk
Lots of ideas for indoor and outdoor cooking.

www.skratch-pad.com/kites
Instructions for making kites.

www.facepaintingdesigns.co.uk
Plenty of ideas for face painting.

SPECIAL NEEDS

www.P2PUSA.org
P2PUSA's mission is to provide access and assure quality in parent-to-parent support for all US families with children who have a special health need or disability.

www.cafamily.org.uk
Contact a Family works with families of children with all kinds of disabilities, providing information, a helpline, and support groups in regions and on social networking sites.

www.addiss.co.uk
The Attention Deficit Disorder Information and Support Service has information for parents, teachers and sufferers of ADHD, with products and book reviews.

www.nas.org.uk
The National Autistic Society offers practical help for people with autistic spectrum disorders and their families, carers, partners and the professionals who look after them.

www.autismusa.net
An information resource about autism, giving access to research, books and services in the US.

Mental wellbeing

www.youngminds.org.uk
Advice line 0808 802 5544

Young Minds is a national UK charity aiming to promote the mental health and wellbeing of children and young people. Advisers give information and advice about the mental health of a child or young person and can refer you to a specialist professional for one hour of free telephone advice.

www.lift-depression.com
A self-help website sponsored by the Human Givens Institute with some good ideas, based on the latest thinking about depression.

www.bacp.co.uk
0870 443 5219

The British Association for Counselling and Psychotherapy have a 'seeking a therapist' section for the UK and internationally, with explanations about different types of therapy.

www.mind.org.uk
08457 660 163

Mind works to create a better life for all who have experienced mental distress. They have some good online leaflets including 'How to deal with Anger' and 'How to Parent when you are in a Crisis'.

www.mentalhelp.net
A US based site giving information about psychological research and services. They have a therapist search service for adults and children.

ANGER

www.angermanage.co.uk
Well-designed, lively site with helpful information and a video.

www.apa.org
The American Psychological Association website has a good list of resources for anger management.

SUBSTANCE ABUSE

www.talktofrank.com
Advice line 0800 776600

UK government sponsored site about drugs aimed at young people. Information and advice, email service and links to local services.

www.drugfree.org
A US site for parents which has a good 'Guide to the Teenage Brain'.

www.quit.org.uk
0800 00 22 00

Helpline for smokers who want to stop, they also offer workshops in schools and a website aimed at young people.

SEX EDUCATION AND BODY IMAGE

www.brook.org.uk
0808 802 1234

Services and information for young people, plus interactive website with quizzes and games.

www.bbc.co.uk/barefacts
An excellent website for parents, giving approaches for talking about sex with children and young people.

www.dove.com
Dove has a 'Campaign for Real Beauty' with online self-esteem workshops and excellent short films challenging the effects of the beauty industry on young girls.

BULLYING AND ABUSE

www.childline.org.uk
0800 1111

A 24-hour helpline for children in the UK which also answers emails.

www.childhelp.org
1 800 4-A-CHILD

A 24-hour helpline for children in the US and Canada.

www.bullying.co.uk
A UK charity which provides information and advice for pupils and parents. They have a special section for primary schools.

www.bullying.org
A website started in Canada, collaborative and with comprehensive resources including 'webinars' for teachers and parents.

www.kidscape.org.uk
08451 205 204

Campaigns against bullying and child abuse. A section for parents and carers includes advice on assertiveness for children being bullied and they also run assertiveness workshops.

RELATIONSHIPS, DIVORCE AND SEPARATION

www.thecoupleconnection.net
An excellent interactive self-help site to help couples improve their relationships.

www.relate.org.uk
Relate offers advice, relationship counselling, sex therapy, workshops, mediation, consultations and support face to face, by phone and through its website. Their section for parents has good advice on contact issues.

www.itsnotyourfault.org
Site with sections for children, young people and parents involved in separation and divorce. Easy to navigate.

www.helpguide.org
An extensive US mental health site with good sections on helping children through a divorce and on 'co-parenting' with your ex.

BEREAVEMENT

www.crusebereavementcare.org.uk
0844 477 9400

Website with many resources, helpful hints for parents and also a link to www.RD4U.org, an interactive site for young people about bereavement. Cruse also helps bereaved military families.

www.dougy.org
US site for an organization that provides services for bereaved children. Good ideas for activities.

www.winstonswish.org.uk
Winston's Wish, as well as extensive resources aimed at bereaved children and their carers, has a good section on helping children cope with a serious illness in the family.

Childcare

www.ncma.org.uk
The National Childminding Association has a search facility to find childminders all over the UK.

www.nannysuccess.com
A comprehensive website offering advice and action plans to help parents find and manage a nanny or au pair. Good checklists for better interviews and choices.

Internet safety

www.nextgenerationlearning.org.uk
A government sponsored site with a good quiz for parents on 'e-safety'. Good links to other useful sites.

www.isafe.org
A US site which provides online training for schools, parents and children on internet safety.

Booklist

Steve and Shaaron Biddulph, *The Complete Secrets of Happy Children: a guide for parents*, Thorsons, 2003

Steve Biddulph, *Raising Boys: why boys are different and how to help them become healthy and well balanced men*, Thorsons, 2003

Robert Brooks and Sam Goldstein, *Raising Resilient Children: fostering strength, hope and optimism in your child*, McGraw Hill – Contemporary, 2002

Elizabeth Crary, *Pick up Your Socks: a practical guide to raising responsible children*, Parenting Press, 1990

Adele Faber and Elaine Mazlish, *How to Talk so Kids will Listen and Listen so Kids will Talk*, Piccadilly Press, 2003

Adele Faber and Elaine Mazlish, *Liberated Parents, Liberated Children: your guide to a happier family*, Collins Living, 1990

Adele Faber and Elaine Mazlish, *Siblings without Rivalry: how to teach your kids to live together so you can live too*, Piccadilly Press, 2001

Sue Gerhardt, *Why Love Matters: how affection shapes a baby's brain*, Brunner-Routledge, 2004

John Gottman and Joan Declaire, *Raising an Emotionally Intelligent Child*, Simon and Schuster, 1998

Joe Griffin and Ivan Tyrrell, *Release from Anger: practical help for controlling unreasonable rage*, Human Givens Publishing, 2008

Edward M Hallowell and John R Ratey, *Driven to Distraction: recognizing and coping with ADD from childhood through adulthood*, Touchstone, 1995

Suzie Hayman, *Be a Great Single Parent*, Hodder Education, 2010

Suzie Hayman, *Be a Great Step-Parent*, Hodder Education, 2010

Richard Layard and Judy Dunn, *A Good Childhood: searching for values in a competitive age*, Penguin, 2009

Mel Levine, *The Myth of Laziness: how kids – and parents – can become more productive*, Simon and Schuster, 2003

Helen Likierman and Valerie Muter, *A Parent's Guide to Dyslexia, Dyspraxia and other Learning Difficulties*, Vermilion, 2008

Helen Likierman and Valerie Muter, *Top Tips for Starting School*, Vermilion, 2008

Gael Lindenfield, *Managing Anger: simple steps to dealing with frustration and threat*, Thorsons, 2000

Ed Mayo and Agnes Nairn, *Consumer Kids: how big business is grooming our children for profit*, Constable, 2009

Nicola Morgan, *Know your Brain: feed it, test it, stretch it*, Walker Books, 2007

Sue Palmer, *Detoxing Childhood: what parents need to know to raise bright balanced children*, Orion Books, 2008

Judy Reith, *Be a Great Mum*, Hodder Education, 2010

Martin Seligman, *The Optimistic Child: a proven programme to safeguard children against depression and build lifelong resilience*, Houghton Mifflin, 2007

Daniel Siegal and Mary Hartzell, *Parenting from the Inside Out: how a deeper self-understanding can help you raise children who thrive*, Tarcher-Penguin, 2004

Margot Sunderland, *What Every Parent Needs to Know: the incredible effects of love, nurture and play on your child's development*, Dorling Kindersley, 2007

Georgina Walsh, *How to find the Childcare your Child will Love, Manage it Properly and Make it Work for You*, Foulsham, 2008

Anthony E Wolf, *It's not Fair, Jeremy Spencer's Parents Let Him Stay Up All Night!: a guide to the tougher parts of parenting*, Noonday Press, 1996

New titles in the '**Teach Yourself**' parenting section come out regularly. Check www.teachyourself.com

Index

Image credits

Notes

Notes

Notes

Notes